JUSTICE
FOR THE JUDGE

JUSTICE
FOR THE JUDGE
JUDGE

An Autobiography

RANJAN GOGOI

RUPA

Published by
Rupa Publications India Pvt. Ltd 2021
7/16, Ansari Road, Daryaganj
New Delhi 110002

Sales centres:
Allahabad Bengaluru Chennai
Hyderabad Jaipur Kathmandu
Kolkata Mumbai

ISBN: 978-93-5520-188-1

Fourth impression 2022

10 9 8 7 6 5 4

The moral right of the author has been asserted.

Printed at Sanat Printers, India

Dedicated to my mother, Shanti Gogoi,
who taught me to live with courage,
conviction and compassion

❧

CONTENTS

CONTENTS

PROLOGUE

1970, New Delhi. A boy aged 15 and a half from the district town of Dibrugarh in north-eastern Assam arrived in India's capital to study at Delhi University (DU). He was in for a shock. He was told he could not be admitted as he was underaged. The teenager persisted, finally secured a relaxation in the age guideline and joined St Stephen's College, from where he graduated. After eight years in the national capital, the youth returned to Assam with a law degree. He spent long hours at the study table, burning the midnight oil, and achieved a degree of success in the legal profession, which led to his elevation as a High Court judge at the relatively young age of 46. This was followed by appointment as chief justice of the Punjab and Haryana High Court in Chandigarh. Very soon, he retraced his steps back to the national capital to serve as a judge of the Supreme Court of India, and subsequently as its chief justice. This is the story of that boy, Ranjan Gogoi. *My* story.

Forty-eight years after I first set foot in New Delhi, on 3 October 2018, at 10.45 a.m., President Ram Nath Kovind administered the oath of office of the Chief Justice of India (CJI) to me at a glittering ceremony in the Durbar Hall of Rashtrapati Bhavan. In less than a minute, my life had changed. Heading the judicial institution of the world's second most populous country was a huge challenge. After the ceremony, I went to meet my mother, Shanti Gogoi, who had come from Assam for the occasion. She told me that the people of India had placed me in the highest chair in the judiciary with great hope and expectations and that I had to ensure that all this is not lost when I demitted office.

Justice for the Judge traces my journey from my hometown, Dibrugarh, to 5, Krishna Menon Marg (the official residence of the CJI) and the first court of the country and thereafter my rather unusual passage to Parliament. The memoir chronicles both and proffers the reader insight into the reasons for my entry to the temple of India's democracy.

The first part of the book describes my formative years in a traditional, middle-class Assamese family helmed by my far-sighted mother and sans any display of male superiority by the breadwinner (my father), himself an accomplished lawyer who later enjoyed a successful career in politics. This is followed by a detailed account of the events during my tenure as a High Court judge, as a judge of the Supreme Court, and, finally, as the CJI. I would like readers to judge for themselves if I managed to fulfil my mother's wish that carried with it the hopes of millions. It is for these millions that I write—to enable them to know how judges live and work, and decide whether judges in India get justice in life.

This book is a frank revelation of what transpires behind the majesty of the courtroom; what goes into the process of rendering path-breaking judgments that mould the life of the nation and its citizens; how appointments to high judicial office are made and how decisions affecting the vitality of the judicial system of the country are taken. The contents are revealing because it is necessary for the average citizen to have more than a glimpse of the working of the institution of the judiciary. Readers will also find an account of what lies behind the glitter and glamour of the high office of a judge of the Supreme Court or of the CJI and derive a better understanding of the life of a judge or chief justice. My attempt is to reach out, and in doing so I have been as forthright as always.

Misplaced apprehensions about the contempt law make silence a viable option for the right-thinking majority, while its efficacy or lack of it provides adequate opportunity to disseminators of misinformation to accuse judges of committing wrong in every sphere of activity; for the latter know no fear, a phenomenon that has been growing of late at an alarming rate—to the detriment of the system. An accurate perspective of the working of the judicial system and clearing of the fog of misinformation is the imperative need of the judiciary and this is what the book for the major part seeks to accomplish.

A tenure in the Supreme Court of a little over seven-and-a-half years is undoubtedly a considerable period. Many important decisions, both judicial and non-judicial (administrative), had to be taken. Some of these decisions had their own ramifications, significance and consequences though to me they were all routine decisions taken during the course of performing my duties as a judge. To me, all cases and questions that came before me in court were equally important. Yet, after retirement, I was made increasingly aware that some of my decisions were of great significance and in reaching them, I had veered away from the traditional path of judicial decision-making. Ayodhya, Rafale and electoral bonds, among others, are the frequently mentioned cases in which the judicial verdict is alleged to have been consciously rendered to favour the government in power. This book candidly lays forth my inability to comprehend the basis for such perceptions.

The book narrates how I dealt with the most formidable challenge that came my way during the almost two decades of judicial tenure: the Ayodhya case. I chose not to shirk what I inherited from my predecessors but to bite the bullet and to lead the adjudication of one of India's oldest-standing disputes.

While the contribution of my brother judges, the registry, as well as the co-operation of the lawyers, must be acknowledged, what cannot be lost sight of is that without the iron will of the CJI as the leader, the culmination of the matter would not have been possible.

The closure of the case, regardless of the way the decision went, was a matter of great personal satisfaction, not for any other reason but for being able to surmount the most challenging task that had ever come before me.

I do not for a moment regret the negativity created and the personal attacks that I had to withstand, and continue to withstand, owing to the outcome of the case. All sorts of malignant things about me and my integrity have been said, and will continue to be said, by certain sections. But there is the other side—the respect of the huge neutral populace, which convinces me of the shallowness of social media and the importance in life of having the courage to take decisions true to one's conscience, without favour and without fear of consequences or brickbats from certain quarters. The Ayodhya chapter deals with all this in vivid detail.

The refusal of a section of rather vocal people to accept the Bobde Committee's report, which held as wholly unsubstantiated some quite unsavoury personal allegations against me by a female employee of the Supreme Court, is another aspect I have delved into. This is bewildering, especially as the in-house inquiry procedure is what is established by law. Equally perplexing is the contradictory stand of this group of people in accepting the proceedings and the report of another, similar in-house inquiry conducted subsequently during the tenure of Justice S.A. Bobde as CJI. This inquiry was with regard to a complaint by the chief minister (CM) of a state. I am utterly clueless as to why this group of people has been raking up the issue periodically, continuing the tirade non-stop till date. I have attempted to unveil the truth on all the above matters for the benefit of the vast silent majority. For this section of the citizenry, my book also reveals what they ought to know—why from one perspective the institution may appear to be shrouded in opacity and why, at the same time, this may be necessary. I also disclose that opacity or lack of transparency is not synonymous with absence of correct and cogent reasons for decisions taken.

Free speech is a hallmark of democracy and I have chosen to exercise it in the next 300-odd pages. Readers will judge the aptness of the book's title from what I have to say and decide for themselves whether justice is being done to judges who, on account of the office they hold, have to perpetually remain silent and stoic, even when life shoots bullets at them. Should the wheels of justice stop moving? Should judges not perform in the manner they are required to just to keep at bay adverse opinion and criticism? I have attempted to answer these contentious questions and more in the pages that follow.

I hope you will have an illuminating read.

One

MY ROOTS IN ASSAM

In the early 1950s, Assamese youth grew up in a highly congenial atmosphere within the home and out. Family bonding and values were strong, consciously cultivated and lauded, and social disapproval acted as a strong deterrent and propagated purity of thought, belief and actions. A deep-seated sense of righteousness was all-pervading and aberrations were frowned upon.

It was in this harmonious and nurturing milieu that I was born to Keshab Chandra and Shanti Gogoi on 18 November 1954 in Dibrugarh, a sleepy but picturesque district town on the banks of the Brahmaputra and in the heart of the tea belt of Assam. In a way, it was a 'westernized' town with planters' stores which stocked everything from needles to Ford cars. This was to cater to the British population living in the tea gardens in neighbouring locales. Even after the British planters had left and ownership of the tea estates had passed to Indian companies or individuals, the colour that Dibrugarh had acquired in the preceding years remained unchanged. To add to this was the cool, rainy weather for which Dibrugarh was often referred to as the second Shillong of Assam (Shillong was then the state capital). Golf, polo and tennis were popular. Dibrugarh was the district headquarters of what today are three districts—Dibrugarh, Tinsukia and North Lakhimpur.

My father belonged to a family of cultivators in a village in Sibsagar (Sivasagar) district. His father had worked as a clerk in a tea estate and retired as head clerk. The family was not wealthy by any means though the notion generally was that my father was born with a silver spoon in his mouth. Others said he found a bag full of gold coins while felling a tree for firewood! The reality, as happens, was quite different. My father started practice in Sibsagar court and lived in the village home, which was a couple of miles from the town. My mother would often describe to us their struggles during the initial days of my father's legal practice; he would go on a bicycle to Sonari, 20 miles away, in the morning and return in the evening with ₹20–30, which he would hand over to her with pride. Being a man of few words perhaps helped him in cross-examination of witnesses, which with time became legendary—permitting him to shift his practice to Dibrugarh.

He soon built an extensive practice, and even rose to become president of the Dibrugarh District Bar Association—a Bar rich not only in talent, but also in earnings—for more than one term. In those days, the president of the Bar usually had the last word in any matter of controversy. He was a true leader of the Bar and always a successful lawyer in the real sense of the term. My father was designated as a senior advocate by the High Court in 1970. This was a rare honour for a person who did not practise in the High Court but was exclusively a trial court lawyer.

My father never dictated our career graphs but always supported my siblings and me in our decisions. By the time I joined St Stephen's College in 1970, my father had a large practice and a reasonable income; yet, when I would opt to travel between Dibrugarh and Delhi (72 hours) by Class III 'sleeper' with student concession (total cost of about ₹50), never once did he suggest that I should travel by air though there was an airport next door and a daily flight from Dibrugarh to Delhi via Calcutta. Food during this train journey was from platform vendors and water was from the taps. It was only on rare occasions that my mother would persuade him to let me travel by air.

In the late '70s, my father joined politics. In March 1978, during the Janata Party wave, he became a Member of the Legislative Assembly (MLA). He was appointed finance and law minister of the state. He later switched to the Congress, the party which was his home for long, but was forced to leave it when he felt he was being persistently denied a ticket to contest the Assembly elections from Dibrugarh.

He had a meteoric rise in politics, becoming CM of the state in early 1982. But the game of numbers, inherent in the game of politics, played its role and he had to step down in about three months while recommending dissolution of the Assembly. What followed was the highly controversial 1983 elections that the All Assam Students' Union (AASU) and other affiliated bodies, who had spearheaded the 'foreigners movement', urged the people to boycott.

As my father had decided to contest, we had to face the fury of the agitators (mainly women), who gathered outside our Dibrugarh house and raised all kinds of unsavoury slogans. This was perhaps a strategy to dissuade my father from contesting and to pressure the family to persuade him to withdraw. The elections in March–April 1983 were a farce, if for nothing else than the poor voter turnout.

On being elected, my father was naturally in contention for the chief minister's post. The Congress elected Hiteswar Saikia as leader of the legislature party. My father was offered a ministerial berth. My mother was dead against his accepting as, according to her, after chief ministership, being a minister was a comedown. My father had a different perception. He did not consider his three-month tenure as CM, that too in somewhat fortuitous circumstances (the Assam agitation on the foreigners issue was at its peak), to be any kind of impediment to joining the Cabinet. Eventually, he took the oath of office and continued as a minister until the Assembly was once again dissolved following the signing of the Assam Accord on 15 August 1985. Thereafter, the Asom Gana Parishad (AGP), consisting mainly of the erstwhile student leaders of AASU, swept to power.

On the day my father demitted office, I visited him in his official residence in Dispur. I went straight to his bedroom. He was combing his hair. Without looking away from the mirror, he told me he had realized that politics was not his cup of tea and leaving the legal profession to join politics had not been the right decision. How accurate he was! He was singularly unfit for politics. Would you ever find a politician returning unutilized election funds to the party high command? My father did precisely that and handed over a large amount to N.D. Tiwari, then a powerful name in the ruling Congress party. My father's values and beliefs around a career in politics, at least for himself, found manifestation in a book, *Gauhati High Court: History and Heritage,* in which it is mentioned that, as the CM, he was asked by the then law minister, Abdul Muhib Mazumdar, whether I would also become CM one day. My father replied that I would certainly not join politics and therefore would not become chief minister, but I did have the potential to become the CJI.[1]

Coincidentally, that book was released on 29 August 2018 when speculation was rife surrounding my elevation as the CJI to succeed Justice Dipak Misra. After I had become CJI, this prophetic statement was much discussed.

THE WIND BENEATH MY WINGS

The person who really foresaw my future was my mother who, till her death at the age of 87, lived all by herself in our ancestral home at Dibrugarh. A fiercely independent woman, she ran an NGO called Socio Educational Welfare Association (SEWA), an organization she had established and nurtured on her own after my father's death in 1998. This venture was her rejoinder to the suggestions offered by her children that she should consider living with us instead of

---

[1]Arup Kumar Dutta, *Gauhati High Court: History and Heritage,* Publications Division, Ministry of Information and Broadcasting, Government of India, 2018.

Ranjan Gogoi

being alone in Dibrugarh. One of the most reputed NGOs in the Northeast today, it is involved in activities as diverse as running ambulances and crèches for children to undertaking HIV-related projects in tea gardens.

My mother was born in a political family. Her father, a Congress MLA in the pre-Independence era, died prematurely in tragic circumstances. A diabetic suffering from a wound that refused to heal, he was unable to secure a life-saving dose of penicillin as the stock in Dibrugarh had been diverted to meet the needs of the Army fighting the Second World War. After his death, my grandmother took over and went on to become an MLA and then a Cabinet minister in the B.P. Chaliha government.

My mother was married at an early age, in February 1951, and passed her matriculation examination two months later. After marriage, she had to shift to the village where my father lived. She would often tell us that while in Dibrugarh she had access to a bathroom, there was none in the village. It was the overwhelming support she received from her seven sisters-in-law that enabled her to adjust to life in a rural environment during those early years.

Even as my mother began planning to start a family, she passed the intermediate examination followed by graduation. She did not remember her graduation year, perhaps because she did not go to receive the degree, but I recall being fairly grown up when she appeared for the BA exams. Each time, on reaching home after an exam, she would immediately look up a few books on her study table. I reckon she was trying to see if she had written the answers correctly. On most occasions, she appeared satisfied.

Though chronologically young, my mother possessed a great deal of wisdom. It was primarily on account of her foresight that my father invested his initial savings in a plot of land instead of a car and started construction of our house in Dibrugarh in 1958. It was complete, if construction of a house can ever be complete, sometime in the 1980s.

She meticulously plotted the career graphs of her children and was instrumental in my going to Delhi for graduation. She encouraged my elder brother, Anjan Kumar Gogoi, to join the newly established Sainik School in Goalpara from where he went to join the National Defence Academy (NDA). He was commissioned in the Indian Air Force in 1973 when I was still in college. I would spend my weekends with him during his initial postings in Bareilly and Chandigarh as a pilot officer (now the first rank after successful completion of training is flying officer). He was lavish in his hospitality in the Air Force mess, particularly the bar. I used to carry some liquor (courtesy of my brother) back with me to Delhi. And so my return to the college residence was eagerly awaited by some of my friends in anticipation of the treasure I would bring back! My brother retired as an air marshal while serving as the Air Officer Commanding-in-Chief (AOC-in-C), South Western Air Command (SWAC).

My mother had plans of seeing my youngest brother, Nirjan Gogoi, as a doctor. One day, she invited one of his friends, Dr Moloy Chakravorty (now a renowned neurosurgeon in Siliguri) to come and stay with Nirjan in our house. She did this as my brother was apparently showing less interest in studies and more interest in a girl, which my mother thought was an unnecessary distraction at that age. The plan worked. I firmly believe that she was similarly responsible for my two sisters—Indira and Nandita—joining the Assam Civil Services. In fact, Indira joined service (after qualifying in the competitive examination) after she had become a mother.

My mother was also the woman behind the man, my father, once he stepped into politics. My father had ambitions of becoming a minister when we were still very young; my mother succeeded in persuading him to defer his plans until we grew up. Though I was not in Dibrugarh at the time of the 1978 elections, when he was elected to the Assembly for the first time (I was a law student in Delhi), in the subsequent elections that my father contested, I found her planning, strategizing and executing every move in the election campaign. My father, I must confess, was a helpless spectator to the events that were being orchestrated around him. But, knowing my father as I did, I am sure he was enjoying the spectacle and had no qualms about taking a back seat.

Though born to politician parents and despite my father being in active politics for nearly 20 years, holding key portfolios in the state Cabinet, my mother's opinion of a career in politics was largely pejorative. She thought there were other professions more worthy of engaging in. After my retirement as CJI, when rumours swirled of me being the Bharatiya Janata Party (BJP) candidate for the CM's post in Assam (after the April 2021 elections), my mother called me late one night, saying, 'Don't even think about it!' She hung up only after I convinced her that I had no such plans and that the news was nothing but a rumour.

THE SIMPLE LIFE

Dibrugarh offered a simple, uncomplicated lifestyle and we grew up in a milieu with a consistent feel-good ambience. In addition to the occasional evening visits to the Planters' Clubs in the neighbourhood, a good part of our summer vacations were spent in Kaziranga, where my father's elder brother was posted for several years as a forest officer. Our visits had become so regular that we came to know quite a few of the elephants who used to ferry tourists inside the sanctuary by name. The interiors of the sanctuary, barred to tourists, became easily accessible to us. The experience and opportunity, in retrospect, was a godsend. Later, as we grew older, the summer holidays came to be spent in Shillong where our maternal grandmother worked as a minister and lived in a sprawling bungalow in Stoney Land. She was a very affectionate person who cooked excellent meals, but had a weakness for gambling and would return home late at night after several rounds of rummy. *Teer* was her favourite pastime, a game in which the last two digits of the number of arrows that strike the target are declared the winning number. For example, on a given day if 1,000 *teers* or arrows are shot by 20 archers, and 526 strike the target, then 26 is the winning number of the day and bets placed on 26 on that day will return several times the initial investment. I recall that the gains were fairly high: at least 20 times the wager.

My school education took place in Don Bosco, the premier English-medium school in Dibrugarh. We engaged seriously in academics as well as sports. School was a preparatory ground for higher studies and consequential achievements in life. I did reasonably well, securing first division in the matriculation examination of 1969 which, at that time, was quite an achievement.

I enrolled in Cotton College, Guwahati, for pre-university education (equivalent to Classes XI and XII today) at the age of 14. My preferred field of study, humanities, surprised many (though not my parents) as first divisioners were expected to head for the science stream to become engineers and doctors. People tried to discourage me from pursuing a course in humanities and advised me to opt for science but I was resolute. I spent only five to six months in Cotton College as the pre-university course was a short one but have fond memories of it. It was nice to be in college. I secured the fourth rank in the merit list of Gauhati University. Now it was time to make my next life's decision: choosing a career.

Two

CAPITAL CALLING

My mother was adamant that I go to Delhi for graduation even before the results of the pre-university examinations were declared. She mentioned an Irwin College she had heard about and insisted I should try to secure admission there. My father did not object, but I sensed he would have been happier had I continued my studies in Guwahati. Around this time, Hem Barua, a Member of Parliament (MP) from Assam, was in Dibrugarh and staying with Lalit Hazarika, an advocate friend of my father's. Barua and his wife visited us one evening and told me I could stay in their house in Delhi until my admission.

Thereafter, I boarded a flight at Mohanbari Airport (now called Dibrugarh Airport) for Delhi via Calcutta with an air bag that had all my belongings and a chest of tea which Barua had requested me to carry for him. The chest, weighing about three to four kg, must have been gifted to him by somebody in Assam. I reached Delhi on the evening of the same day, flying between Calcutta and Delhi in a Caravelle jet. In those days, there used to be only one flight in the morning and one in the evening—operated by Indian Airlines—between Calcutta and Delhi.

The next day, I went to Irwin College only to realize that it was a women's college. Both of Barua's sons were studying in

St Stephen's which, I was told, would be a good choice for me. I filled the admission forms and had to face an interview. I also had to plead for relaxation of the lower age limit as I was 15 and a half whereas the minimum age for admission to DU was 16. During the interview, the board members engaged me in very friendly conversation. I recall a person of another nationality telling the others that my marks percentage was 72. That was Dr David Baker, who was to be my history teacher and later my block tutor. He passed away only recently.

Before the list of successful candidates was put up on the notice board, the results of the interview could be queried at the window manned by one Mr Roberts, who later turned out to be St Stephen's one-man army. It was dark when I reached the college. There was a long queue of candidates who had come to find out the interview results. As I advanced in the queue, I came within earshot of the conversations between the students and Mr Roberts. I could hear him telling the four candidates ahead of me, '*Apka nahin hua*' (You have not been selected). When I gave my details, he looked at the papers before him and said, '*Apka ho gaya hai. Kal tak* fees *jama kara dijiye*' (You have been selected, please pay the fees by tomorrow). I asked about my hostel admission. Without looking at me, he said, '*Apka dono ho gaya*' (You have secured both). That was my entry into St Stephen's College in June–July 1970. I opted for BA (Hons) in history.

My residence in college (in St Stephen's, the hostel is referred to as residence) was H7, on the first floor of Allnutt North Block. On the day of my arrival at the residence, a short, fair man with a huge moustache and a white uniform came up to me and introduced himself as Bansi, my 'gyp'. He informed me that he would clean my room every morning, make my bed and otherwise look after me. I was impressed. As soon as Bansi left, a man in the room opposite beckoned me over. He then started asking all kinds of strange questions and told me to do strange things, like sitting on an invisible chair and eating an imaginary meal. I realized that he was ragging me. His name, I gathered, was Shantanu Consul and he was a postgraduate student of history.

St Stephen's was known for ragging, which is prohibited by law today. New students were ragged both physically and mentally. This went on for over a month. After the period of ragging ended, everyone became good friends. My personal experience of ragging, which was considerable, was largely fine.

Soon after joining college, one day many students, including a few from my own state, disappeared from the residence. Later, I found out they had gone underground and joined the Naxalite movement led by Kanu Sanyal. The college had a strong undercurrent of indoctrination in Naxalite philosophy and many impressionable minds succumbed, even to the extent of quitting college and going to far-flung areas of the country. Most of them, of course, returned to the mainstream later and did well in the careers they chose.

BEING A STEPHANIAN

St Stephen's College was a cosmopolitan institution with students from different parts of the country, speaking various languages. Once in college, there were no regional groups. In fact, there were no groups at all as is usual in a college. Everybody was everybody's friend and you could be as friendly with one as with all. The Stephanian bond is very strong and one feels this particularly after leaving college. There were Stephanians working on plantations in Assam, in the civil services, in the judiciary and also in the corporate world. Notwithstanding the diversity in the country, there was always a common bond—*he is from college*. The bond remains undiminished even today. You always have a soft corner for somebody *from college*. My stint in St Stephen's lasted five years—three years in Allnutt North and two in Mukherjee East (for MA). I cherish the memory of each moment of those years.

St Stephen's offered infinite opportunities for growth. Afternoons could be spent participating in any of the events organized by one of the more than 30 societies, ranging from the Shakespeare Society to the Gandhi Study Circle. High tea at the end of the event ensured decent attendance. Sports of all kinds, including tennis and basketball, were available. Eminent names like Professor Mohammed Amin (Senior), Dr Krishna Mohan Shrimali, Professor Dwivedi and Dr Baker embellished the faculty line-up of the history department.

Life in St Stephen's was abundant. The café was a world apart from usual college cafés. Scrambled eggs, buttered toast (if you were broke, the 'slice' would do) and the mutton mince-stuffed aloo tikkas were exemplary. Fifty years on, I still recall the taste. The mess food was also quite good. Breakfast was, as the first meal of the day is supposed to be, excellent. Vegetarians used to get dosas and samosas for breakfast. For non-vegetarians, mutton served in dongas (pots) was available at every meal in unlimited helpings. The after-dinner dessert was a delicious surprise every night.

For my out-of-pocket expenses, I used to get ₹100 every month from home by money order. In those days, a money order took about a week from Assam to Delhi. ₹1 went as a tip to the postman who would hunt you down to deliver the remaining ₹99, at times even after his normal working hours. He once located me in the university coffee house and once even at the university cricket ground during a match.

Delhi of the 1970s was vastly different from the city today. A metered taxi ride cost ₹5 from the university to Connaught Place. The minimum fare of auto-rickshaws when the meter was activated was 50 paise. The Oberoi (then known as the Oberoi Intercontinental) and the Ashok were the only five-star hotels. These places, of course, were beyond our reach. The Oberoi Maidens near Indraprastha (I.P.) College, which was more affordable, also housed a discotheque called Sensation that stayed open until the early hours. For old time's sake, after retirement, on my first visit to Delhi, I stayed at the Maidens.

Notwithstanding the fact that I had spent a good part of my time in St Stephen's in pursuits other than studies, I was the proud recipient of the prestigious Westcott Memorial History Prize that is awarded to the student in the third year BA (Hons) class who has secured the highest marks in the second-year final exams. The credit, however, should really go to my friend, R. Balakrishnan or Bala, IAS (Retd), whose notes I had used for the exams. In the BA final examinations, I secured the highest marks in the college—ensuring me a room in residence for the MA course, a difficult proposition otherwise. The MA classes were held in the Arts Faculty building and students of other colleges enrolled for a particular course would attend the lectures together. So one got to see the DU that lay beyond St Stephen's.

LIFE AT LAW SCHOOL

After completing MA in 1975, I was unable to secure any meaningful employment. I was not yet 21 and so was too young to write the civil services examination. It was at this stage that my father, who had never intervened in my plans for life, suggested I study law and become a lawyer. I agreed because I had no option. I have little recollection of how I secured admission in DU's Faculty of Law, since in those days I think anybody could walk in and gain admission. Thirty years later, when I went for the admission of my son and daughter to the same law faculty, they had to appear in an entrance examination with thousands of others.

However, I do remember very clearly how I secured a bed in Jubilee Hall (the university hostel), which was the first step to securing a room. My entry into Jubilee Hall was initially in a guest room shared by four people. This I managed with the help of Dev Kant Barooah, the then president of the Indian National

Congress (INC). I did not know Barooah, but I hardly hesitated in approaching him to secure accommodation in Jubilee Hall by virtue of being a fellow Assamese. I thought he was duty-bound to help a student from his home state—a completely wrong notion as I was to realize as I grew in life. Barooah, dressed in an impeccable white dhoti and kurta, was seated on a large sofa with white covers in his office at 24, Akbar Road. I do not recall how I secured entry into the room. When I put the request to him, he looked at me, picked up the phone next to him, dialled and said to the person at the other end, 'I am sending a boy to you, please help him'. The person at the other end was V.P. Dutt, pro-vice-chancellor of DU, who was later nominated as a member of the Rajya Sabha (1971–80). I went to meet Dutt immediately and he assured me that he would try his best to help me. Soon, I was offered a place in the guest room from where I shifted to a regular room within a month.

Life in Jubilee Hall was rather different from St Stephen's. Residents lived in a compact two-storeyed building. The cosmopolitan crowd comprised some easygoing and fun-loving students doing law as well as serious students of science and medicine, who were mainly engrossed in their books. Jubilee Hall had a unique practice of allowing 'permanent guests' to stay with a resident. What the expression really meant was that if a resident was willing to share his room with another, he was permitted to do so. The other person acquired the status of a permanent guest but not that of a resident. The expression was so common that its implications in a lighter vein were missed. I never understood the logic of having guests who would never leave. The food was surprisingly good. Jubilee Hall was the only hostel in the university which boasted of a tandoor. Hot tandoori rotis were served to the residents at every meal.

Even today, Delhi University's law faculty stands out as one of the best institutions of legal learning, notwithstanding the mushrooming of innumerable national law schools as well as five-star private law universities with 'imported' faculty. When I studied in the law faculty, nearly five decades ago, we learnt law in the case study format where we dealt with legal principles on the basis of the facts in a case rather than from textbooks. Unlike today, law students were primarily taught and trained to become lawyers, an objective that was ironically the basis for the setting up of the first National Law School of India University (NLSIU) in Bengaluru. The Delhi Law Faculty boasted of eminent names among the faculty, including successful lawyers who taught the first class in the mornings and went to court thereafter. I recollect that many principles of law that came before me either as a lawyer or as a judge, were actually taught in the law faculty. The principles were so firmly ingrained that I had no difficulty in finding solutions. This undoubtedly made my task as a lawyer and a judge easier.

The method of teaching, the fact that some of the faculty were in active legal practice, and the aspirations of the majority of the students to become practising lawyers made them eminently suitable for the legal profession. They were mentally attuned to becoming practising lawyers at least a couple of years prior to joining the Bar. In fact, most looked forward to the day when they would be lawyers. The law faculty, thus, gave a head start to its students as far as legal practice was concerned. No wonder many of the country's successful lawyers, including several very prominent names in the Supreme Court Bar, are products of the institution. Many High Court judges all over the country are law faculty alumni. I recall that at one point of time, six judges of the Supreme Court were Delhi law faculty alumni.

While at the law faculty, I also appeared for the civil services examination and qualified for the interview. All went well until I reached the last person on the interview panel—Dr Sarup Singh, former vice-chancellor of DU. I gave a reply that made Dr Singh considerably agitated. I sensed that I had been eliminated; I was proved right when the results were declared. On my next attempt at the examination, I qualified for the interview for selection to the Indian Police Service (IPS). I was uninterested in that and skipped the interview. Soon after, I was back home in Assam—armed with a law degree and ready for battle in court.

Three

FROM CLASSROOM TO COURTROOM

In the summer of 1978, after writing the final-year LLB paper, I arrived back in Guwahati. By then my father had become a minister and naturally, I stayed with him in the ministerial bungalow. He told me two things. First, that I should move out as quickly as possible. He said he owned a plot of land in Guwahati, the precise location of which he was unsure about except for the fact that it was along Zoo Narengi Road, next to the residence of one Dr Mukti Gogoi. He promised me ₹50,000 to construct a small house on the plot. He insisted that I begin construction immediately and complete it as soon as possible. Second, he would take me to the most successful lawyer in Guwahati, J.P. Bhattacharjee, and request him to take me on as his junior.

Within a few days, I had located the plot and an architect-cum-engineer, Tulen Konwar. He was extremely helpful and work commenced for the construction of a three-room, single-storey house of about 700 sq. ft in a corner of the relatively large plot of a bigha (1,600 sq. yards). Alongside, J.P. Bhattacharjee, who was then and for years later one of the most renowned lawyers of Guwahati, told me that I could come to his chamber/office every evening and read books. This was his way of saying that he had agreed to take me on.

J.P. Bhattacharjee's first junior was S.N. Medhi, who later became law minister of Assam. He was an excellent draftsman. One day, he complained to J.P. Bhattacharjee that the judge before whom he was arguing a rent matter was being troublesome. The judge had asked Medhi the meaning of bamboo. The question of law involved was whether a structure made of bamboo was a permanent structure so as to entitle the tenant/occupant to protection from eviction. Medhi said that despite his best efforts, he was unable to elucidate the meaning of bamboo to the judge's satisfaction! J.P. Bhattacharjee instructed Medhi to say, when the hearing resumed the following morning, 'My Lord, bamboo is what your Lordship is giving me' [in Guwahati 'giving bamboo' means giving trouble]. I believe the strategy worked. On another occasion, Medhi was moving a writ petition before a particular judge. He had no case but told his junior that he was optimistic as on the morning of that day he had helped the judge get an LPG refill cylinder (cylinders were in short supply). The judge had no gas to cook food in his house. When the matter was called, the judge told Medhi that he had no case and the petition deserved to be dismissed. Strange are the ways of the judicial system!

Having just entered the profession and being part of the team of J.P. Bhattacharjee, reputed to be a very hard taskmaster, complying with the multiple demands suddenly being made on me became difficult. I lived with my father in the state capital at Dispur. In the mornings, I would visit the construction site at Zoo Narengi Road. Thereafter, I would go to court. In the evenings, I would go to J.P. Bhattacharjee's office around 6–6.30 p.m. and be there until closing time, which was around 10.30–11 p.m. My mode of travel was public transport. I would change into my advocate's dress after visiting the construction site at a cousin's house near the High Court from where I walked to the Court. My change of clothes post-court was in the same house. My journey home and thereafter to and from J.P. Bhattacharjee's office late in the evening was by bus. I remember at least one occasion when I fell off the bus and hurt myself as it was overcrowded.

The relation between a senior advocate and his junior/juniors in the Gauhati Bar was then a little different from what it is in Delhi now. Juniors were not paid salaries, but would receive a fee for every case in which he/she was engaged. The bond between the senior and the junior over a period of time used to become exceedingly strong and juniors did not leave a senior's association until they had put in several years of practice and managed to build their own practice. J.P. Bhattacharjee's office was a unique example. In addition to briefing by other counsel, clients would drop into the office of their own accord. Such clients were given over by J.P. Bhattacharjee to one of the many juniors (usually by rotation). The client would become the junior's client. All work pertaining to the case including drafting (if a case was made out) had to be done by the junior and only after the draft was prepared was it put up before J.P. Bhattacharjee. In between, the junior could always consult him. The clients never conferred or dealt with J.P. Bhattacharjee directly in any manner. All monetary transactions and receipt of instructions, papers and the like were handled by the juniors.

Most offices of senior advocates in Guwahati, at that time, were not only places of legal work, they were also schools where professional ethics, principles, etiquette and manners were discussed and inculcated. J.P. Bhattacharjee's office was always considered an epitome in this regard. No wonder that office produced at least four judges of the Supreme Court—Dr Justice Mukundakam Sharma, Justice Amitava Roy, Justice Hrishikesh Roy and me.

COURTROOM CHRONICLES

My first day in court was extraordinarily pleasant and memorable. Many senior members of the Bar and other successful lawyers came forward to compliment me on my choice of the legal profession and found time to talk to me. They did not do this because I was the law minister's son. I later found out from others my age who had joined the Bar around that time that such welcoming gestures were also extended to them. I understood this to be part of the Gauhati High Court convention. Obviously, such good practices had to end as the number of new entrants to the Bar began to increase and in time, reached deluge-like proportions. But it was very much in evidence in those days. In sharp contrast was the absence of any welcome or felicitation by the Gauhati High Court Bar on my becoming a Supreme Court judge in 2012 or the first-ever CJI from the Northeast in October 2018. Not once did the Gauhati High Court Bar invite me to its premises during this period. This is odd and makes me cherish all the more the welcome I received in 1978 on joining the Bar in Guwahati.

On my very first day in court, J.P. Bhattacharjee moved two writ petitions before Court No. 1, presided over by the then Chief Justice, C.M. Lodha. One was a labour matter. I did not understand much except that both the petitions were summarily dismissed—a rare occurrence for J.P. Bhattacharjee, I was told. Yet he took the dismissals with grace, with a notable absence of rancour.

Later that day, I went to Court No. 4 where a single Bench of Justice K.M. Lahiri was in session. Justice Lahiri had joined the Bench after great success in the Bar, particularly as a criminal lawyer. Once again, I did not understand much of the proceedings except that there was some discussion on 'thumbs up'. Seeing a new face in court, Justice Lahiri called me to the front of the courtroom and told me that I was being appointed the amicus curiae in the case. I did not know what the expression meant. Later, comprehending the purport of my appointment and on reading the case papers, I learnt that the matter pertained to a claim for compensation by a workman under the Workmen's Compensation Act, 1923, for an injury resulting in the loss of a thumb.

Justice Lahiri had a great sense of humour. One day, while sitting on a division Bench in Court No. 2, he noticed that the second judge had fallen asleep, even as the arguments were on. Justice Lahiri quietly sent for his usher and started to rise from his seat. The second judge woke up and began to fumble for his shoes. But, importantly, everything was in good humour.

Justice B.N. Sarma, appointed an ad hoc judge under Article 224A of the Constitution of India after completion of his tenure, used to hold court on the first floor of the High Court building. Requests for adjournment were met with Justice Sarma's retort that he had been appointed to decide cases, not adjourn them. Appointment of such judges under Article 224A could be a solution to deal with the huge pendency of cases in our courts. As Chief Justice, I had made a similar recommendation to the law minister to tackle the ever-increasing back-log. The suggestion to the government was that ad hoc judges should be appointed on a selective basis, keeping in mind the previous performance and track record of the judge and not as a matter of course. The proposal is yet to be approved or perhaps it has not found favour with the government.

My greatest satisfaction as a lawyer was the help that I could render to my father outside the court when he faced a disqualification under the Tenth Schedule of the Constitution in 1994. The proceedings were initiated at the instance of the then CM of Assam, Hiteswar Saikia, who had faced a no-confidence motion in the House. The Speaker had asked members supporting the motion to stand. My father remained seated. The Speaker then asked members against the motion to rise. My father remained seated as, according to him, he had already indicated his stance by remaining seated the first time.

When my father was served a notice seeking disqualification, he challenged it in the Gauhati High Court.

P.K. Goswami, a senior advocate and a legendary figure in the Assam Bar, represented my father. Amitava Roy (later a judge of the Supreme Court) and Hrishikesh Roy (at present a judge of the apex court), who were then members of the Gauhati Bar, assisted Goswami. I stayed away from the hearings to avert any embarrassment. One person who often sat through the proceedings was Himanta Biswa Sarma, then a young lawyer, who later became CM Sarma, around that time, had joined the Congress under Saikia after severing all links with the AASU with which he, I am told, was closely associated during the 'foreigners movement'. I believe his presence in court was on account of keen academic interest, much of which he displayed when he had briefed me in several income tax cases involving a lottery baron. I feel he would have been a successful lawyer had he chosen to remain in the profession.

The disqualification proceedings against my father dragged on and eventually the 1996 elections to the Assembly rendered them futile. In our legal system, prolongation of litigation or early resolution are conflicting interests that dominate any legal proceeding.

ON THE PERSONAL FRONT

My house on Zoo Narengi Road was more or less complete in record time. I had spent ₹63,000 of my father's money. I remember the figure because I had kept accounts. When I moved into the house, the electricity connection was yet to be provided and so I lived without power for about two weeks. There was no running water either and a ring well was the source of water for the house. In fact, running water came to the house just before my marriage in 1981 as my mother insisted that her daughter-in-law should have this minimal comfort.

I got married to Rupanjali on 9 October 1981. She had been born and brought up in Shillong where her father had worked for the Assam government. The family had shifted to Guwahati after 1978. After the wedding, we went to Darjeeling, the Queen of the

Hills, which was bright and sunny in October. We stayed in the West Bengal Tourist Lodge which was surprisingly well-kept and served excellent food. I remember visiting the nooks and cranies of Darjeeling; the evening walks on the Mall which was never too crowded. There were several good British-era eateries on the Mall, since Darjeeling had been the summer getaway of the British.

My return to work after marriage was almost immediate. For Rupanjali, the days were periods of endless waiting. With the passage of time, my return from J.P. Bhattacharjee's office grew more and more delayed as work increased. My next-door neighbour Dr Mukti Gogoi used to joke with his friends that the whistle of the pressure cooker cooking dinner in Ranjan's house would sound when he was waking up in the morning. Dr Gogoi, of course, was a very early riser. Around this time, I also managed to acquire a scooter out of my earnings. Going to the court and to the office became easier, though my wife was very reluctant to travel with me on the scooter.

In 1982, we rejoiced at the birth of our son, Raktim. Life continued at a steady pace until October 1984 when, on the eve of our family holiday in Kathmandu, I had my first attack of acute pancreatitis. I was taken to the All India Institute of Medical Sciences (AIIMS) and remained there for a long time. I had to undergo a complex surgery. However, I recovered which, I am told, is rare. Very soon, I was back to work and raring ahead with vigour and enthusiasm.

Rashmi, our daughter, was born in December 1985. Both my children went to school in Guwahati—Raktim to Don Bosco and Rashmi to St Mary's. Raktim completed graduation from Christ College (now University) in Bengaluru, while Rashmi graduated from I.P. College, Delhi, after two years at St Bede's College, Shimla, for plus two. Both graduated in law from the Delhi Faculty of Law, my alma mater. Both are happily married and well-settled in life. They have been my strongest supporters during every chapter of my life. They are the ones, besides their respective spouses, to whom

I turn when in doubt. In hindsight, I feel that their upbringing was a little too strict; often, I feel that they deserved much more than what they received. Today, I cannot give them anything for they have everything.

Ranjan Gogoi

Four

ELEVATION TO THE BENCH

Sometime in the early part of May 1993, I received a call from the Principal Private Secretary (PPS) to the Chief Justice of the High Court, asking me to meet Chief Justice U.L. Bhat at his residence. During the meeting, Justice Bhat conveyed to me his decision to recommend my name for appointment as a judge of the Gauhati High Court. I was not yet 39 years old at that time. Justice Bhat told me that though the preferred age for appointment as a High Court judge was 45 years, he had spoken to the then CJI, Justice M.N. Venkatachaliah, about my case, and the latter had informed him there could always be exceptions.

Justice Bhat left Guwahati on transfer to the Madhya Pradesh High Court as the Chief Justice in December 1993. One or two evenings prior to his departure, I made a courtesy call on him at his residence. During the course of our conversation, Justice Bhat, on his own, informed me that my case for elevation as a High Court judge had not been fairly dealt with and that the CM of Manipur, after having initially agreed to the proposal, had later objected on grounds of my age.[2] Justice Bhat said that all the other states had no objection to the proposal and further that the change of stance

---

[2]Appointment to the Gauhati High Court required consultation of all the seven Northeastern states as the High Court was the common High Court.

on the part of the CM of Manipur was at the instance of Hiteswar Saikia, the then CM of Assam, who happened to be a political rival of my father's. At that point in time, my father, though in the Saikia Cabinet, belonged to the dissenters' camp.

I left Justice Bhat's residence after wishing him the very best. I was disappointed and dejected not so much at not becoming a judge but because of the way the matter had been dealt with. Faced with the solitary opposition offered by one state out of seven, CJI Venkatachaliah thought it fit not to process the file, though he had earlier suggested to Justice Bhat that exceptions to the age requirement could always be made. Those were the pre-collegium days. When I view the matter in retrospect, what I find novel about the episode is that at no point of time between the date when the proposal of appointment was mooted by the Chief Justice of the High Court, i.e. May 1993, till the date I called on the Chief Justice prior to his departure from Guwahati (sometime in December 1993), was the matter of my proposed appointment and the progress of the case thought fit for any kind of discussion between the recommendee and the Chief Justice or any other person. Today, casual and informal discussions with regard to progress of files relating to appointments are a common affair and what exactly is happening to a particular case recommended for appointment is an open secret.

After this 'fiasco', I returned to practice. Luck was on my side: my practice grew in reasonable measure. I started charging higher fees; yet there was no dearth of cases and clients. I managed to build up a reasonable reserve of funds and this continued till sometime in October 1999 when the then Chief Justice of the High Court, Justice Brijesh Kumar, sought my consent to recommend my name, once again, for elevation as a High Court judge. On the offer being made by the Chief Justice this time, I debated in my mind whether after the 'fiasco' of 1993 I should give my consent. Finally, I did so. The Chief Justice told me that he was aware of the fact that I was not yet 45 and that he would be sending the recommendation once I crossed that age, which was to be on 18 November 1999.

Prospective High Court judges of today complain about delays in the matter of appointment. In fact, such delays have been perceived to be one of the major reasons for the reluctance of members of the Bar to opt for becoming High Court judges. Such delays have also been adversely commented upon by 'public spirited' and 'conscientious citizens' as being one of the major drawbacks of the appointment system in the higher judiciary. The position two decades earlier was no different. This is evident from what happened to the recommendations that were sent by Chief Justice Brijesh Kumar in November 1999. Five names (mine being the last at serial no. 5) were recommended. The names were arranged in order of date of enrolment at the Bar. Three out of the five recommendees were appointed judges of the Gauhati High Court on 15 November 2000 (after one year). The names of Justice Amitava Roy (sl. no. 4) and myself (sl. no. 5) were kept pending on the grounds that the slots against which our names had been recommended were earmarked for elevation from the district judiciary. Ram Jethmalani was then the Union law minister. Soon thereafter, there was a change in the Union Council of Ministers and Arun Jaitley became the new law minister. He re-examined the file and found that one Bar vacancy was available to be filled up. Accordingly, both the names, i.e. Justice Roy's and mine, were sent to the Supreme Court Collegium. During the process of consultation, the consultee judge[3], Justice S.N. Phukan, took the view that my name should be considered first, keeping in view my exposure to all-round work, practice and income. This information is based on the official records. Accordingly, my name was recommended though I was at sl. no. 5. In January 2001, I was

---

[3]A consultee judge of the Supreme Court is one who has worked in the High Court in respect of which the recommendations made are being considered by the Supreme Court Collegium. Such a judge is required to be consulted by the CJI with regard to the name(s) recommended.

informed that my name had been cleared for appointment.

The warrant of appointment was signed by the president of India on 23 February 2001 and reached Guwahati on 24 February. The Chief Justice of the Gauhati High Court, Justice N.C. Jain, was holding court in Aizawl, Mizoram, the seat of one of the seven permanent Benches of the High Court. In those days, Aizawl could be reached from Guwahati only via Calcutta and that too after an overnight stay in that city. This was necessary in either direction of the journey. Lengpui Airport at Aizawl has a tabletop runway and that too of the minimal length required for Boeing 737 operations. A Boeing 737 used to service Aizawl from Calcutta three days a week. Aizawl had very unpredictable weather. I was told that pilots (at that time) insisted on visual sighting of the runway before landing. Flight operations to and from Aizawl, therefore, were uncertain and aircrafts often used to return to Calcutta after hovering over Lengpui.

As luck would have it, Justice Jain's flight out of Aizawl was cancelled on successive days and he was unable to administer the oath of office to me. He called me from Aizawl to suggest that the senior most judge available in Guwahati (principal seat) could administer the oath. I refused, saying that I would wait for the oath to be administered by the Chief Justice. Justice Jain tried to convince me that the delay could impact my all-India seniority which could have an adverse impact at a later point in time. I said I did not consider this a good enough reason for the oath to be administered by anybody else other than the Chief Justice of the High Court. Eventually, Justice Jain managed to reach Calcutta from Aizawl on 27 February, and then took the morning flight to Guwahati the next day.

It was only thereafter that at 2 p.m. on 28 February Justice Jain administered the oath of office to me as a judge of the Gauhati High Court.

My mother, mother-in-law and a host of relatives, friends and well-wishers were present at the ceremony. I missed my father, who had passed away a few years earlier in 1998 at the age of 73. He was not ailing in any manner and it was after a full dinner that he complained of uneasiness in breathing. At midnight, he was taken to the Assam Medical College and Hospital at Dibrugarh. He passed away while actually conversing with my mother. Apparently, dawn was breaking and he was telling her that she, not being an early riser, was not used to the sound of morning bird call. Immediately after this affectionate jibe, he stopped speaking and breathing.

My senior, J.P. Bhattacharjee, who had by then left Guwahati to settle in Calcutta, came especially for the occasion. He was proud to see his favourite junior (as I came to be known) taking oath. My wife took good care of the guests, taking time to speak to all who had come to wish us. In the evening, the family had a quiet dinner in a popular Chinese restaurant. Thereafter, I had to attend to the case files that had already arrived, little realizing that I would be doing just that for the next 20 years.

INTERACTIONS OF JURISPRUDENCE AND GEOGRAPHY

A judge of the Gauhati High Court in 2001 was a judge of the High Court of seven states i.e. Assam, Nagaland, Meghalaya, Manipur, Tripura, Arunachal Pradesh and Mizoram. Later Meghalaya, Manipur and Tripura had separate High Courts and today, judges of the Gauhati High Court serve four states, namely, Assam, Nagaland, Mizoram and Arunachal Pradesh. When I became a judge in 2001, the principal seat of the High Court was (and it still is) at Guwahati and the rest of the six states had permanent Benches.

A very complex administrative process was involved in the sitting arrangement for judges in the outlying Benches. A permanent Bench had one permanent judge but actual sitting on the Benches was done by judges going from one seat/state to another by rotation. There was an institutional requirement for frequent changes in the sitting arrangements in the outlying Benches, namely, to enable the litigants to avail of the remedy of filing Letters Patent Appeals (LPAs).[4] Unless the judge who has been in a particular outlying Bench is moved out and another two judges brought in, no appeal can be heard. Sitting arrangements, therefore, used to change every two weeks and though posted at the principal seat, I was required to go to one of the outlying Benches for at least two weeks every month.

Temporary sitting arrangements as well as permanent postings of judges in the outlying Benches are the sole prerogative of the Chief Justice of the Gauhati High Court. A permanent posting in any one of the outlying Benches or any change in such posting works as the transfer of a judge from one state to another. While transfer of High Court judges is made by the Union government on the recommendation of the five-member Collegium of the Supreme Court, a change of posting in an outlying Bench of the Gauhati High Court, which also works as a transfer, is done by the Chief Justice of the High Court acting unilaterally.

The arrangements for visiting judges in the outlying Benches were by and large good but in one or two stations the situation was not very conducive to comfortable living and good work. The second, third and fourth bungalows for visiting judges in Manipur, when I first went there, were far from satisfactory. As I had gone with some senior judges, I was assigned bungalow no. 3 or no. 4. I had one look at the interiors of the bungalow and felt uncomfortable. I called up one of the senior members of the Registry in the principal Bench to explore alternative places of stay. He advised me to adjust, which I did. Gradually, over a period of time, not only did we (my wife always accompanied me to all the outlying Benches at great personal discomfort) get used to things, but things themselves improved. Later in my career as a judge of the Gauhati High Court,

---

[4]Letter Patent Appeal (LPA) is an appeal by a petitioner against a decision of a single judge to another Bench of the same court.

I found the living arrangements for visiting judges at all stations reasonably satisfactory.

Some of the cases in the Gauhati High Court had peculiar features. The Code of Civil Procedure, 1908 and the Code of Criminal Procedure, 1973 were excluded from application in the hill states where the Rules for administration of justice framed by the British Government held the field. Cases had to be decided in accordance with justice, equity and good conscience and not by strict adherence to the mandate of the procedure provided under the codes. Cases from tribal areas had to be decided by the application of customary laws, on which texts of law were rare. Settlement of disputes by the panchayats and by a process of conciliation was usual with limited rights of appeal to higher forums.

In many states like Nagaland, Arunachal Pradesh and Mizoram and the hill districts of Assam i.e. Karbi Anglong and North Cachar, the judiciary was yet to be separated from the executive. Ministers wrote the Annual Confidential Reports (ACRs) of the judicial officers. Pressure from the executive to write judicial orders in a particular manner, therefore, was not unknown. All these posed major challenges to the judges of the High Court both on the judicial as well as the administrative side. When the judges of the Gauhati High Court visited the National Judicial Academy (NJA) at Bhopal and the peculiar features of the justice delivery system in the Northeast were narrated, it came as a surprise to the brother judges in other High Courts of the country. They were blissfully unaware of the prevailing scenario in the Northeast.

There was a considerable amount of work in the outlying Benches at Agartala (Tripura) and Imphal (Manipur). Two or three judges, therefore, used to be posted in these two stations. Kohima (Nagaland), Aizawl (Mizoram) and Itanagar (Arunachal Pradesh) had few cases and usually one judge was made available in each of these three Benches. At times, two judges used to go to these places to hear LPAs that may have accumulated. While Agartala, Imphal and Aizawl were accessible by air, reaching Kohima and Itanagar involved a long and arduous road journey (10 hours). We had a Chief Justice who prepared a sitting plan showing the presence of a judge in Itanagar on one day and in Aizawl the next which was impossible whether the judge travelled by road (700 km) or by air. Therefore, the first thing that a Chief Justice of the Gauhati High Court needs to know is the geography of his jurisdiction before familiarizing himself with the unique laws administered in the Northeastern region of the country.

While work could keep a visiting judge busy in stations like Agartala and Imphal, life used to get monotonous in Kohima and Aizawl where Benches had to rise before lunch. Post-lunch sessions were rare. In winter, 4.15 p.m., which was the official rising time for the High Court, could be quite late as not only dusk would have set in, but life itself would be coming to a close for the day. This was/is particularly true for Kohima and Imphal where shutters come down by 5–6 p.m. in the evening, perhaps as part of the lifestyle carried over from the troubled years of extremist violence. In this kind of situation, a two-week sitting in any of the outlying Benches could prove to be a punishment for a judge who had lived his life in a relatively bigger place like Guwahati. For judges with young children who had not yet completed their education or with aged parents, going to an outlying Bench was a solitary and lonely exercise. In contrast, Guwahati (principal seat) had plenty of work. In my days, between thirty to forty thousand cases were pending in the principal Bench at Guwahati, calling for the urgent attention of the judges.

During my tenure, cases involving schoolteachers of Assam created major problems. A huge number of cases filed and pending in the High Court, at any given time, pertained to the education department. In a state where there was no or little industry, appointment of teachers became an industry in itself. The bulk of these cases pertained to illegal appointments and consequential nonpayment of salary. Appointments were made against non-existent posts, far exceeding the number of posts for which recruitment was advertised. Each incumbent held a valid appointment order signed by the same competent authority and it was very difficult to distinguish one from the other. This created problems in the matter of payment of salaries as the budgetary allocation was against the specified number of posts advertised but appointments had far exceeded that number. I found that in many cases the problem of illegal/excess appointment was sought to be brushed under the carpet by resorting to payment of salary by rotation, namely, monthly salaries were rotated amongst teachers where salary would be paid to all every alternate month. Excess appointments of teachers against non-existent posts in government-aided schools also gave rise to what came to be known as the concept of 'dropped teachers'—teachers who could not be regularized at the time of regularization of services of the employees of an erstwhile aided school taken over by the state. This exercise in Assam was known as 'provincialization' of schools.

As there were a large number of cases on the same issues pertaining to the education department, I resorted to the process of 'bunching' or 'grouping of cases.' This resulted in a situation where one judgment of the Court would take care of several hundred similar cases. Bunching/grouping of cases was extended to other pending cases wherein same or similar questions were in issue. This resulted in a sharp increase in disposal of cases by the Gauhati High Court and a corresponding decline in the number of pending cases—a situation which every court seeks to achieve.

In 2004–05, the Government of Assam undertook an exercise involving appointment of about 6,000 police constables. Each district was allotted a specified number of posts and the selection was held district-wise. A group of writ petitions came to be filed, challenging the selection in practically all the districts. The cases were assigned to my Bench by the Chief Justice. The consequential judicial exercise was a mammoth one, requiring scrutiny of a large number of documents. Sitting on a single Bench, I decided the matter, upholding the selections in some districts while setting them aside in several other districts.[5] The matter was carried in appeal before the division Bench and dismissed.[6] Eventually, the Supreme Court reversed the judgment and the selection and consequential appointments in all districts were upheld.

While the matter was pending before me, a preposterous and unpleasant incident occurred. My mother, who was then nearly 70 years old and lived all alone in our family home in Dibrugarh, received a telephone call from the then CM, Tarun Gogoi, requesting her to meet him in Guwahati. The distance between Dibrugarh and Guwahati is considerable; while a road journey takes about 10 hours, it is an hour by flight. My mother, who otherwise was fit, mentioned the matter to me and asked whether she should undertake the journey. I told her, in good faith, that it is an honour to be invited by the CM and she must not refuse. She, therefore, bought a ticket and came to Guwahati and met the CM at his official residence the next day. During the course of the meeting, to her utter shock, the CM requested her to speak to me to secure a favourable order in the 'constables' case', namely, that the selection and appointment of constables in all districts be upheld. Perhaps noticing her discomfiture, Gogoi reportedly told her that though he personally valued judicial independence, it was at the instance of the 'young boys' (young ministers holding positions and portfolios of importance) that he had been compelled to speak to her on the issue. My mother left the chief minister's residence, telling him that she had no control over me in official matters and that she could not comply with the request. When she informed me about what had transpired, I was disappointed as I had held the person concerned in very high esteem.

---

[5]When a High Court judge sits alone, the sitting is called a single Bench sitting.
[6]When two judges sit together, the sitting is called a division Bench sitting.

Apart from this solitary instance and another involving the NRC matter (mentioned later), my tenure of almost two decades as a judge, including my term as the CJI, has been free from any kind of external/extraneous requests or influence. It was a dream run where all that mattered was my conscience and its dictates to do or not do something in a particular manner. I believe this is so in the case of most judges and that the 'freedom to think and decide' is the singular attraction that inspires the best talent in the Bar to join the Bench. Such an environment, therefore, needs to be nurtured and even consciously cultivated because a truly independent judge answerable to himself and to nobody else is a national asset. Every citizen, whether he/she is in politics, business, industry or any other kind of public life, and above all, the vast multitude of the country's population that lives below an artificially drawn poverty line, need 'good' judges to secure their life, liberty and property and to oversee their welfare.

A NEW CHAPTER

My transfer to the Punjab and Haryana High Court was on the basis of a 'Horizontal Transfer Policy' that the then CJI, S.H. Kapadia, had thought fit to introduce. Under that policy, senior judges of a High Court in line to become Chief Justices were to be transferred to the High Court of which he/she would eventually become the Chief Justice. Such transfers were to be made a couple of months ahead of the due date, i.e. the vacancy in the office of Chief Justice of the High Court occurring, so as to enable the person concerned to acquaint himself/herself with the High Court which he/she would eventually head as the Chief Justice. Justice Arun Mishra and I were the first two judges who came to be transferred under that policy. Justice Mishra was transferred from the Madhya Pradesh High Court to the Rajasthan High Court to eventually become the Chief Justice. Justice Kapadia's letter informing me about the said decision had a very interesting last sentence where he made it clear that he was not seeking my views on the merits of the 'Horizontal Transfer Policy', but was only seeking my consent to go on transfer to the High Court mentioned in the letter. I came to know of this development while I was on a holiday and returning from Nainital to Delhi by road.

I readily agreed to go to Chandigarh and was sworn in as a judge of the Punjab and Haryana High Court on 9 September 2010. I was judge number three in an otherwise 'big' High Court having a sanctioned strength of 75 and a working strength of over 50.

Justice Mukul Mudgal was, at that point of time, the Chief Justice of the Punjab and Haryana High Court. Like him, the previous two Chief Justices were also from Delhi—Justice D.K. Jain and Justice T.S. Thakur (his parent High Court was Jammu and Kashmir but he was working in the Delhi High Court). I was therefore surprised at being chosen to head the Punjab and Haryana High Court. On the very evening of my arrival in Chandigarh, Chief Justice Mudgal met me. He was most kind and affectionate. He had a booklet containing the names and photographs of all the serving judges, which he handed over to me to enable me to familiarize myself with my colleagues. He also indicated that a Collegium exercise was due and that I should acquaint myself with the working of the lawyers at the earliest. We had a quiet dinner, thereafter.

A courtroom/hall in the original building of the High Court was allotted to me and land acquisition appeals and criminal appeals were assigned to the Bench, which I shared with Justice Rajan Gupta (now a senior judge of the Patna High Court). Justice Gupta, whom I call Rajan, was again very kind and understanding and though I was several years his senior in age as well as in service, I took his guidance and advice with regard to the practices, procedures and traditions of the new High Court to which I had been transferred. The Bar was extremely polite and cooperative and went out of its way to make me comfortable. Never ever did I have a moment of discomfort with my colleagues on the Bench or the members of the Bar.

Sometime in October 2010 my 'consent' to be appointed Chief Justice of the High Court was formally taken. It was, therefore, expected that my appointment as the regular Chief Justice would be made soon after the retirement of Justice Mudgal on 4 January 2011, on which date I was appointed Acting Chief Justice. As the regular appointment was not forthcoming, enquiries were made and I gathered that the file recommending my name for appointment was not 'traceable'. I was dumbfounded and remembered an oft-repeated story of an appointment file being recovered from the inside of a sofa on which the law minister used to sit. The sofa was being repaired after the minister's exit from office.

Mercifully, the file recommending my name was located and my appointment as the regular Chief Justice was made on 11 February. I was sworn in on 12 February by the Governor of Haryana, Jagannath Pahadia. The oath of office is always administered to the Chief Justice by the senior most governor of the two states, i.e. Punjab and Haryana, which is serviced by a common High Court. Between the recovery/discovery of the file and the date of notification, there was sufficient time for everybody in the family to come from Assam to Chandigarh to be present at the oath-taking ceremony. My mother and my mother-in-law, along with a host of friends and relatives, were present. Several lawyers from Assam also attended the ceremony.

After taking the oath as the Chief Justice of the High Court, things were not much different as I had already been working as the Acting Chief Justice since January that year. In fact, though Acting Chief Justices do not sit in the chamber of the regular Chief Justice and work from the first court, I was made to do so by an 'order' of Justice Mudgal which had the support of all the judges of the High Court. Such was the kindness, affection and respect shown to me by all the judges. I looked forward to a meaningful tenure as the Chief Justice. However, that was not to be.

On 27 April, Justice Jasti Chelameswar, who was then the Chief Justice of the Kerala High Court, had come to Chandigarh to meet some of his friends in the city. He had been my Chief Justice in the Gauhati High Court for almost three years. We had planned a dinner in the evening and, in fact, my wife had left to meet Mrs Chelameswar while I was still in court. That day, I sat in court for about 15–20 minutes beyond court hours, as I wanted to complete a judgment that was being dictated in open court. After completion of work, I felt a little abdominal discomfort. I went home, the discomfort became acute and soon I was in pain. I informed Justice A.K. Goel, my neighbour and the senior most judge. He rushed to my residence. I was advised to go to the Postgraduate Institute of Medical Education and Research (PGIMER), Chandigarh. Within an hour, I was in a deleterious state with acute pain.

After some tests and scans, I was told that I had had an attack of acute pancreatitis (this was the second attack). After spending a day or two in PGI, for 'better management' I decided to go to Sir Ganga Ram Hospital, New Delhi, under the care of Dr Samiran Nundy, who had earlier treated me while he was working in AIIMS. The then CM of Haryana, Bhupinder Singh Hooda, who had come to visit me in the hospital (Parkash Singh Badal, the then CM of Punjab, had also come to the hospital), offered the services of the state aircraft to fly me to Delhi which, in the given circumstances, I gratefully accepted. I got admitted to Sir Ganga Ram Hospital on 29 April. Thereafter, on several occasions, I was discharged only to be readmitted. Finally, I was discharged on 22 July.

Without finding any fault with anybody, I must confess that at the time of leaving Sir Ganga Ram Hospital, I was not fit to be discharged. I could barely walk and find my bearings. Fortunately, I opted to go back to Chandigarh instead of staying in Delhi. Within two days or so of reaching Chandigarh, I was admitted once again in the PGI. Dr Sanjay Jain of internal medicine, Dr L. Kaman of surgery and Dr R. Kochhar of gastroenterology constituted the medical team. I was seriously unwell and faced several life-threatening days in the ICU. I remained in hospital till 9 November and resumed work as the Chief Justice the next day. By that time, I had exhausted all my earned leave and was on half-pay leave, meaning I was drawing half of my pay.

My constant companion during the period of over six months of my illness was my wife. Every night, she slept in the hospital and went home in the morning for an hour or so to freshen up. At all other times, she was by my side. My son and daughter, both of whom were based in Delhi, would come to Chandigarh on weekends and would often stay over at the cost of their professional work.

My first day in court, after resumption of work, amounted to admitting two murder appeals. I had become so weak that on the previous day, I travelled to the chamber of the Chief Justice and climbed the three steps that lead to the podium of the Court. This was for the purpose of testing myself; if I would be able to climb the three steps to take my seat in the Court the following day. I regained strength and confidence slowly, and in no time, I felt like my former self, ready to take on the world and its challenges.

In this endeavour, I received a great deal of help from a remarkable person named Rajbir Singh, who was everybody's man Friday in the High Court. A protocol assistant attached to the office of the Chief Justice by designation, Rajbir had no fixed hours or areas of duty; from driving the car, managing the Chief Justice's establishment, working on the computer to liaisoning with all kinds of authorities, he did everything. Rajbir enjoyed the confidence of successive Chief Justices. Another unique quality of the man was his ability to maintain confidentiality. On each day of my prolonged illness, he was around like a shadow, always available at all hours of the day and night.

◆

A Collegium meeting of the Punjab and Haryana High Court was conducted by Justice Mudgal shortly after my joining as judge number three. Nearly a dozen names from the Bar were recommended. This was after a very long time and most of the names were cleared and the incumbents appointed. As the Chief Justice, I had sent one or two lists consisting of about 10 names. The persons recommended were relatively young. The majority of the names did not get cleared due to the remarks made by one of the consultee judges of the Supreme Court who, in the process of consultation with the CJI, mentioned that he did not recollect the persons recommended. Obviously he could not have, as by that time several years had elapsed since he had left the Punjab and Haryana High Court.

A similar fate awaited the list sent by Justice Arjan Kumar Sikri as the Chief Justice and thereafter by Justice Sanjay Kishan Kaul. Similar remarks were made by the same consultee judge in his letter(s) to the CJI in respect of the names recommended by Justices Sikri and Kaul. The total number of persons who had to be excluded because of the stance of the particular Supreme Court judge would roughly be about 15 to 20. If that many persons considered eligible by three Chief Justices of the High Court get excluded because a consultee judge in the Supreme Court, who had worked in the High Court a decade earlier, fails to recognize the names, the next Chief Justice has to fall back on names which are, naturally, not the first choice. This adversely affects the quality of the Bench.

One day, an unknown senior lawyer appeared before me on behalf of the Tatas in connection with a housing project that had got involved in litigation because of the proximity of the construction to the Sukhna lake. The gentleman wanted an early hearing and did not feel the date suggested by the Bench was early enough. As he was requesting an earlier date, I asked if he wanted a date or a hearing. I told him that if he wanted a date, he could have any date but if he wanted a hearing it would be on the date that the Court would give him. My Court Master, a seasoned man, whispered to me that the lawyer in question was Mukul Rohatgi. Unacquainted with the Delhi legal circle, I replied, 'So what?' as I had only vaguely heard the name. This is when I first came across Rohatgi whom I got to see and hear practically every day in the Supreme Court for over seven years. I acknowledge him as one of the finest lawyers of the country with a razor-sharp mind and excellence in court craft besides being always polite and courteous to the Bench.

In the Punjab and Haryana High Court, sitting commences at 10 a.m. whereas 10.30 a.m. was (is) the time of commencement of sittings in the Gauhati High Court. Most High Courts commence work at 10.30 a.m. Since the pre-lunch session in the Punjab and Haryana High Court used to be three hours instead of two-and-a-half hours, as in most High Courts, the judges used to break for a cup of coffee at about 11.45–12 noon. Curiously, many of the Benches did not resume work and after lunch,[7] the judges used to go home. As the Chief Justice, I tried to discourage this practice. My success, however, was limited as the coffee break had become quite popular and a part of the work culture of the High Court. I do not know if the 'coffee break' still continues in the High Court.

Before I had become the Chief Justice, I was told by many of my well-wishers that I must listen to the grievances of my colleagues. One day, a judge came to me. He spoke in Punjabi, complaining about a person. He refused to speak in any other language but Punjabi. I understood his complaint to be in respect of some judicial officer. I therefore called one of the registrars, who informed me that the judge was complaining to me about the conduct of his personal peon.

Social interaction amongst the judges was abundant as there used to be regular parties in the evening. You really did not need a reason for a party and many of these parties were penalty parties; penalties imposed by the 'marshal' (normally the second judge in order of seniority) during the course of lunch. A penalty could

---

[7] In the Punjab and Haryana High Court the judges bring their own lunch but eat together in the Judges' Lounge.

be imposed for the strangest of reasons including if the 'marshal' felt you were looking happy or good, though the most common reason was for coming late to the lunch room. There was no 'appeal' against the marshal's decision(s). In fact, the High Court had the infrastructure and the manpower to organize a full-fledged party at the shortest notice, say, two to three hours. The said infrastructure was put to frequent use, as I could see.

One interesting and 'adventurous' exercise that I undertook during my tenure was to visit the trial courts in Chandigarh as well as the neighbouring districts. On a working day I used to go incognito (mine was an unknown face). I succeeded in visiting three to four courts in the subordinate court building located in Sector 17 of Chandigarh. I was able to go up to the dais and at times had to answer queries from the policeman on duty or court staff regarding the nature of my business. I remember paying an incognito visit to the court of an Additional District and Sessions Judge somewhere near Chandigarh where I found evidence being recorded on three tables. Here the judge recognized me. He did not know what to say or do.

On the whole, my tenure in Chandigarh was immensely satisfying. My only regret is that my illness prevented me from doing more.

Five

IN THE SUPREME COURT

In September 2011, I became the senior most judge of the Gauhati High Court after Justice Mukundakam Sharma, who is from Assam, retired from the Supreme Court. My turn for consideration for elevation to the Supreme Court had become due. But since I was in hospital (PGI) at that time, struggling to regain my health, there was a lot of speculation on whether I would be able to discharge the duties of a judge of the Supreme Court, if I were to be elevated. Even my ability to continue as the Chief Justice of the Punjab and Haryana High Court was being doubted in certain quarters. At one point of time, I was written off and the focus turned to the next judge of the Gauhati High Court, in order of seniority, to fill up the 'Assam slot' in the Supreme Court. But this was not to be. Divine will was otherwise.

On 10 March 2012, Justice Altamas Kabir, who was then the senior most judge of the Supreme Court, had come to Chandigarh in connection with some National Legal Services Authority (NALSA) meetings. My J1,[8] Justice M.M. Kumar, advised me that I should go and receive Justice Kabir at the airport along with him. I told Justice Kumar that it was not a part of protocol for the Chief Justice of the High Court to receive a judge of the Supreme Court at the airport

---

[8]Senior most judge after the Chief Justice.

and that protocol permitted a reception by the Chief Justice of the High Court only in the case of a visit by the CJI. As far as Justice Kumar's going to the airport was concerned, I left the matter to him but I informed him that I would receive Justice Kabir at the entry to the High Court when he reached the High Court premises. I acted accordingly and remained present with Justice Kabir throughout the day in various meetings until he left Chandigarh for Delhi that evening.

Justice Kabir had apparently informed the Collegium members that I had been with him throughout the day and that I would be fit to discharge my duties, if I were to be elevated to the Supreme Court. Promptly, the matter was taken up and the Supreme Court Collegium recommended my name for elevation on 22 March 2012. Thereafter, on completion of all formalities, I was sworn in as a judge of the Supreme Court on 23 April. CJI S.H. Kapadia administered the oath of office to me in the first court of the country (Court No. 1). It was a brief but solemn event.

To me, personally, my appointment as a Supreme Court judge was the fulfilment of a promise that I had made to myself way back in 1978 when I had returned to Assam from Delhi after completion of my studies at the Delhi Law Faculty. I had promised myself that I would return to Delhi one day in a different capacity. I fulfilled that promise three decades later in April 2012. The 15-and-a-half-year-old boy had returned to the capital as a judge of the Supreme Court of India.

My elevation is worthy of mention for certain other reasons. I do not know why Chief Justice S.H. Kapadia was determined that I should be appointed a judge of the Supreme Court. Justice Kabir's visit to Chandigarh was a step in this exercise which was initiated by Justice Kapadia to satisfy all members of the Collegium that I had recovered from illness and was fit to discharge my duties, contrary to the gossip that was spreading. Ironically, I was not even aware of the 'real' purpose of Justice Kabir's visit to Chandigarh and did not either receive or see him off at the airport.

Collegium meetings are always treated as sacrosanct and decisions are required to remain confidential. Detailed reasons for the decisions taken are not recorded. This is for a wide variety of good reasons, though it has given many the opportunity to call the procedure opaque. What would have been the extent of embarrassment for the late Justice S.N. Phukan, a respected judge from Assam, if the proceedings of the 2001 Collegium meeting wherein my name was recommended by him in preference to Justice Amitava Roy (whose name appeared higher in the list of recommendees) had been made public? He would have certainly come under criticism from one section of people who could have gone to any lengths. This is one example why the confidentiality of the process is required to be maintained to enable due discharge of duties.

In my case, the news of my recommendation made on 22 March was published in *The Hindu* on 29 March.[9] It is on reading this news report that I came to know that, if appointed pursuant to the recommendation, I would have a chance of becoming the CJI after Justice Dipak Misra. At no point of time earlier had any such possibility been a part of my calculations.

CALLED TO JUSTICE

My first day in the Supreme Court was on the Bench presided over by Justice Kabir. Justice Jasti Chelameswar was also a member of the Bench. I had learnt earlier that the mentioning[10] in Justice Kabir's court, particularly on a miscellaneous day, used to go on for several hours. My first day in Court was a miscellaneous day. Mondays and Fridays are miscellaneous days in the Supreme Court

---

[9]J. Venkatesan, 'In Ranjan Gogoi, northeast will have representation in Supreme Court', *The Hindu*, 29 March 2012, https://bit.ly/2YqUf6Q, accessed on 10 September 2021.
[10]See glossary for meaning

and Wednesdays and Thursdays are set out for regular hearings. Tuesday is mixed business—some after-notice matters and some regular cases. The mentioning went on till around 12.30 p.m. Effective orders were, in fact, passed at the mentioning stage.

The situation, at times, was chaotic. I cannot help but compare the experience of that day with the mentioning on my first day as the CJI. I told the members of the Bar, who had assembled for mentioning, that it would not be allowed except if a man were to lose his life or his home. In retrospect, it was an ill-advised and impractical move on my part and that too on the first day as the CJI. Mentioning had taken such firm root in the unwritten practices followed in the Supreme Court that no CJI or judge has been able to stop it, let alone control it. While I admit that mentioning cannot and should not be done away with, it is my opinion that it is for the Bar to carve out the occasions when mentioning should be made. Nothing of that kind has been done and today mentioning goes on very freely and merrily.

The 10.30 a.m. mentioning is usually for listing of cases which, according to the advocates, have not been listed though due and ready for listing. A good percentage of such mentioning is for listing of fresh cases. I had noticed that in many cases, the mentioning was for no apparent reason except, perhaps, 'professional' reasons. Cases where there are defaults/defects in filing and which therefore cannot be listed were mentioned before the Bench. In other cases, the fault lay with the Registry who may have failed to act as promptly as required. On the whole, there was a virtual collapse of the system which was running on an everyday basis with firefighting operations constantly at work instead of working to a well evolved plan.

The working in the High Courts is much more orderly. Though the volume of filing of new cases in the High Courts is much higher than in the Supreme Court, listing of cases is more streamlined. True, judges of the High Courts sit on single Benches and, therefore, more Benches are available. But now Supreme Court judges can also sit on single Benches. The non-availability of Benches (inadequate number of judges) in the Supreme Court is not the real reason for the delays in listing. The problem lies elsewhere; many cases are filed with defects. Defects are not corrected despite repeated opportunities to do so. Cases, therefore, do not get listed. This is the principal reason for delay in listing of fresh cases which, however, does not become known either to the litigant or the public. The general impression, therefore, is that it takes a long time to get cases listed in the Supreme Court. It is actually not so.

Mentioning, obviously, is always for a fee. 'Successful' mentioning has certain practical and tactical advantages. If you can make the CJI agree to have the matter listed earlier than scheduled, it is an advantage gained. If the CJI orders the matter to be listed on the next day, the advantage could be more as the judges who would hear the matter will hardly have the time to read the brief as the paper books will reach the judges' residential offices very late at night, say, around 10 or 11 p.m. by which time the judge(s) may have retired for the night. Compare this with the usual cases listed in the regular manner where the paper books come to the judges at least two to three days in advance, affording them time to read the briefs.

◆

Within a few days of my joining the Supreme Court, I realized that the working environment in the Court is very different from what one experiences in the High Courts. Being the last Court, naturally, no chance is taken by either side and all matters are fiercely contested. Each issue in a case is adequately documented and every argument finds full exposition with a free flow of supporting literature. This makes the task of reading for the judge considerable and decision-making extremely difficult. Some of the paper books of the cases (case files) are voluminous, running into several (14/15) volumes, often leaving the judge at the mercy of the lawyer who will take the judge through only those pages that he would want to unless, of course, the judge has read up all the volumes which often is difficult. The miscellaneous work on Mondays and Fridays also poses a tremendous challenge.

As far as I am concerned, I remember starting my reading of Monday matters on Saturday morning and Friday matters on Monday evening. Even on occasions when I had to leave Delhi during the weekends, the paper books of the Monday board always accompanied me. I had to read these paper books wherever I was and whatever the reason of my visit. While or after reading a case, I used to make copious notes on the blank papers that were attached to the paper book. It is to these notes that I turned to, to refresh my memory in the course of the hearings of the case. This practice is followed by nearly all judges. The practice in the Supreme Court of a case coming before the same judge(s) who had dealt with it initially is a worthy practice for a Court which is otherwise heavily overburdened. It saves time for the judge. A look at the notes he may have prepared earlier refreshes his memory. But the burden is enormous. I believe the experience of most of the judges of the Supreme Court was no different and is the same even today.

◆

The miscellaneous board, consisting of about 60 to 65 matters (with about 30 fresh matters) gets over in most courts before lunch; in some courts even by 11.30 a.m. All such courts, thereafter, rise for the day. Many chief justices have tried to ensure that some regular cases are heard after miscellaneous work is over. I subscribe to such a view. Such efforts, however, have not succeeded and have, at times, met with stiff resistance from judges as well as lawyers. While some judges claim exhaustion and fatigue after the hard work and extensive preparation required to be undertaken to face the miscellaneous boards, lawyers say that as the progress of the miscellaneous board in different courts varies, they do not get free for regular work in courts where the miscellaneous board may have got over early as they continue to have miscellaneous work in other courts.

On the days earmarked for miscellaneous work (Monday and Friday), in some courts there is a spillover of miscellaneous matters which are longish and urgent. These matters are fixed for the next day i.e. Tuesday or even on a Wednesday or Thursday (regular days) with priority over regular matters. Consequently, even on regular days, the regular board does not move in many courts. New cases, on the ground that they are urgent, get disposed of whereas old, regular matters (as if they are not urgent) get sidelined. This is the bane of the working of the judicial system, both in the Supreme Court and in the High Courts of the country, which I have noticed— old cases getting older and new cases getting priority attention.

◆

Presiding over a Bench has its own charm. However, before becoming a presiding judge, I had sat as the second/third judge on a number of Benches. One of my earliest judgments, in Pranab Mukherjee's election case, was a dissenting judgment in the very year of joining the Supreme Court (2012). Yet, I believe that ordinarily differences of opinion amongst judges should not arise unless, of course, the majority on the Bench fails to see what is obvious. Dissenting opinions have been celebrated by the next generation and they have, on many occasions, acted as path finders. But that is how it should be: dissent in the best traditions of judicial values and principles— inability to agree with the majority view born out of real, deep and sincere conviction. So far as concurring judgments are concerned, the trend is increasing; if you agree with the judgment authored by another judge, there may not be any pressing need to write a separate judgment to concur with the conclusions. I remember one judgment where the opinion of Justice V.D. Tulzapurkar was reported by a law journal as a concurring opinion and by another as a dissenting opinion. 'Concurring' opinions, at times, require another judgment to explain the true meaning, which often leads to uncertainties.

The Supreme Court of India must not be an academic institution; not only must it act in a business-like manner—quick, responsive and effective—it must also be understood by the average citizen. This is a view that I entertain very strongly. Judgments of the Supreme Court must be understood by the layman. Today, at times, even members of the legal fraternity find it difficult to immediately comprehend some of the text. It was my constant endeavour to keep my judgments simple, to be read and understood by everybody.

Sometime in 2013, I was inducted onto the forest/environment Bench which was then presided over by Justice Aftab Alam. Justice K.S.P. Radhakrishnan was the second judge. The forest/environment Bench used to meet at 2 p.m. on a particular day every week. The time allotted was grossly inadequate though the issues before the Bench were of great importance. There were just too many cases and lawyers wanting to argue their cases. No meaningful transaction of business was possible within the allotted time. Mining was a key subject dealt with by the forest/environment Bench, and for the Bar, mining had/has some other connotation. Mining cases brought rich dividends to the arguing counsel.

On the first day of my participation on the forest Bench, the proceedings were to be conducted in Court No. 5 which is opposite the Judges' Lounge. The three of us—Justice Alam, Justice Radhakrishnan and I—met in the Judges' Lounge shortly before 2 p.m. Justice Alam had a lot of affection for me as I am a good friend of his younger brother who now lives in the US. He warned me that I would be walking into proceedings akin to a Diwali mela. We entered the court. Sure enough, there was not an inch of space available. Court No. 5, which could accommodate hardly 50 to 60 lawyers (including those standing), was packed with probably three or four times that number. Surprisingly, all the seniors, not only designated seniors but also seniors in terms of age, had managed to occupy chairs in the first two rows. There were about 20 lawyers arguing at the same time. At one point of time, Justice Alam asked where the Solicitor was. At that time, Justice Rohinton Nariman was the Solicitor General. Justice Nariman, in his booming voice, replied that the Solicitor was here (near the entrance door) but was unable to enter! We gave up and left the courtroom.

I do not know whether I should have done it, but I asked Justice Alam to request the CJI to continue the Bench for some time so that some urgent and important matters like the Odisha and Karnataka mining cases, which had resulted in closure of a large number of mines, could be argued and decided. I think Justice Alam spoke to the then CJI as the forest Bench had been constituted to sit continuously for a couple of days. We managed to hear both the Odisha and the Karnataka mining cases. The Odisha ones were assigned[11] to Justice Radhakrishnan for writing the judgment.

Justice Alam did not mention anything about the Karnataka matters. I, therefore, presumed that he would be writing the judgment. The hearing of the Karnataka matters was completed on 21 March 2013 and judgment was reserved. Justice Alam was due to retire on 18 April that year. Four or five days before his retirement, Justice Alam came to my residence and asked me how the judgment was progressing. I asked, 'Which judgment?' He replied, 'The Karnataka mining judgment.' I was dumbstruck. There had been some communication gap. I knew that the case was voluminous and the records that would be required to be looked into and the issues addressed were simply too many to be marshalled within the available time. But I assured him that it would be done and we would be delivering the judgment on his last working day.

The next four to five days were hell for me. My staff helped tremendously. They worked overtime. There were files lying all over the floor of the office at my residence. I do not know how many

---

[11]The senior most/presiding judge decides who will write the judgment and accordingly assigns the task.

hours of arduous work I put in, but I could complete the judgment to my satisfaction. The judgment, reported in (2013) 8 SCC 154 *(Samaj Parivartana Samudaya & Ors. vs State of Karnataka & Ors.)*, was delivered on the last working day of Justice Alam's tenure. At the farewell dinner the previous evening (by that time the judgment had been circulated), Justice Alam took me aside and complimented me for the judgment. It felt good. Even though the Karnataka mining judgment has been delivered, many peripheral issues, including follow-up action on the directions issued, are still pending before the Supreme Court in a number of IAs filed.

◆

The presiding judge is not the master of the show. Every presiding judge should and does consult the second or third judge who may be on the Bench before any effective orders are dictated in the courtroom. In fact, such consultation and consent are natural because the order, though dictated in open court by the presiding judge, is the order of the Court i.e. passed by all the judges constituting the Bench. Judgments that are kept reserved for pronouncement on a later date are pronounced only after full and complete discussion amongst the judges and after circulation of the draft judgment by the judge authoring it. The practice (particularly in the media) of referring to an order or judgment of the Court as that of the presiding judge does not appear to be correct. Every order/judgment is a judgment of the Court i.e. of all the judges on the Bench, regardless of who authored it or who presided over the Bench.

By the time a judge gets elevated to the Supreme Court, he would have presided over a Bench in the High Court for a very long time. But once he comes to the Supreme Court, he would be the second/third judge on the Bench. In the normal course, it would take him about two and a half to three years to preside over a Bench. Therefore, when I first came to know that I would preside over a

Bench, I was overjoyed. But I did not know how to react to the other part of the news, namely, that the second judge on the Bench would be Justice Madan B. Lokur, my Chief Justice in Guwahati for seven to eight months. Justice Lokur was my contemporary in St Stephen's College. I had known him since 1971, first as a Stephanian and thereafter as a lawyer and finally as a High Court judge. Madan, as I call him, displayed no emotion as the second judge on the Bench. We completed our business for the day (it was a miscellaneous day) very quickly and without any difference of opinion on any of the cases listed before us.

It may appear a little surprising that I became a Supreme Court judge before Justice Lokur despite being junior to him as a High Court judge and as the Chief Justice of a High Court. But such developments occur as a matter of course. Being a federal court, representation in the Supreme Court, subject to suitability, has to be given to all the states. For example, if you have two judges from Delhi in the Supreme Court, a third judge from Delhi who is senior to, say, a Guwahati judge will not be preferred if the Gauhati High Court does not have representation in the Supreme Court. In such circumstances, it is the Guwahati judge, though junior, who would be considered for elevation and not the Delhi High Court judge.

There is much logic in this practice for if elevation to the Supreme Court is to be made purely on the basis of all-India seniority, the Supreme Court may be filled with judges belonging to one or two High Courts to the exclusion of all other High Courts and the states represented/serviced by such High Courts. In fact, very interestingly, after I was appointed to the Supreme Court in April 2012, as many as 16 Supreme Court judges appointed after me for the next four years (up to 13 May 2016) are/were senior to me as High Court judges. I have compiled a list reflecting the above position which readers may find interesting (Table 1). I, therefore, do not know why, at times, the government raises the issue of all-India seniority of a High Court Chief Justice recommended by the

Supreme Court Collegium for elevation to the Supreme Court and objects to the recommendation on that basis. All-India seniority has always been only one of the parameters for consideration for elevation to the Supreme Court.

TABLE 1

S.No.	Name of Hon'ble Judge	Date of appointment as judge in the High Court	Date of appointment in the Supreme Court
	Myself	28.02.2001	23.04.2012
1.	Justice Madan B. Lokur	19.02.1999	04.06.2012
2.	Justice M.Y. Eqbal	09.05.1996	24.12.2012
3.	Justice V. Gopal Gowda	11.06.1997	24.12.2012
4.	Justice Vikramajit Sen	07.07.1999	24.12.2012
5.	Justice P.C. Ghose	17.07.1997	08.03.2013
6.	Justice Kurian Joseph	12.07.2000	08.03.2013
7.	Justice A.K. Sikri	07.07.1999	12.04.2013
8.	Justice S.A. Bobde	29.03.2000	12.04.2013
9.	Justice Shiva Kirti Singh	29.12.1998	19.09.2013
10.	Justice C. Nagappan	27.09.2000	19.09.2013
11.	Justice R.K. Agrawal	05.02.1999	17.02.2014
12.	Justice N.V. Ramana	27.06.2000	17.02.2014
13.	Justice Arun Mishra	25.10.1999	07.07.2014
14.	Justice A.M. Sapre	25.10.1999	13.08.2014
15.	Justice A.M. Khanwilkar	29.03.2000	13.05.2016
16.	Justice D.Y. Chandrachud	29.03.2000	13.05.2016

In August–September 2016, when I was judge number six in the Supreme Court, a three-judge Bench was constituted to hear death penalty matters. Justices U.U. Lalit, P.C. Pant and I were on the Bench. One of the cases posted before us was a death penalty case from Kerala. After an extensive hearing, we acquitted the accused of the offence of murder but held him guilty of the offence of rape and maintained the life sentence imposed. The death sentence was consequently set aside. Our judgment, dated 15 September 2016, is reported in (2016) 16 SCC 295.

Markandey Katju, a retired judge of the Supreme Court, posted a blog stating that the judgment was legally flawed (he is entitled to say that). But he went on to say more: that the 'intellectual level' of Supreme Court judges, barring Justices Nariman and Chelameswar, was extremely low. The language used by Katju in his blog was extremely undignified. Individual judges were named and derogatory statements made, which is evident from the following extract from the blog:

> The present Chief Justice of India, Justice Thakur, in the BCCI case chose to ignore binding precedents that there is broad separation of powers in the Indian Constitution, and it is for the legislature, not the judiciary, to legislate. By acting thus he displayed total lack of judicial discipline, seeking only popular adulation, and throwing the Constitution and the law to the winds. The number 2 in seniority, Justice Anil Dave openly said that the Bhagavad Gita should be made compulsory in all schools in India, thus violating his oath to uphold the secular Constitution. Justice Gogoi, who is in line to become the Chief Justice of India on the basis of seniority, has shown that he does not know an elementary principle of law, namely that hearsay evidence is not admissible (see paragraph 16 of his judgment in the Soumya murder case). I can go on and on about most of the present Supreme Court judges to show how low is their intellectual level, but that is not necessary. Suffice it to say that they have reached their positions not because of merit but only by dint of seniority. Justice Deepak Mishra, in line to become CJI, was appointed a Judge in Orissa High Court at a very young age because of the influence of his relative Justice Ranganath Mishra, former CJI, who was one of the most corrupt judges in

India. Justice Ramanna, who is also in line to become CJI, was appointed as a High Court Judge in Andhra Pradesh at a very young age due to his political connections, and later became Supreme Court Judge not because of merit but purely due to seniority.[12]

As Katju had stated his reasons for holding the view that the judgment of the Court was legally flawed, the Bench decided to treat the blog as a suo motu review petition and issued notice requesting Katju to assist the Court in the matter. There were connected review petitions filed by the state of Kerala and others. Katju came to court and, I understand, was received by the Secretary General who escorted him with all courtesy and respect to Court No. 6. This, coincidentally, happened to be the courtroom from where Katju had retired. All the review petitions were argued and Katju also raised his contentions with great force. I felt he could have been more polite while addressing the Court.

Be that as it may, after conclusion of arguments, the order dismissing the review petitions, including the suo motu review petition, was dictated by me in open court. Thereafter I, as the presiding judge, gave a copy of the blog to Katju and asked him to read it. I also gave a copy of the same to Mukul Rohatgi, the then Attorney General, and asked him what he thought of it. Rohatgi, who was present in the court probably for some other matter, instantly and spontaneously said, 'My Lord, this is contemptuous.' When he came to know that the blog was written by Katju, Rohatgi looked worried and tried to find a way out by offering alternative views.

Katju became furious. He told the Bench that though he had been a judge for several years, he was not being treated politely and with respect by us. Look at the irony! Katju as a retired judge

---

[12]'Supreme Court Issues Contempt Notice to Katju. If the Fence Eats Away the field, Who Saves the Crop?' Bharatkalyan 97, https://bit.ly/3wlNeRn; accessed on 15 September 2021.

expected respect from sitting judges while, at all times, he showed utter disrespect and contempt for them. This was evident from his blogs, including the one cited in the previous pages. He said nothing about its contents. Had he even expressed a little regret about it or even in respect of the language used in the blog, perhaps we would not have pursued the matter. But he accused the Bench of misleading him to come to court and of laying a trap to initiate contempt proceedings against him. He was insulting in his language and disposition; his conduct in court together with the language of the blog left us with no choice but to proceed and issue a contempt notice to him. The event was widely published—for the first time in judicial history, a former judge of the Supreme Court was being proceeded against for contempt by the Supreme Court itself.

Thereafter, one day, I received a phone call from the senior advocate representing Katju saying that the former judge would like to apologize and whether, if he did so, the Bench would accept the apology. I was surprised. I told the senior advocate that Katju was free to do whatever he thought proper, but I could not immediately say anything with regard to the response of the Bench as that would be a matter of judicial consideration and orders. I further told the senior advocate that I would love to invite him home for a cup of tea after the case. That promise remains unfulfilled at my end.

On 6 January 2017, the suo motu contempt petition against Katju was listed for consideration before a Bench of Justice Lalit and me. (Justice Pant, who was the third judge on the Bench, had recused himself from the case.) In the meantime, Katju had filed an affidavit dated 30 November 2016 tendering an unconditional apology for writing and publishing the blog. The Bench accepted the apology and closed the matter.

For nearly two years thereafter, Katju remained silent as far as I was concerned. But after my elevation as the CJI, he started posting tweets containing nasty, factually incorrect and undignified comments about me as a person and my role as the CJI. He became extremely vocal after my retirement. His language was regrettable. In an interview with one of the national TV channels after my nomination to the Rajya Sabha, I was asked to comment on Katju's tweets. I maintained that Katju was not relevant to me anymore.

I do not think I needed a greater vindication of my view than the press reports that had appeared a few months earlier to the effect that Katju had tendered evidence denigrating India and its judiciary in a magistrate's court in the UK in the matter of the extradition of Nirav Modi. Katju is reported to have said, amongst other things, that in India it is not possible to secure justice as the judiciary is not free from the executive. The UK Court where Katju had tendered evidence recorded its view on his statements and observed, inter alia, in its judgment dated 25 February 2021:[13]

> 139. Despite having been a former Supreme Court Judge in India until his retirement in 2011 his evidence was in my assessment less than objective and reliable. His evidence in Court appeared tinged with resentment towards former senior judicial colleagues. It had hallmarks of an outspoken critic with his own personal agenda...

> 140. ... He made bold assertions about corruption across the judiciary in India (including former Chief Justices) and that the Supreme Court had surrendered itself to the executive. Of note, despite being critical of a former Chief Justice passing a verdict in a Supreme Court in exchange for a nomination to the upper house of Parliament of India on his retirement on a quid pro quo basis, suggesting collusion and corruption, Justice Katju himself secured appointment by the Government

---

[13]In the Westminster Magistrate's Court before District Judge (MC) Sam Goozée Appropriate Judge, *The Government of India (Requesting State) vs Nirav Deepak Modi (Requested Person)*, JUDGMENT.

to Chairman of the Press Council of India following his own retirement.

144. ... There is no cogent or reliable evidence that the judiciary in India are no longer independent, or capable of managing a fair trial even where it is a high-profile fraud with significant media interest.

Do I need to say anything more?

◆

I worked as the executive chairman of NALSA from 28 August 2017 until I became the CJI. Thereafter, as the CJI, I was the patron-in-chief of NALSA. Legal service was largely rendered in the form of quick resolution of disputes through Lok Adalats and by spreading awareness of legal rights through public interactions. I do not believe in Lok Adalats as a viable and judicious means of dispute resolution except in petty criminal cases where, on admission of guilt, a fine of ₹10–20 is imposed, paid and the case closed. In matters like compensation under the Motor Vehicles Act 1988 or other such statutes or even in serious family disputes relating to property, I always understood awards by Lok Adalats to be depriving one party of something that he may have been entitled to if the case were adjudicated. I always viewed Lok Adalats as an expression of the helplessness of the litigant who agreed to less favourable terms on account of his inability to wait for the 'endless' legal process to run its course. Lok Adalats are not an alternative to regular adjudication and gained prominence primarily because of the inability of the system to deal with cases on merits.

Therefore, as chairman of NALSA, while continuing with all ongoing work, I introduced what I would unhesitatingly call a new facet of legal service i.e. to ensure that a person entitled to some benefit under some legal scheme gets what is due to him. This we ensured by holding legal service meets where the giver of the benefit and the recipient thereof were brought face to face through the Legal Services Authorities to enable exchange of benefits due under the law i.e. under a duly framed scheme. Such camps were held in various places in Assam, Jammu and Kashmir, Madhya Pradesh and a couple of other states. Unfortunately, due to lack of time, I could not extend such programmes to other parts of the country but I had the satisfaction of organizing such camps in places like Kargil and Leh and in several tea gardens of Assam.

Making prosthetic limbs available to needy persons in a situation where voluntary organizations were ready to offer such services free was an ongoing process of the activities undertaken by NALSA through the various state organizations during my tenure as chairman. Justice Ajit Singh, former Chief Justice of the Gauhati High Court, was instrumental in this exercise as he had done some work in this area as the Acting Chief Justice of the Rajasthan High Court through an agency called Bhagwan Mahaveer Viklang Sahayata Samiti, Jaipur, headed by Devendra Raj Mehta. The joy of a person being able to walk or ride a bicycle after years of inability is something to behold. It brings a depth of satisfaction that outweighs owning all the gold in the world. These are some of the most satisfying moments of my judicial career.

To spread joy among a large number of the deprived, the Union government was persuaded to increase the budgetary allocation for NALSA from ₹100 crore (2017–18) to ₹150 crore (2018–19). Unfortunately, it was reduced to ₹140 crore (2019–20) and further to ₹100 crore (2020–21). While on the subject, it will be worthwhile to mention that in the Union Budget only about 0.2–0.4 per cent of the allocation is for the judiciary (meant for the Supreme Court, National Judicial Academy, National Legal Services Authorities; for creation and upkeep of courts under special schemes, etc.). Administration of justice being a state subject in List II of the Seventh Schedule of the Constitution, establishment of regular courts, creation of posts to man them, annual salaries, and so on are the responsibility of the state governments. Shockingly, the average allocation of funds for the judiciary in the state budgets is again a negligible percentage of the total allocation. Budgetary allocation, both by the Union and the states, will have to be meaningful if India's court system is to be brought in tune with our visions of social and economic justice and to face the challenges of a trillion-dollar economy. Flexibility of allocation of earmarked funds from one head of expenditure to another, whenever and wherever necessary, could be one 'small' step to begin with.

◆

Life as a Supreme Court judge was hectic, fast-moving and entirely taken up by Court work. Rupanjali, as usual, was most understanding and supportive; never for a moment did she complain about anything. In fact, she appeared very happy if I had worked particularly hard on any day. When I used to dictate a judgment and return to my official residence, she would invariably ask whether things had gone to my satisfaction. Though she did not even pretend to understand the nuances of legal work, she would give a very patient hearing to all that I had to say. She was naturally unable to proffer her conclusions on the subject, but that did not matter; I had spoken my heart out and there was somebody to listen to me. These thoughts could not have been shared with anybody and I had the satisfaction of sharing them with her. Rupanjali was not too interested in going out or meeting friends who were, in any case, very few in number. She was not too interested in shopping either. I remember, during our initial days, once she disapproved of my bargaining with the shopkeeper. Her logic was perfect—we are coming out after such a long time. How do a few rupees matter? The only passion that Rupanjali has, which I can confidently share, is for shoes. She will not refuse an offer of footwear and at any given time she would have at least 20 to 25 pairs, most of the collection being inexpensive.

Though India is the second most populous country in the world, its judge-population ratio of 19 per million (10 lakh) is one of the lowest. The total judge strength in the country consists of 34 judges in the Supreme Court, a little over 1,000 in the High Courts and around 25,000 judges at the district level. At any point of time, a large number of these posts lie vacant for a wide variety of reasons. Though numerically the pendency of cases is very high in each court, my understanding of the situation is that a large number of the pending cases can easily be put in the category of 'non-essential', 'not contested' or 'infructuous' matters. The truly contested cases or cases of substance would be perhaps not more than one-third of the total pending cases which in the subordinate courts today is 3,92,45,090, in the High Courts 58,46,668 (as on 5 July 2021 according to data available on the National Judicial Data Grid [NJDJ] portal) and in the Supreme Court 69,212 (as on 2 July 2021—mentioned on the Supreme Court website). (The overall number of cases is believed to have gone up by a crore during the pandemic period.) One-third of the above pendency is still a considerable number.

The number of judges available to handle these cases is grossly inadequate. As there are no immediate prospects of increasing the judge strength in the country to any significant levels, the judiciary must continue its task undaunted and with the available tools. A little priority for commercial cases, those involving senior citizens and a few effective meaningful changes in some areas of litigation (more effective than what we have had in the form of the Arbitration and Conciliation Act, 1996 and the Commercial Courts Act, 2015) will go a long away. Though the Codes of Civil and Criminal Procedure are cast in letters of gold, giving litigants on both sides equal opportunities to contest their respective cases, some modifications particularly with regard to service of summons, etc.

and curtailment of time for pleadings and arguments are matters that require immediate attention. The '*Tarikh pe Tarikh*' reputation and endless arguments of lawyers must be curbed to reasonable levels. Regretfully, the required initiative in this direction has not even commenced. Also, a little improvement/quality control at the time of recruitment of judges, at all levels, is urgently required. This reform can be initiated, supervised and ensured by the judiciary itself at no extra cost. No approval, sanction or consent of any other authority is required.

A judge, at whatever level he is working, must be a totally committed person. Commitment is to be understood as synonymous with a mission to render quick and effective justice. Hard work and labour must become a way of life. Judicial office is not a 10 to five job, but is a lifelong and daily commitment. To try out, on certain occasions, I had gone to court without doing any homework. I found it extremely difficult to perform. A judge who reads the briefs of the next day is able to tackle the business of the day in a more constructive and efficient manner. Superfluous and unnecessary arguments and requests for adjournments can be dealt with in a more confident way. Such commitments and values can also be inculcated in a judge by his illustrious seniors in service as well as through regular in-house training programmes which today all State Judicial Academies hold.

As a High Court judge, whenever I had gone to the NJA at Bhopal, I had found serious inadequacies in the training modules designed which included discussions on the laws of the Sea (undoubtedly important) but not on judicial values and ethics (equally, if not more, important). As a young judge, I remember telling Professor (Dr) N.R. Madhava Menon, who was then the director of the NJA, my views on the matter. He took my suggestion seriously and introduced some changes. The 'business' of deciding cases requires planning and strategy at the micro level in tune with such macro level planning that may be in force. Unfortunately, I do not think the Indian judiciary has drawn up any plan or strategy to handle its huge business. Everything is ad hoc. It appears to me that there is complete helplessness, if not lack of awareness or desire, to tackle these issues which are the institution's greatest challenge.

◆

The tenure of the judges of the Supreme Court, including the CJI, more often than not, is very short. Judges are known to have retired even without presiding over a Bench. I do not think I would be wrong in saying that the average tenure of a judge of the Supreme Court is about four years and that at times it has taken judges more than three years to get the chance to preside. The average tenure of a CJI is about a year. Such short tenures do not provide adequate opportunities to the judges and the CJI to make the sort of contributions that would ordinarily be forthcoming with longer tenures. If prospective High Court judges, both from service and the Bar, are expected to have a minimum period of tenure, I do not see why such a requirement for Supreme Court judges should be absent. The maximum age for a Bar entrant to the High Court Bench under the Memorandum of Procedure (MoP) is 55 years, meaning that if appointed, he should have a tenure of at least seven years as a High Court judge. Similarly, a district judge due for elevation to the High Court must not have crossed 58 and a half years on the date the vacancy in the High Court, against which his case is to be considered, occurs. But when it comes to the Supreme Court, there are no rules, no norms—written or unwritten. After interacting with members of the political branch on this issue, mostly informally, the impression I gathered is that, by and large, the thinking is that Supreme Court judges should not have long tenures and the CJI, in particular, should not remain in office for more than a year.

◆

The Bar in the Supreme Court is, undoubtedly, of very high calibre with talent flowing vertically to lawyers who are relatively young. But the appearance of stalwarts in the Supreme Court for regular matters on regular days of hearing is rare, whereas the galaxy present on a miscellaneous day is eye-catching. The logic is simple: if the fee (which is 'astronomical' by any standards) can be earned in a minute or two on a miscellaneous day, why work for hours on a regular hearing day to earn the same amount? The fee is charged for an appearance, regardless of the time taken.

To 'remedy' the situation, a unique practice, I understand, has developed. On a regular day, the fee is charged by the hour or by the clock. How far this practice has permeated the Court, I do not know. But you do find mostly young lawyers arguing the few regular hearings that take place on a regular day. Ironically, it is at these regular hearings that the law is expounded and developed after a full hearing. Fortunately, there is a lot of talent amongst the young lawyers of the Supreme Court to enable the judges to expound and develop the law in the right direction with their help and assistance.

◆

The registrars of the Supreme Court who run and supervise the administration of the Supreme Court are drawn from two sources—State Judicial Service and Supreme Court Service. I tried to keep the representation in equal proportion i.e. 50:50. While the registrars who come from the Supreme Court Service continue till their retirement with changes in portfolios from time to time, State Judicial Service officers, who come on deputation to the Supreme Court, have tenures which seem to be coterminus with the CJI's. With every change of the incumbent in the office of the CJI, I have noticed a corresponding change in the registrars coming from the State Judicial Services. This is avoidable. After assuming office as CJI, I retained some of the registrars coming from this stream who had worked with my predecessor. My successor, Justice Bobde, did better. He did not make any changes and additional hands came in as officer(s) on special duty (OSDs) of the rank of registrars. Those who worked as registrars during my time, by and large, continued to work under the next CJI. This is most desirable for the better administration of the Supreme Court.

Yet another issue that merits attention is that of Public Interest Litigations (PILs), which take up a lot of time of the Supreme Court Benches. A PIL is an innovative and path-breaking mechanism for bringing issues of great public importance before the Court by any socially conscious citizen, acting bona fide in a representative capacity. Many issues of vital social and economic and at times political importance have been addressed through the medium of PILs. Unfortunately, in course of time, the philosophy behind PIL jurisprudence seems to have been lost, as observed by the Supreme Court itself in several of its pronouncements. Many PILs are an attempt to invite the Supreme Court to get into matters of governance and other areas of executive functioning. Challenging executive and legislative actions in legal guise, these PILs seek to lure the Court into areas with which it should ordinarily have no concern. Some are intended to put the lawyers behind the PILs into circulation for 'professional reasons'. Many PILs raising utterly ridiculous issues, like banning of Sardar jokes, bringing back the Kohinoor to India or banning wearing of red dresses all over the country, have been filed and some of them have actually been entertained by the Supreme Court. After all, the cost of filing a PIL in the Supreme Court on any issue arising anywhere in the country is a few hundred rupees. And you always have some newspaper, portal or publication ready to publicize such PILs.

PILs have become the life and soul of the Supreme Court as they bring the issues raised and the persons raising them into public focus. PILs bring power. A section of lawyers is therefore willing to go to any lengths to bring vexed and at times inappropriate issues for adjudication as PILs, thereby taking up valuable judicial time. All these shortcomings and pitfalls must be overcome and PILs must serve as a vehicle to achieve social and economic justice as in the case of bonded labour, environmental issues and Vishaka guidelines, to name a few.

LIVING IN LUTYENS' DELHI

Residential accommodation for the judges of the Supreme Court, in spite of more or less an adequate number of bungalows being available in the Supreme Court Judges Pool, is a problematic issue, causing serious inconvenience to judges in due discharge of their judicial functions. The procedure for allotment under which option to shift to a vacant bungalow is given to all the judges in order of seniority needs to be streamlined to quicken it, as delay in allotment causes untold hardships for a newly appointed judge who has to stay either in the State Guest House or the Supreme Court Guest House. As of July 2021, there is one sitting judge of the Supreme Court who, though appointed in September 2019, is still living in the Supreme Court Guest House. In many High Courts, the practice of placing the accommodation file in the Judges' Lounge has been adopted with good results. Options are being exercised at a much quicker pace, leading to faster movement of files and, consequentially, allotments.

When I joined the Supreme Court, there were 28 judges in office. Therefore, in the afternoon of my first day in office, I was informed by the registrar concerned that 1, Rajaji Marg was available for allotment. Rajbir informed me that the bungalow, though nice, was overrun by monkeys who at times posed a serious problem for the occupants. This is, perhaps, why at some earlier point of time 1, Rajaji Marg was the official guest house of the Supreme Court. Rajbir, as usual, was right but I had no choice in the matter. The next day, my wife, along with Mrs Chelameswar with whom she had a strong bond from the Guwahati days, went to see the bungalow and thereafter we together visited it. I then informed the Registry that I would be opting for it. The bungalow needed minimal repairs and we did not insist on any extra work. In no time the CJI approved the allotment and 1, Rajaji Marg was made available to me. I occupied it within 10 days of allotment. It proved lucky for me in some ways and unlucky for some other reasons.

My grandson, Maharth, was born to my son, Raktim, and daughter-in-law, Kakoli, on 19 October 2014. This was just a week before the marriage of my daughter, Rashmi, with Tanmaya Mehta, son of Justice Valmiki Mehta. I remember seeing Maharth as a tiny infant, a few days old, when he reached 1, Rajaji Marg from the hospital. Today, he is a bubbly youngster all of seven years old who is extremely talkative. How time has flown!

Rashmi is a law graduate. After graduation, during the initial years, she was not particularly keen on litigating in the courts. She joined the law firm, Luthra & Luthra, at Barakhamba Road and lived in a rented room in Defence Colony. Soon after I became a judge of the Supreme Court, she moved in with us at 1, Rajaji Marg.

She had just turned 26 and Rupanjali and I were naturally anxious about her marriage. Though she had a huge circle of friends, she was yet to find a match for herself. Parental search for a 'suitable match' did not meet with any success either. I remember waiting up for her on nights when she was out partying—always in the hope that we would get some affirmative answer to our usual question: 'Anyone?' However, to our disappointment, the answer was always in the negative!

As the popular adage goes, marriages are made in heaven, and this was pretty much the case with Rashmi. One fine day in February 2014, Justice Alok Singh (then a judge of the Uttarakhand High Court) and his wife came to meet us at home. I had known Justice Singh for a while as he had served in the Punjab and Haryana High Court before being transferred to his parent court via the Jharkhand

High Court. Justice Singh informed me that Justice Valmiki Mehta had a son of the same age as Rashmi who was also a lawyer. He enquired if we could get Rashmi and Tanmaya to somehow meet and see how things worked out.

I remember calling Rashmi to my room that evening and asking her, somewhat hesitatingly, if she was interested in meeting up with Tanmaya. To my surprise, she agreed. Before there could be any change of mind, so to speak, I passed on Tanmaya's number (which I had received from Justice Singh) to her. Thereafter, both my wife and I stepped back and waited (with bated breath) to see how things progressed. To our delightful surprise, everything worked out in ways we had never imagined—their engagement took place in July followed by their wedding on 26 October 2014.

In the last week of August, barely two months before the marriage, Rupanjali underwent a major surgery. With the marriage date fast approaching, she had not fully recovered from the surgery and was very weak. She is a very strong person though built delicately. She displayed no signs of ill health to others and, mercifully, everything passed off very pleasantly. Rupanjali, by the grace of God, recovered slowly but surely and is well today.

We stayed at 1, Rajaji Marg until January 2015 when we shifted to 10, Tees January Marg. The new premises were more sprawling, the lawns were larger and peacocks were frequent visitors to the house. Rupanjali looked after the peacocks and arranged special feed for the birds, which was lavishly spread out in the evenings. This attracted a large number of birds of different species, including tiny birds, the likes of which I had not seen before. Many of the trees that stand at 10, Tees January Marg were home to these birds.

Raktim, Kakoli and Maharth came from 1, Rajaji Marg to stay with us at 10, Tees January Marg, though somewhat reluctantly. I remember telling Raktim that the money which he would save on rent, if he continued to stay with us, was my contribution to helping him build a base to enable him to survive in Delhi after my retirement. I could not give him anything else. He agreed and that is how we were able to watch our grandchild growing up. Finally, and as agreed to earlier, around the time I entered the Collegium (November 2016) Raktim, Kakoli and Maharth left 10, Tees January Marg to live in a rented apartment in Defence Colony. They, of course, continued to visit us almost on a daily basis. So did Tanmaya and Rashmi.

While we were comfortably tucked away in the sprawling bungalows in Lutyens' Delhi, on a visit to Dibrugarh during the summer break of 2015, my mother, in whose name the land on Zoo Narengi Road, Guwahati, stood transferred after my father's death, insisted that I should get it transferred in my name. This is what she had been repeatedly insisting on after my father's death in 1998. I had been avoiding the issue for reasons not entirely logical. This time she was adamant and came with us to Guwahati to get the gift registered. Things were arranged, but to my horror, I was told that I would have to spend about ₹16 lakh (a small fortune for me) on account of stamp duty and registration fee. My mother found the development very funny: I had to pay ₹16 lakh for the plot on which I had an existing house in my name; the property was known to all as belonging to Justice Gogoi. Yet I had to pay a small fortune for the legal recognition. I really had to pay for my own property, which I did by means of a withdrawal from my Provident Fund account. In fact, it was my mother's suggestion that I should recount this event in my memoirs to let people know how little the former CJI knew about the realities of life.

After I became the CJI, I had to shift to 5, Krishna Menon Marg, the official residence of the CJI. Rupanjali and I visited the premises after Justice Dipak Misra had vacated it. All the registrars were in attendance. We all agreed that the bungalow needed a complete overhaul which was going to take several months and cost a large amount. The question was not one of personal comfort or individual likes and tastes—5, Krishna Menon Marg is the official residence of the CJI and therefore must befit the status of the office. I, therefore, asked for thorough repairs and complete renovation to be carried out. We finally moved into 5, Krishna Menon Marg on 17 January 2019. We vacated it two days after the end of my tenure i.e. on 20 November 2019.

Six

COLLEGIUM AND THE RULE OF LAW

The word 'collegium' in the context of judicial appointments in the Supreme Court often raises eyebrows. It simply means a forum of the first three to five judges of the Supreme Court, including the Chief Justice, which makes binding recommendations for appointment in the higher judiciary. The Collegium is the product of a judicial verdict equating consultation with the judiciary by the executive, as mandated by the Constitution, with concurrence and primacy. Consequently, what we have in practice is a system of judges appointing judges with the executive playing a less than dominant role.[14]

I entered the Collegium of the Supreme Court a day after my 62nd birthday i.e. on 19 November 2016. This was following the retirement of Justice Anil Dave from the Supreme Court. Justice T.S. Thakur was the CJI and was due to retire on 4 January 2017, i.e. immediately on reopening of the Court after the winter vacation, which was about a month away. During this time, as the CJI, he had summoned three Collegium meetings (Collegium of five judges)

---

[14]*Supreme Court Advocates-on-Record Association and another vs Union of India* (1993), 4 Supreme Court cases 441 (nine judges), https://bit.ly/31s1RqH, accessed on 1 October 2021.

to consider names for elevation to the Supreme Court. Justice Chelameswar had, at that point of time, refused to physically participate in the Collegium meetings on account of differences on certain issues with the Chief Justice. So only four members of the Collegium—the Chief Justice, Justices Khehar, Misra and I—participated in these meetings.

What transpired in these meetings was both perplexing and confusing; any name proposed by the Chief Justice met with a response from either Justice Khehar or Justice Misra that they needed time to consider it. Justice Thakur had no choice but to adjourn the meeting and fix another date. In the last meeting just before the winter break, even before opening the papers, Justice Thakur asked the members if they were interested in conducting any business. I expected the first response would be from Justice Khehar or Justice Misra. It was useless for me to speak as the silence of the other two judges answered the question and settled the issue. We parted on a pleasant note after the customary cup of coffee and walked out of the Supreme Court, using the same staircase to go down from the first floor to the ground floor. Justice Thakur was the first to descend the stairs. I could see a little stoop in his shoulders; perhaps he had realized that there would be no more Collegium meetings. Perhaps he had regrets over not being able to make any headway in finalizing the recommendations for elevation to the Supreme Court that he may have had in mind.

The winter recess of the Court came thereafter. In anticipation of Justice Khehar becoming the Chief Justice, I along with Justice Madan Lokur tried to remove the impasse created by the absence of Justice Chelameswar from the meetings of the Collegium. We talked to him and invited him along with Justices Khehar and Misra to Justice Lokur's house. One evening, during the winter break, all five of us who were to constitute the Collegium once Justice Khehar took over as the CJI met at Justice Lokur's residence. Though I do not precisely remember the specific area of disagreement which had led to Justice Chelameswar's exit from the meetings of the Collegium, he was rather sore and agitated. Coming to specific issues, Justice Chelameswar informed the Collegium that he saw no reason as to why Justice K.M. Joseph had not been recommended. Justice Khehar, due to become the Chief Justice shortly, promised to do so. Justice Chelameswar then agreed to attend the meetings of the Collegium. Immediately after Justice Khehar assumed office, the Collegium recommended four names for elevation. But the case of Justice Joseph was not taken up as promised. Justice Chelameswar once again was very upset.

Eventually, in January 2018, when Justice Misra was the CJI, Justice Joseph was recommended along with Justice Indu Malhotra, a leading member of the Bar, for elevation to the Supreme Court Bench. However, the proposal of Justice Joseph ran into rough waters. There were objections in writing from the Government of India with regard to the all-India seniority of Justice Joseph to justify his appointment as a judge of the Supreme Court. The government was all set to notify the appointment of Justice Malhotra and exclude Justice Joseph. Here, I must give full credit to Chief Justice Misra. I have reasons to believe that he used strong-arm tactics i.e. threatening to resign, if Justice Joseph was not appointed.

Finally, on 3 August 2018, the appointment of Justice Joseph as a judge of the Supreme Court was notified by the Government of India. But, contrary to practice, his name appeared below Justice Malhotra's in the warrant of appointment. Again, a controversy erupted. There was some speculation and a few reactions in the social media that Justice Joseph should not and would not take the oath of office. By that time, Justice Chelameswar had retired. I spoke to him to gauge the authenticity of the rumours. He scoffed and said that Justice Joseph would certainly take the oath, which he did on 7 August.

◆

The working of the Collegium system has been adversely commented upon by its critics as well as its proponents. Even in the National Judicial Appointments Commission (NJAC) judgment delivered on 16 October 2015 [reported in (2016) 5 SCC 1],[15] individual judges coming to a different or the same conclusion found fault with the working of the Collegium. Justices Chelameswar, Lokur and Kurian Joseph all had very negative views on the functioning of the Collegium system and some of its decisions. Most of the criticism revolves around the ultimate decision, namely, the recommendation(s) made. Over-representation of a particular High Court, under-representation of another, and overlooking of seniority are some common objections. 'Opacity' of the system has invited sharp and persistent criticism.

My views on the matter are somewhat different. Inadequacies and inconsistencies in the system, which do exist, have to be resolved by those who work the system, until a 'better' system is evolved. Some of the shortcomings are self-inflicted and, therefore, avoidable. Zealous adherence to the principle of seniority at times creates problems of different kinds; delays in making recommendations (as experienced since November 2019 to June 2021 in the Supreme Court) and slow and sluggish movement of names recommended are issues which can be sorted out in-house without much difficulty. But solutions that appear to be simple are not forthcoming; there is need for more dynamism at all times.

From my experience as a member of the Collegium and as the CJI presiding over the Collegium meetings, I believe the system worked reasonably well during my tenure. There was no dissent, opposition or friction. Every decision taken was unanimous and backed by reasons considered satisfactory and justification

---

[15]By a constitutional amendment, the Collegium system of appointment of judges in the higher judiciary was sought to be replaced with appointment by the NJAC. The amendment was struck down by the Supreme Court (NJAC judgment) primarily on the ground that it infringes on the independence of the judiciary, a basic feature of the Constitution.

considered adequate. Whether others agree with the decisions taken is a different matter. No two persons can think alike. But I have full satisfaction that every decision of the Collegium during my tenure as the CJI was taken in the best interests of the institution. I would like to cite a few instances that would show how the system worked during my tenure.

A RINGSIDE VIEW

In a Collegium meeting held on 12 December 2018 and presided over by me as the CJI with Justices Madan B. Lokur, A.K. Sikri, S.A. Bobde and N.V. Ramana, we agreed to recommend the names of Justice Pradeep Nandrajog, the then Chief Justice of the Rajasthan High Court, and Justice Rajendra Menon, the then Chief Justice of the Delhi High Court, for elevation to the Supreme Court. The next day, the smaller Collegium (first three judges) was to meet to consider the names to be recommended for appointment as Chief Justices of High Courts.[16] The first three judges had, amongst others, informally decided to recommend Justice Ravindra Bhat as the Chief Justice of the Rajasthan High Court. Thereafter, at a social gathering that took place on the evening of the 12th, I came to know that the decisions taken at the five-judge Collegium meeting had been discussed and congratulatory messages had been sent to those who had been recommended. The decision regarding Justice Bhat, whom we had informally agreed to recommend for appointment as Chief Justice of the Rajasthan High Court but the matter was yet to be formalized as the meeting of the smaller Collegium was scheduled the next day, also became known. I talked to Justice Lokur, the senior most judge, and expressed my strong disapproval of the leakage of the Collegium decisions and that too (in the case

---

[16]Recommendations for appointment to the Supreme Court and for transfers are made by the larger Collegium i.e. five judges whereas recommendations for appointment of Chief Justices and judges of the High Courts are made by the smaller Collegium of the first three judges.

Ranjan Gogoi

of Justice Bhat) even before the meeting of the Collegium had taken place. Justice Lokur was equally disturbed.

Though we had agreed on them at the Collegium meeting, the names of Justices Nandrajog and Menon had not been sent to the law minister as per procedure. In fact, the letter to the law minister was yet to be drafted. Having talked to Justice Lokur, I decided to keep the matter in abeyance. The meeting of the smaller Collegium scheduled on the 13th was postponed. The winter break started from 15 December (Saturday) and status quo was maintained. In the meantime, Justice Lokur completed his last working day and was due to retire on 31 December 2018.

While the matter was so situated, I received a written communication in respect of a case [RFA (OS) 92/2012 titled *F. Hoffman—La Roche Ltd. & Anr. vs Cipla Ltd.*] decided by the Delhi High Court on 27 November 2015 by a Bench presided over by Justice Nandrajog. It was an appeal against grant of injunction by a single judge of the Delhi High Court in a suit involving grant/ infringement of patent right. I had stated in one of my interviews that the CJI receives about 300 letters, complaints, mails on an average every day. There is a unit in the Supreme Court which handles these complaints very confidentially. Each letter, postcard and mail is numbered, read and dealt with in accordance with a set procedure. When this information concerning the case of F. Hoffmann reached me, I called for the judgment and the related papers. Reading them, I recalled hearing the matter at some earlier point of time on the judicial side. I therefore looked into the matter a little deeper.

I found that though the case was decided by a judgment dated 27 November 2015, there was another order/judgment dated 8 December 2015, which had deleted paragraphs 4 to 38 of the judgment of 27 November while retaining the rest of the paragraphs. In the order dated 8 December, it was mentioned:[17]

---

[17]Order of the Delhi High Court of 8 December 2015, https://bit.ly/3CSR8nf.

2. ...a law intern associated with the Bench offered to make a precise of the impugned judgment, and so well was the draft of the precise submitted that the Bench decided to incorporate the same in the judgment as was submitted to us by the intern

3. The attention of the Bench was thereafter drawn to an Article published in the year 2013 where the impugned judgment had been pen profiled and it dawned on the Bench that paragraphs 4 to 38 of our judgment were a virtual verbatim copy of the Article published.

4. This has constrained the Bench to pass a suo moto order offering apology to the learned authors of the Article and simultaneously taking corrective action.

5. Our reasoning commences from paragraph 39 onwards of our decision dated November 27, 2015, wherein we have dealt with the arguments advanced with reference to the issues which arose and said part of our judgment from paragraph 39 onwards is distinctly severable from paragraphs 4 to 38 ....

7. Deleting paragraphs 4 to 38 of our decision and retaining the rest but as renumbered, we replace paragraphs 4 to 38, with two paragraphs....

From the above the following facts are clear:

1. That the judges had permitted a law intern to be associated with the judgment writing. According to me, law interns/ law clerks can be asked to research on issues arising in the judgment but they should not have a direct role in the preparation of the judgment.
2. That paragraphs four to 38 of the judgment dated 27 November 2015 was a verbatim reproduction from an article on the subject published in some journal earlier in 2013.
3. Paragraphs four to 38 were 'drafted' by a law intern so well

that the said paragraphs were inserted in the judgment dated 27 November 2015.

4.   The judgment also mentions a *suo moto* apology by the Bench to the learned authors of the article; in other words, an apology was offered for plagiarism in a judicial order.

When these facts along with the information that an appeal (C.A. Nos.1136-37/2016) had been filed before the Supreme Court against the judgment(s) in question were brought to the notice of the other members of the Collegium, an opinion was expressed that Justice Nandrajog's elevation to the Supreme Court could even come in the way of an appropriate decision in the civil appeal filed against the aforesaid order by one of the aggrieved parties (this was the matter dealt with by me on the judicial side at an earlier stage). However, on further enquiry, I learnt that the said civil appeal came to be closed on withdrawal by an order of the vacation Bench dated 22 June 2017. I was not a party to the order.

While these developments were going on in the case of Justice Nandrajog, it was brought to my notice that the Collegium of the Patna High Court headed by the then Chief Justice, Rajendra Menon, had on 18 January 2018 recommended four names out of which three did not meet the income criteria and therefore could not have been recommended. The Supreme Court Collegium on 24 October 2018 remitted the said proposal to the High Court for reconsideration. Six more names were recommended by the Patna High Court Collegium headed by Chief Justice Menon on 20 July 2018, out of which three names, once again, did not meet the income criteria. My discreet enquiries in the matter indicated that Chief Justice Menon may not have made the above recommendations fairly and on merit.

The CJI makes enquiries in different ways; some of these are unique and at times rather unconventional methods are also used. There are no set parameters in this regard and wide discretion is vested in the Chief Justice to choose an appropriate method to unravel the facts and come to a reasonable conclusion. These discreet enquiries are conducted informally. My enquiries in this matter revealed that a former CJI who had served as the Chief Justice of the Patna High Court may have suggested the names of the recommendees to Justice Menon.

Against this background, the Collegium reconsidered the names earlier proposed for elevation to the Supreme Court (Justices Nandrajog and Menon) and as Chief Justices of High Courts. Collegium meetings were held on 5 and 6 January 2019 and finally on 10 January 2019 the Collegium resolved to forward the names of Justice Dinesh Maheshwari, Chief Justice of the Karnataka High Court, and Justice Sanjiv Khanna, a judge of the Delhi High Court, for elevation to the Supreme Court.

Justice Maheshwari had been superseded by Justice Ajay Rastogi on 2 November 2018, as at the time some verification concerning Justice Maheshwari was pending. As neither Justice Rastogi nor Justice Maheshwari would go on to become the CJI or even come into the Collegium (Justice Rastogi would have entered the Collegium for a day), we took the decision that if Justice Rastogi were to be elevated, pending receipt of the verification report in the case of his senior, Justice Maheshwari, no substantial damage or harm would be caused. It was in these circumstances that we decided to go ahead and recommend Justice Rastogi though he was junior to Justice Maheshwari. In the meantime, the verification with regard to Justice Maheshwari was completed and the matter was duly clarified. We were, therefore, in a position to recommend Justice Maheshwari and we acted accordingly.

So far as Justice Khanna was concerned, if elevated, he was to supersede Justices Nandrajog, Gita Mittal and Bhat. I proposed and the Collegium accepted that Justice Khanna be elevated since if he were elevated at that point of time, he would go on to become CJI for six months. Delhi High Court would have a CJI in 2025 (when Justice Khanna is due to become CJI), after a gap of almost 20 years;

the last CJI from the Delhi High Court was Justice Yogesh Kumar Sabharwal who demitted office in 2006. I must say, in this regard, that Justice Sikri, a member of the Collegium whose parent High Court is Delhi, was particularly happy about this.

Justice Gita Mittal was next in line and then serving as Chief Justice of the Jammu and Kashmir High Court. Her case was duly considered by the Collegium. Her judgments as a judge of the Delhi High Court and her overall performance were also considered. As for Justice Bhat, he would have a short tenure and would not have come either to the Collegium or become the CJI if he was not elevated at the time Justice Khanna's name was proposed and accepted. The Collegium, therefore, decided that it should wait and consider Justice Bhat's name in the next round which we did and he assumed office as a judge of the Supreme Court on 23 September 2019.

BALANCING CONFIDENTIALITY AND TRANSPARENCY

I wonder how much of the above reasons and grounds that weighed with the Collegium in taking its decisions in these matters should have been recorded for public scrutiny for the sake of so-called transparency. All the judges who had been bypassed i.e. Justices Nandrajog, Menon and Mittal have successfully completed their tenures and have all retired from the high office of Chief Justice of a High Court. Could they have continued to function as Chief Justices of the High Courts in the manner they did had the Collegium recorded its reasons for not elevating them to the Supreme Court?

Another instance worth mentioning in connection with the Collegium's functioning during my tenure is the case of seven names for elevation as judges of the Kerala High Court. Three out of the seven names were cleared by the Collegium headed by me sometime in October–November 2018. One name was not approved. The remaining three recommendees did not meet the requisite income criterion. One member of the Collegium (from Kerala) requested that the three names be cleared. The other member and I had our reservations. At this stage, these three recommendees filed revised income tax returns which were also submitted to the Supreme Court.

In the light of this development, I sent the matter to a sitting judge of the Delhi High Court known for his wide exposure to taxation law, seeking his opinion. The opinion was that the revised returns were time-barred and could not be considered. The Collegium, therefore, could not clear the three names. The particular member of the Collegium kept requesting, even after his retirement, that we should find a way out. We could not. He was not happy about the Collegium's rejection of the three names in question.

◆

Justice Surya Kant, a judge of the Punjab and Haryana High Court, was elevated as Chief Justice of the Himachal Pradesh High Court before his senior, Justice Ajay Kumar Mittal. Consequently, Justice Surya Kant was elevated to the Supreme Court in preference to Justice Mittal (since retired as Chief Justice of the Madhya Pradesh High Court). The basis for this decision was an earlier view recorded by Justice Chelameswar in writing during the Collegium proceedings which had recommended Justice Mittal as Chief Justice of the Delhi High Court during the tenure of Justice Khehar as CJI. Justice Chelameswar recorded in the minutes of the Collegium meeting that Justice Mittal, to his knowledge, was not fit to be a Chief Justice. CJI Khehar did not forward the name of Justice Mittal to the government for reasons unknown. In these circumstances, did my Collegium do anything wrong in opting for Justice Surya Kant over Justice Mittal? Justice Mittal was later (during my tenure as CJI) elevated as Chief Justice of the Meghalaya High Court and thereafter transferred as Chief Justice of the Madhya Pradesh High Court from where he retired. If the view of Justice Chelameswar had been made public, could Justice Mittal have become a Chief Justice at all? The extent of avoidable embarrassment that the so-called 'lack of transparency' prevented is evident. Populist notions will necessarily have to be consciously guarded against.

◆

Justice R.S. Reddy, the then Chief Justice of the Gujarat High Court, took the oath of office as judge, Supreme Court of India, on 2 November 2018. Justice Akil Kureshi, the senior most judge of the Gujarat High Court, was transferred to the Bombay High Court by a notification dated 1 November 2018. He was to join on or before 15 November 2018. Being the senior most judge of the Gujarat High Court and entitled to remain in that High Court until 15 November, Justice Kureshi was required to be appointed the acting Chief Justice of the Gujarat High Court. Instead, his junior, Justice A.S. Dave, was appointed by a notification dated 1 November 2018. This led to an uproar in the Gujarat Bar.

I spoke to the law minister on the morning of 1 November itself and insisted that the order appointing Justice Dave as the acting Chief Justice be recalled and a fresh order appointing Justice Kureshi be issued. This was followed by a communication in writing the next day. The 'error' was rectified and a fresh notification dated 2 November 2018 was issued, superseding the earlier notification and appointing Justice Kureshi. Thereafter, before the due date, Justice Kureshi moved to the Bombay High Court.

On 10 May 2019, Justice Kureshi was recommended by the Collegium for appointment as Chief Justice of the Madhya Pradesh High Court. In the process of consultation, the law minister in his letter dated 23 August 2019 expressed the objection of the Union government to the recommendation. The objection was based on a negative perception flowing from certain judicial orders passed by Justice Kureshi.

It would have done nobody any good if the objection of the government had come into the public domain. The learned judge, at that time, still had several years of service left. I, therefore, requested a senior member of the Collegium to take up the matter with the government. It is to the credit of all concerned that we could avoid a confrontation between the two constitutional bodies. Justice Kureshi's recommendation was modified and he was appointed Chief Justice of the Tripura High Court on 8 November 2019.

A Chief Justice, regardless of the size of the High Court, is a Chief Justice and becomes eligible for consideration for elevation to the Supreme Court. Justice Kureshi thus continues to be eligible for consideration for elevation to the Supreme Court until the end of his High Court tenure in March 2022.

One may agree or disagree with the factors that weighed with the Collegium. But to say that the decision taken is arbitrary merely because the reasons behind it are not made public would be incorrect. We should repose some trust in the judges. All that they do is not necessarily wrong, as is sought to be projected. But I doubt if reason will ever prevail. At times, I am haunted by the thought that if a perception develops in the next generation of judges that they must tailor their work or decisions with the aim of avoiding a negative report card at the end of their tenures (report cards have become the order of the day), what would that portend for the future of the judiciary as an institution?

Let me cite a specific instance to show how the Collegium is required to finely balance the need for transparency with the requirement of confidentiality. Prior to October 2017, Collegium resolutions recommending names for elevation to a High Court or the Supreme Court were not put up on the Supreme Court website. To satisfy the requirement of transparency, Chief Justice Misra felt that the Collegium decisions along with the reasons for them should be posted on the website. However, some members of the Collegium and other judges who were consulted had a different view. Eventually, on 3 October 2017, the Collegium resolved that, henceforth, its decisions would be put up on the website. Accordingly, decisions on some elevations that were taken on that date were, for the first time, uploaded on the website.

One resolution pertained to a recommendation for elevation to the Madras High Court. Amongst the persons considered was a district judge-rank officer from Puducherry, who had earlier served as a registrar of the Supreme Court (I shall refer to him as 'Mr X'). The Intelligence Bureau (IB) in its report on Mr X had commented adversely. I had never considered the IB reports on prospective judges as the ultimate word. But a negative/adverse report in writing from the IB creates difficulties for the Collegium. It could not recommend Mr X for elevation to the Madras High Court.

I left for Hyderabad on a private visit after the Collegium meeting on 3 October. Apparently, many judges including Collegium members had requested Chief Justice Misra not to post the Collegium decision on the website. Chief Justice Misra was undeterred. As soon as I reached Hyderabad, I received calls from some colleagues requesting me to speak to Justice Misra not to go ahead. I attempted but failed.

Mr X, who was known to me, met me personally over the issue. He told me that the adverse report of the IB had caused serious problems for him within his family. Besides, it could also affect his continuance as a district judge beyond the age of 58 (a district judge-level officer is usually allowed to continue for two more years i.e. upto 60 years of age on reaching the age of superannuation which is 58 years).

Mr X's apprehensions proved true. Though he continued in service beyond 58 for some time, eventually the continuance was refused by the Madras High Court, acting on its administrative side. It is commonly perceived that the adverse IB report and the decision of the Supreme Court Collegium not to elevate him on its basis were the reasons. This is how transparency worked in the case of Mr X. Those who clamour for transparency in the administrative process of the judicial wing of the state must realize that the incumbents of judicial posts are differently placed from their counterparts in government and the sanctity of the administrative decisions affecting judicial officers cannot be judged by application of the same norms and parameters that govern government servants.

Mr X's case was an eye-opener. Modifications and rectifications were made in recording the decisions of the Collegium subsequently. Yet, difficulties cropped up from time to time. Consultee judges (a judge of the Supreme Court who is consulted by the Chief Justice while making recommendations for elevation to the High Court(s) where he had earlier worked) had serious reservations about their views, particularly negative views, regarding the suitability of a particular name being put in the public domain. Many felt that reasons for supersessions need not be recorded, or if recorded, must not be put in the public domain as it may reflect on the judge superseded who may still have some time to retire.

With such views slowly gaining ground, from October 2019 the text of the Collegium resolutions stood altered to record only the conclusion reached—bereft of reasons or details, a practice followed by my successor CJI and by the present CJI till date.

SANCTITY UNDER THREAT

Routine matters, at times, become events of substantial importance. As Collegium decisions do not enter the public domain, the press, at times, plays a role in this regard. The contribution of *The Times of India* and its senior correspondent, Dhananjay Mahapatra, in this regard has been noteworthy. His article, 'Preaching retired judges seldom look back at their conduct during judgeship', published on

5 August 2019, makes for interesting reading.[18] He writes:

'...Justice [Ajit Prakash] Shah became Chief justice of Madras HC on November 12, 2005, and on May 7, 2008, he was appointed CJ of Delhi HC, the constitutional post from which he retired on February 12, 2010. As CJ of Delhi HC, he shot into fame with his pioneering judgment in July 2009 decriminalizing Section 377 of Indian Penal Code, which for more than a century punished the LGBT community.

After the judgment, he became the most talked about judge in the country and a darling of social activists, activist lawyers and, of course, the media. Despite the brilliant judgment and years as chief justice of two prominent HCs, he failed to earn a berth in the Supreme Court as a judge.

By the time he entered the zone of consideration for selection as an SC judge, the collegium system was well entrenched and appointments to the apex court were made collectively by the CJI and his four senior most colleagues. The collegium considered his name a few times, but not favourably. We do not know whether it riled him. But the two categories of activists lost no time in making a villain out of Justice S H Kapadia for opposing Justice Shah's elevation. Activists circulated stories of alleged differences between Justices Kapadia and Shah from their Bombay HC days as the reason for the former's opposition to Shah's elevation to the SC. Only a few knew what actually dissuaded the SC collegium from recommending Justice Shah's name to the government—a four-page letter dated September 12, 2008, by advocates of Madras HC giving details of allegations against Justice Shah and opposing his appointment as an SC judge.

---

[18]Dhananjay Mahapatra, 'Preaching retired judges seldom look back at their conduct during judgeship', *The Times of India*, 5 August 2019, https://bit.ly/3onunlp, accessed on 16 September 2021.

The advocates had sent the letter to then President Pratibha Patil, then Vice-President Hamid Ansari, then PM Manmohan Singh, then CJI K G Balakrishnan and his colleagues Justices B N Agrawal, Ashok Bhan, Arijit Pasayat and Kapadia. What holds true for the 2008 complaint against Justice Shah is his own statement in the recent lecture, 'Without passing judgment on the truth or falsity of the allegations, I must admit there are certain stark facts that stand out which demand consideration.'

The 2008 complaint talked about a film actress and also about chamber hearing, instead of open court hearing, in a case relating to a builders' lobby and how a property worth hundreds of crores of rupees was sold for a song. The advocates had earnestly requested for 'a proper in-house inquiry or proper investigation' into the allegations. Then CJI Balakrishnan did not order an inquiry.

No social activist or activist lawyer ever demanded an inquiry, as it would have dimmed the judge's halo that was shining bright with effusive praise for his LGBT judgment. No doubt, he was a fine judge. But didn't he have his failings?

That is why Justice Shah probably said in his lecture, 'Judges must be constantly reminded of what is appropriate behaviour throughout their career, so that the role that is cast upon them— of administering impartial justice—is never compromised ... '[19]

A.P. Shah's reply was also published in *The Times of India* dated 7 August 2019. Some extracts are as follows:

> ... Besides this, I must add that I am deeply anguished by Mr Mahapatra's insinuations about my alleged past. He relies upon a letter that he claims was allegedly sent in 2008 by some lawyers to the then Chief Justice of India, which supposedly cast aspersions on my character. He also adds that only a limited number of

---

[19]Ibid.

persons knew of this letter, and that the then CJI took no action. (I also wonder as to how the journalist obtained access to this letter in the first place.) On my part, this is the first time I have heard of such a letter, and in any event, I deny all the allegations made by your reporter with all the contempt it deserves.

One would have thought that someone as credentialed as Mr Mahapatra would have stuck to basic journalistic principles of verifying sources, and checking facts, and asking for an opinion from the other side, before filing a report. None of these were done. In many respects, this article could even be construed as being defamatory ....[20]

Shah questioned the journalist's source of information but did not volunteer to have the allegations, if they exist, duly verified. A complaint of the kind referred to in the news item does exist in the records of the Supreme Court. I am not commenting on the merits, truth or falsity or otherwise of the complaint and the allegations made. But Shah's public utterances on a host of issues may have acquired greater credibility if he had volunteered to have the allegations against him duly verified.

Coincidentally, I have also noticed that out of a few names which were not cleared by the Collegium of the Supreme Court for appointment as Delhi High Court judges during my tenure as CJI, some have become prolific anti-establishment writers, violently criticizing the Supreme Court. Is it not a case of the grapes becoming sour? What a pity!

TRANSFERS IN JUDGES' INTERESTS

Transfer of judges has often been alleged to be a weapon of revenge used by members of the Collegium. I do not wish to comment

---

[20]'Judiciary's sanctity under threat, I'll continue to speak', *The Times of India*, https://bit.ly/3qiUzzZ, accessed on 16 September 2021.

except to talk about three transfers made during my tenure as CJI to set the record straight. The first was the transfer of Justice V.K. Tahilramani, Chief Justice of the Madras High Court, to the Meghalaya High Court. Information, adverse in nature, pertaining to the learned Chief Justice, including her irregular and infrequent sittings in court, was received by the members of the Collegium. On cross-checking, some authenticity was found in these complaints. We, therefore, took the decision on 28 August 2019 to transfer Chief Justice Tahilramani to Meghalaya where there was less work. She declined to go to Meghalaya and on 6 September preferred to resign. For some time the issue was in the news and the Supreme Court was under attack for committing injustice and harm to a good judge. The transfer was termed arbitrary and vindictive. I believe the time has come to lay bare a few facts.

A complaint dated 25 August 2019 filed by one Traffic Dr K.R. Ramaswamy[21] was received by the CJI's office on 17 September 2019 (after Justice Tahilramani had resigned) and placed before me. The complaint contained allegations of illegal acquisition of immovable property in Chennai by Chief Justice Tahilramani. The complaint also mentioned a more than necessary official interaction with the law minister of Tamil Nadu and visits by the Chief Justice to Puducherry by making a detour while going to Madurai, and visiting unknown places using private vehicles while staying in the Raj Bhavan at Puducherry. Questionable exercise of administrative powers of the Chief Justice, including change of the judge in the sensational idol theft cases, was also part of the complaint.

I could have ignored the allegations as Justice Tahilramani had resigned on 6 September 2019. But, given the hue and cry created over the transfer issue and the decision of the Collegium having been labelled arbitrary and vindictive, I decided to have the allegations verified, particularly when much of the oral and

---

[21]Name of the complainant as mentioned in the complaint.

discreet information received by me with regard to the judge, which had formed the basis of the decision to transfer her, found mention in the written complaint of Dr Ramaswamy. Besides, the allegations, being very serious, may have called for further action, notwithstanding the resignation of the judge.

The complaint was, therefore, handed over by me personally to the director of the IB at my official residence. He was instructed to verify and submit a report. The director initially reported orally. Prima facie, some truth in the allegations was reported. I insisted on a written report. The director submitted an unsigned report dated 24 September 2019, which he again personally handed over to me at my residence. I was told that this (unsigned report) was the normal practice of communicating the results of an inquiry conducted by the IB in such circumstances. The disclosure of the report of the director, IB, would not do any good either to the system or to the concerned Chief Justice.

On receipt of this report, on my instructions, the Secretary General of the Supreme Court drew the attention of the director, Central Bureau of Investigation (CBI) to the matter by way of a letter dated 26 September 2019. To set all speculation at rest, the letter of the Secretary General dated 26 September 2019 is reproduced:

Sanjeev S. Kalgaonkar
Secretary General
Supreme Court of India

Tel.: 23384661
Fax: 23386178

September 26, 2019

Dear Shri Shukla,

As instructed by Hon'ble the Chief Justice of India, I am to address you as under:

A complaint dated 25.8.2019 of one Shri Traffic Dr. K.R. Ramasamy has been received in the office of Hon'ble the Chief Justice of India on 17.9.2019. The complaint pertains to certain allegations in respect of Hon'ble Mrs. Justice Vijaya Kamlesh Tahilramani, former Chief Justice of Madras High Court.

I am directed to inform you that the aforesaid complaint dated 25.8.2019 was brought to the notice of Director (Intelligence Bureau) by Hon'ble the Chief Justice of India and a copy of the same was made available to the Director(IB). An unsigned Report dated 24th September, 2019 has been received by Hon'ble the Chief Justice of India from the office of the Director(IB).

As directed, I am forwarding a copy of the complaint and the Report dated 24th September, 2019 for necessary action in accordance with law. The action initiated may be informed at the earliest so that the matter can be placed before the Hon'ble Chief Justice of India.

With regards,

Yours sincerely,

Sanjeev
26.9.2019
[Sanjeev S. Kalgaonkar]

Encl.: As above

Shri Rishi Kumar Shukla
Director
Central Bureau of Investigation,
Plot No. 5-B, 6th Floor,
CGO Complex, Lodhi Road,
New Delhi – 110 003.

Ranjan Gogoi

I was not informed by the CBI director of the action, if any, taken by him pursuant to my above letter at any time until my retirement.

In the second instance, a very senior judge of the Delhi High Court (now a Chief Justice of a High Court) was proposed for transfer and he was informally given the option of choosing the High Court to which he would like to go. The proposal for his transfer was initiated by me as the CJI in the following circumstances.

An order dated 29 August 2018 was passed by a bench of the Delhi High Court in W.P. (Crl.) No. 2453 of 2018 (*Neeraj Singal vs Union of India and Ors.*) granting bail to the petitioner therein who was arrested by the Serious Fraud Investigation Office (SFIO) in the course of an investigation into the affairs of Bhushan Steel Ltd. and associated companies. The bail order was passed in a writ petition filed challenging the provision of law under which the investigation was ordered. A special leave petition (SLP) was filed by the Union of India against the said bail order dated 29 August immediately. A mention was made before the CJI's Court and the matter was fixed for 30 August. Notwithstanding the fact that the matter was to be heard by the Supreme Court on 30 August, the Bench headed by the judge concerned passed another order at about 5.20 p.m. of 29 August, which resulted in the bail order being given effect. This was despite the fact that it was brought to the knowledge of the High Court Bench that the Supreme Court was in seisin of the matter and the hearing had been fixed for 30 August.

This is what the Supreme Court had to say in the matter in its order dated 4 September 2018:

> 3. At the outset, when the matter was taken up for hearing Mr Maninder Singh, learned Additional Solicitor General of India appearing for the appellants, brought to our notice the fact that despite being informed that this Court had listed the case for hearing on 30.08.2018 upon urgent mentioning on the previous day (i.e. on 29.08.2018), the High Court proceeded to

issue directions on 29.08.2018 at 5.20 P.M., as a result of which Respondent No. 1/Neeraj Singal has already been released and the direction given in the impugned order for his release has been implemented. However, learned Additional Solicitor General appearing for the appellants submitted that they intend to continue with the present appeals as the findings and the observations made in the impugned order will have far reaching effects not only on the case on hand but on other investigations and cases concerning offences punishable under the Companies Act, 2013.

4. We may only observe that urgent mentioning of the case was made before the Bench presided over by the learned Chief Justice of India and hearing thereon continued after court hours on 29.08.2018. The matter was directed to be listed on the next day on 30.08.2018. Propriety demanded that the High Court should have showed deference and awaited orders in the present proceedings. The haste with which the High Court was moved on the evening of 29.08.2018 at around 5:20 P.M. to implement its order, despite this Court being seized of the proceedings would indicate an attempt by Respondent No. 1/ Neeraj Singal to pre-empt the hearing before this Court by securing release. We express our disapproval.[22]

In these circumstances, I listed the proposal for transfer of the presiding judge of the Bench in question before the Collegium. The Collegium was duly informed about the reasons for the proposal. All the members of the Collegium, which included Justice Sikri, agreed to the proposal (Justice Lokur had retired in the meantime). But Justice Sikri requested that the matter be deferred to a date after his retirement which was due on 6 March 2019. I acceded to the request of a colleague and acted accordingly.

---

[22]In the Supreme Court of India, Criminal Appellate Jurisdiction, Criminal Appeal No. 1114 of 2018.

Thereafter, whenever the subject of transfer of the judge concerned was mentioned before the Collegium by me, there was opposition from one member who had joined the Collegium after Justice Sikri's retirement and was not a party to the earlier proceedings. The Collegium therefore could not recommend the judge's transfer during my tenure. His subsequent transfer to the Punjab and Haryana High Court, which attracted a lot of attention, was after my retirement, for reasons not known to me.

Yet another transfer of a High Court judge pertains to a 'young' judge with a long tenure and a bright future in my parent High Court. He had been known to me for a long time. His father, a former Advocate General of Assam, was a close friend of my father's. Reports of the judge's avoidable involvement in many issues both on the judicial and administrative side came to me as CJI.

Sometime in August 2019, I, therefore, proposed his transfer to the Bombay High Court. Before doing so, I had discussed the matter with Justice Bobde and requested him to agree to the transfer (the Bombay High Court was his parent High Court). Both of us felt that the transfer of the judge to the Bombay High Court would do him good and Bombay would be an ideal training ground for his future.

After the Collegium had approved the proposal but before the proceedings were signed, I called up the judge and informed him of the decision of the Collegium. This was done informally because I knew him well. I asked him for his response and told him that I would be signing the proceedings of the Collegium only after hearing from him. He sought some time to discuss the matter with his family and very soon called me back to say that he would be happy to go to the Bombay High Court. I understand that Justice Bobde also spoke to him the same evening. The resolution was thereafter signed and the matter processed. The transfer order was issued.

It appears that, subsequently, on 3 September 2019, the Gauhati High Court Bar Association held an extraordinary general meeting condemning the transfer which was alleged to be on extraneous grounds. The wisdom of the Supreme Court Collegium was severely criticized and the action was termed prejudicial as it would affect the judge's seniority for he would be placed much lower in the Bombay High Court than he was in the Gauhati High Court. This claim of erosion of seniority was inaccurate because a transferee judge always carries along his seniority. In the case of a transferred judge, seniority in the parent High Court is what is taken into account at the time of consideration for career advancement.

I became the target of an attack in my parent High Court and that too in very undignified language by a few voluble people. Some senior advocates whom I acknowledged as good friends informed those present at the Bar meeting that they had met the judge concerned, who had told them that he had not been consulted in the matter. I was shocked. Assuming what the advocates said was incorrect, the judge in question could not have issued any statement in view of the office he was holding. But nothing stopped him from calling me. That phone call never came. This is the price I had to pay for a decision taken in the judge's best interests. I believe that the transfer to Bombay closed many chapters of the judge's tenure in Guwahati which was in his best interests.[23]

---

[23] I have chosen to refer to some of the cases by using the names of the incumbents but have refrained from doing so in other cases on the basis of whether they are in office or have since retired.

Seven

A DEBT TO THE NATION

A very controversial issue of late in the Supreme Court has been that of the master of the roster. The expression simply refers to the performance of administrative duties by the CJI in allocating cases to the different Benches. In the Supreme Court, subject-wise categorization of cases has always been done and assigned to different Benches. The table below illustratively indicates the different subject categories:

TABLE 2

Sub. Cat. Code	Description of the Subject Category
0301-0324	Direct Tax Matters
0401-0436	Indirect Tax Matters
0801-0818	Letter Petitions & PIL Matters & Social Justice Matters
0901-0912	Election Matters
1001-1010	Company Law, MRTP, TRAI, SEBI, IDRAI & RBI Matters
1100-1101	Arbitration Matters
1300	Habeas Corpus Matters
1401-1439	Criminal Matters
1501-1505	Appeal Against Orders of Statutory Bodies

1701-1705	Contempt of Court Matters
2401, 2403-2407	Matters Pertaining to Appointment etc. of Constitutional Functionaries
2501-2504	Matters Pertaining to Statutory Appointments & Appointment of other Law Officers
2801-2811	Matters Pertaining to Mercantile Laws, Commercial Transactions Including Banking
3001	Matters Pertaining to Judicial Officers
3002-3004	Matters Pertaining to Employees of Supreme Court/ High Courts/District Courts and Tribunals and Individual Judicial Officers etc.
3100	Matters Pertaining to Admission to Educational Institutions other than Medical & Engineering
3400	Matters Pertaining to Mines, Minerals & Mining Leases
3700	Matters Pertaining to Commissions of Inquiry
4001-4003	Matters Pertaining to Admission/Transfer to Engineering and Medical Colleges
4201-4205	Matters Pertaining to Leases, Govt. Contracts & Contracts by Local Bodies

From the above table, it is clear that there could be, say, in all twenty different categories into which cases are slotted on the basis of subject. Out of these twenty categories, ten different categories can be assigned to one Bench. An equal or smaller or larger number of subjects can be assigned to another Bench or other Benches. Thus, with different permutations and combinations, subject categories are allotted to all Benches. Each Bench, though, would have its own subject categories clearly indicated; often, the same subject category of cases, for instance criminal cases, would have to be assigned to more than one Bench. This is due to the load of cases pertaining to a particular subject category. The work of creating/making different subject categories of cases from time to time and the allocation of different subject categories of cases to different Benches as well as allocation of cases to a particular Bench when the same subject category is assigned to two different Benches are all done by the CJI. Hence the CJI is called the master of the roster.

The controversy particularly arose during Chief Justice Dipak Misra's tenure over allocation of PILs which normally was the exclusive category earmarked for the Chief Justice's court, meaning all PILs were to come before the CJI's court. With increasing number of PILs being filed, it was becoming difficult for the CJI's Bench alone to hear all the PILs; yet for reasons not known PILs were not allotted to any other Bench. In the normal course, if the Chief Justice wanted to allocate PILs to any other Bench, the choice ought to have been according to seniority i.e. the second court, failing which, for any reason, the third, fourth, fifth court and so on.

The case of Kalikho Pul, a former CM of Arunachal Pradesh, who had reportedly committed suicide in August 2016 while being involved in a controversial litigation in the Supreme Court, is one instance. His wife wrote a letter to the five senior judges (including myself), enclosing a note that was alleged to be his suicide note. The note contained serious allegations against some then sitting Supreme Court judges (all have since retired). The letter was received when Justice Khehar was Chief Justice.

Though the letter was addressed to the administrative side, Chief Justice Khehar assigned it to the judicial side—to a Bench headed by Justice A.K. Goel, a relatively junior judge at that time. This was done by registering the letter as a suo moto PIL. Both the cognizance of the matter on the judicial side and its allocation to the particular Bench created a stir and the lawyer for the complainant (wife of the deceased) told the Court that his client did not wish to pursue the matter on the judicial side. The PIL stood closed and the matter buried.

Similar ad hoc allocation of PILs was being done during Chief Justice Misra's tenure as CJI. As the head of the institution, he would mark some PILs to a Bench or the other without there being any fixed criteria or norm. It was the personal choice of the CJI.

Soon enough, a volcanic eruption took place. Brijgopal Harkishan Loya, a district judge-level officer in Gujarat, was trying the Sohrabuddin Sheikh case of an alleged encounter killing by the Gujarat and Rajasthan Police. Loya died in 2014 in Nagpur where he had reportedly gone for a marriage function. A controversy arose as to whether Loya's death was a natural death. Several PILs were filed in the Supreme Court seeking an inquiry.

Many members of the Supreme Court Bar Association believed that controversial and contested PILs were being randomly allocated to one Bench or another on the whims and fancies of the Chief Justice. There were murmurs amongst the senior judges also. CJI Misra was told about the feelings of his colleagues but did not consider it necessary to do anything and allotted the Judge Loya case to a Bench presided over by Justice Arun Mishra (judge number ten in order of seniority at that time).

On the morning of the day when Judge Loya's case was to be heard, I got a call from Justice Lokur saying that once again PILs on controversial issues were being allocated to Justice Mishra's Bench. Justice Joseph as well as Justice Chelameswar spoke to me and expressed their reservations regarding the matter which had been building up over the past weeks.

All of us—Justices Chelameswar, Lokur, Joseph and I—agreed over the phone that we would go to the Chief Justice at 10 a.m. and tell him that he should withdraw Judge Loya's case from the Bench of Justice Mishra. We accordingly assembled in Justice Chelameswar's chamber and went to meet the Chief Justice who, however, did not entertain our request. Justice Chelameswar walked out. I remained and pleaded with the Chief Justice but to no avail. I had no choice but to leave the Chief Justice's chamber along with Justices Lokur and Joseph. We thereafter went to Justice Chelameswar's chamber; he said that we should address the press on the issue. This was on the spur of the moment. We all agreed.

AN 'EXTRAORDINARY' EVENT AND ITS CONSEQUENCES

12 January 2018 was a Friday, a miscellaneous day. Immediately after miscellaneous work, around 12 noon, I went to Justice Chelameswar's residence. What I saw there shocked me: the press was in full attendance, several cameras were set up on the back lawn of his residence, which was the venue of the meet. Outside, there were several OB vans. I did not expect this; what I had understood by Justice Chelameswar's expression 'let us meet the press' was a meeting with a few/some journalists. Anyway, there was no way out now. Not that I wanted to make a retreat; I had committed to addressing the press and I believe till today that, given the circumstances, it was the right thing to do, though very unusual. We strongly felt that things were not right in the Supreme Court and we were proved correct by a slew of remedial steps taken by Justice Misra himself. Thereafter, he became careful and conscious while exercising the power of allocation of cases.

When my turn came as the CJI, I indicated in the list of subject categories allocated to the different Benches that PILs would henceforth be heard by the first five Benches. The allocation of a particular Bench to hear a particular PIL out of the five Benches earmarked, however, was still required to be done by the Chief Justice. The improvement was that the allocation could not be random. At least a beginning had been made. I understand that the next Chief Justice, Justice Bobde, allocated PILs to the first eight Benches.

The 'infamous' press conference was also attended by senior

advocate Indira Jaising. She posed a question to me as to whether the case in connection with which we had gone to meet the Chief Justice was the Loya case. I could have avoided the question or answered it in a hundred different ways, but I said 'yes'. That set the crowd roaring.

I suspect to this day that it is that answer which brought Sanjay Hegde, senior advocate, to my residence a few days later. He had come to meet me on behalf of *The Indian Express* group in connection with the third Ramnath Goenka Memorial Lecture. There was a nicely composed letter from Raj Kamal Jha, editor-in-chief of *The Indian Express,* inviting me to deliver the lecture. My reply was that while it would be a matter of great honour for me to follow the President of India, Pranab Mukherjee, who had delivered the second Ramnath Goenka Memorial Lecture, we should wait for some time, at least till after the summer recess of the Court. My reason for deferring the lecture was entirely personal. The *Express* group agreed to my request and finally the event was held on 12 July 2018. The venue selected was the Nehru Auditorium in Teen Murti Bhavan. The subject was 'Vision of Justice'.

For about an hour, I spoke about my vision of justice and talked about constitutional morality and delays in the justice delivery system. I stressed the necessity for a revolution and not reforms in the judiciary to make courts available to the common citizen. I emphasized the need for speaking the truth and not bowing to power; and the necessity of the judiciary being more proactive and dynamic. I said that the judiciary should be on the front foot subject, of course, to the constitutional framework. Stressing the need for an independent judiciary, I submitted that it must remain uncontaminated. At some point, I also mentioned that despite the judiciary being the weakest of the three branches of government, it was the least dangerous for civil liberties, a combination of the judiciary with either of the two organs could make it a lethal weapon so far as civil liberties are concerned.

I specifically mentioned the judgment of the Supreme Court dated 11 August 1986 reported in (1986) 3 SCC 615 (*Bijoe Emmanuel & Ors. vs State of Kerala & Ors.*), which is very dear to my heart even today. Before the Court in that case were three children— Bijoe, Benu and Bindu. During the morning assembly in school when the national anthem was played, the three children would rise respectfully but not take part in the singing of it. They belonged to the Jehovah's Witnesses sect. Their refusal to participate in the singing of the national anthem was on the grounds that it was against the tenets of their religious faith. An MLA, having come to know of this, mentioned the matter in the House which then appointed a Commission to inquire into the matter and submit a report. The Commission reported that the children were law-abiding and that they showed no disrespect to the national anthem. Even so, they were expelled from the school. The matter reached the High Court and two forums in the High Court decided against the children. The appeal filed before the Supreme Court was allowed on the grounds that it was a part of the children's freedom of conscience to freely profess, practise and propagate a religion and not join in the singing of the national anthem especially when they had displayed no acts of disrespect or any perversity or unpatriotic sentiments. The Supreme Court's view to the effect that 'the real test of a true democracy is the ability of an even insignificant minority to find its identity under the country's Constitution' is a view that we all applaud.

My lecture was apparently well received. This is what eminent jurist Fali Nariman had to say: 'I think the lecture was fantastically reasoned and well thought out, he expressed what many of us feel, and are not in a position to say.'[24] Similarly, former Attorney General of India Soli Sorabjee commented:

---

[24]Ramnath Goenka Memorial Lecture: A Vision of Justice, *The Indian Express*, https://bit.ly/3kdPNjE, accessed on 17 September 2021.

'He spoke up for the need for independent judges to come with solutions, not the usual things—we can't do this, we can't do that—sometimes, we have to be an active judiciary as well.'[25]

I do not think I said anything unusual or out of the ordinary. No judge in the country could have said anything different. Did I preach anything? I do not believe I did. Did I deviate from what I had said? I did not.

I am reminded of two other memorial lectures given by me, amongst several others, during my tenure as a judge of the Supreme Court. One was the Justice P.D. Desai Memorial Lecture on 'Constitutional Realism and Constitutional Idealism—Is the Supreme Court on the Cusp of Evolution?' delivered on 10 March 2018 in Ahmedabad. What I said on the occasion was a prelude to my views expressed at the Ramnath Goenka Memorial Lecture.

On 15 April 2018, I delivered the third Justice G.P. Singh Memorial Lecture in the auditorium of the National Law Institute University (NLIU), Bhopal. The lecture was dedicated to the future generation present in the auditorium in large numbers. My thoughts expressed in the speech were in no way different from what I had said on 12 July at Teen Murti Bhavan. I did not say anything in either of the other two lectures which I did not at the Ramnath Goenka Memorial Lecture. Yet, both the events, important though they were, went largely unnoticed. Why? Because the other two lectures were delivered at places other than the national capital and media focus/coverage was minimal. On the other hand, the third Ramnath Goenka Memorial Lecture was an event connected to the *Express* group. The lecture was attended, amongst others, by persons who felt delighted when I mentioned that the judiciary in the country needed a thorough shakeup, a revolution and not mere reforms. It was also attended by eminent columnists like P. Chidambaram and Abhishek Manu Singhvi, both reputed lawyers

---

[25]Ibid.

of the country. The event was co-sponsored by the Jindal Global Law School. Clearly, it was 'marketed' very well and I became the hero, the saviour, the knight in shining armour who had come to rescue the system from all its evils.

As time passed, I 'failed' in the eyes of some of the vocal and powerful. The hero of the lecture did not act as per their expectations. But should or could I have? I continued to do and act as I believed to be correct, true to my conscience, not the perceptions of anyone else.

MASTER OF THE ROSTER: CJI AND NOT THE COLLEGIUM

There is a convention in the Supreme Court that when the first Court is sitting in a Constitution Bench, no mentioning is made before it. Chief Justice Misra was sitting on a Constitution Bench sometime in November 2017. Advocate Prashant Bhushan, therefore, mentioned a medical college admission matter[26] (which later turned out to be a highly controversial case) before the court of Justice Chelameswar (senior most judge) who ordered it to be heard by a Constitution Bench without Chief Justice Misra. He had probably indicated a date too. Justice Misra did not take this kindly and sought to negate the order by constituting a larger Bench which reiterated by a judicial order that it is the Chief Justice who is the master of the roster and he alone can direct listing of a case before his or any other Bench. The above position was reaffirmed by the Supreme Court in July 2018 in *Shanti Bhushan vs Supreme Court of India*, wherein the contention that it is the Collegium which is the master of the roster and not the CJI, was rejected.[27]

Perhaps to ensure that no mentionings are made before any other Bench except the Chief Justice's Bench, Justice Misra resorted

---

[26]A case involving allegations of judicial corruption in connection with which a retired High Court judge was arrested.
[27](2018) 8 SCC, 396, *Shanti Bhushan vs Supreme Court of India* through its Registrar and Another.

to a strange practice. While the Constitution Bench headed by Chief Justice Misra continued to sit, at 10.30 a.m. and 2 p.m., before the sitting of the Constitution Bench, the CJI along with one or two other judges would sit on another Bench, primarily to take up mentionings. To say the least, it was very odd.

During my tenure, while hearing the Ayodhya case for nearly four months, all mentionings were made in Justice N.V. Ramana's court, as he was the senior most judge available. There was never any friction over this.

The medical admission matter did not die down and eventually led to the unsavoury move for impeachment of Chief Justice Misra. In this regard, one evening, a senior judge of the Supreme Court telephoned to inform me that a Congress Member of Parliament, who is also a leading Supreme Court lawyer, would be coming to see me in the morning in connection with the impeachment issue. I replied that he may be advised not to come. Yet, the following morning, I was informed by my office staff that the personage was waiting at the gate of my residence (10, Tees January Marg). I told my staff that I would not be meeting him. I believe they acted accordingly. I informed Justices Lokur and Joseph about this incident in my chamber in the Supreme Court that very morning.

The impeachment issue fizzled out with the Chairman of the Rajya Sabha refusing to entertain it. But it certainly did not do the institution of the judiciary any good.

Eight

....

THE CHIEF

O n the evening of 12 January 2018, I received a call from one of the other three judges who had participated in the press conference earlier in the day. He said, 'Brother,[28] I salute you. You did not let your career come in the way of doing what was right.'

The press conference attracted attention nationally and internationally. It was a most unusual event, going by the traditions of the judicial institution in a democracy, disapproved of by many on account of the perceived role of the judicial system and the conventions inherent in the institution. There was a lot of criticism. Irreparable institutional harm was perceived to have been caused by the judges by openly airing their grievances.

I became the focus of attention in the build-up of the adverse opinion regarding the press conference. It was said that the event gained gravity due to my presence. After all, I was in line to become the CJI later in the year. It was said that, having breached judicial tradition and discipline, I had forfeited my 'right' to become the CJI. A more vocal section even said that it was a highly irresponsible act on my part, as the future CJI; so irresponsible that I was not fit for elevation to the high office.

---

[28]'Brother' is an expression used by a judge while speaking to another judge.

Critics who always found fault with the Supreme Court did not come forward to defend the judges who at the press conference had 'faulted' the manner in which the Supreme Court was being administered. As time progressed, speculation became rife about my chances of becoming the CJI. The government of the day was dragged into the matter. Many sympathizers and well-wishers appeared from nowhere to tell me that people in power were sceptical. I was amused, to say the least. Knowing how the system of appointment of the CJI worked, I found no reason to take any serious note of the 'concern' expressed which, even if justified (I was sure it was not), hardly bothered me.

Around this time, another story was doing the rounds. As the son of a Congressman, it was speculated that my sympathies were with the Congress party. A judge with such leanings could be a dangerous proposition as the CJI. My newly found friends and sympathizers again offered solutions to the 'problems'.

The icing on the cake for them came in the form of the third Ramnath Goenka Memorial Lecture. As if to lend credence to the prevailing speculation, it was pointed out that here was a judge who wanted a revolution in the judicial system. Gogoi would be a high-risk CJI and such risk must be avoided at all costs.

The people who had been circulating the rumours and fuelling the speculation were unaware of the actual process of appointment of the CJI. The appointment of a CJI is made by the government on the recommendation of the outgoing CJI who normally makes the recommendation at least a month before the end of his tenure so as to give sufficient time to the government to process the matter and issue the warrant of appointment. I do not think that under the norms the government has an option to ignore the recommendation of the outgoing CJI. Therefore, the outgoing CJI plays a vital role in the appointment of his successor. The role of the government, contrary to popular perception, is extremely limited.

In view of the constitutional norms and practices, therefore, what was more important was the role of the outgoing CJI, Justice Dipak Misra, in this regard. Here, once again, the outgoing CJI is bound by convention which is deeply rooted in our constitutional framework. Unless there are very strong reasons, the senior most judge cannot be ignored and has to be recommended for elevation as the next CJI. It is almost mandatory and any exceptions will require the outgoing CJI to consult his senior colleagues. Except for a rare scenario which may be difficult to visualize, the outgoing CJI, according to me, has little discretion in the matter. Even then, many speculated whether Justice Misra would recommend my name in view of my participation in the press conference. Personally, I harboured no doubts.

Sure enough, precisely a month before his retirement, Justice Misra, as per tradition, came to my chamber before commencement of court work and handed over a copy of the letter from him to the law minister recommending my name as his successor. Thereafter, we shared some chocolates which I had brought in anticipation. Both of us then moved to the Judges' Lounge for the morning coffee which all the judges share in the lounge prior to the commencement of court work at 10.30 a.m. But Justice Misra did not make any announcement of the development in the lounge. I, therefore, had to remain quiet. The brother judges came to know of the recommendation from the media. When my turn came to recommend my successor, on the 'appointed' day i.e. a month before my retirement, after handing over a copy of the letter which I had written to the law minister, Justice Bobde and I walked to the lounge for the morning coffee. There I made a formal announcement that I had recommended him as the next CJI. We even cut a cake to mark it.

LORD GANESHA BRINGS CHEER

On 13 September 2018, coinciding with Ganesh Chaturthi, the warrant signed by the president of India appointing me as the

CJI with effect from the due date was brought to my residence at 10, Tees January Marg by the representative of the Department of Justice in the Ministry of Law and Justice. Immediately after the gentleman left, I handed over the warrant to Rupanjali to read. The children were informed and so was my mother who was in Dibrugarh. I had become the Chief Justice-designate. They were, of course, very happy. But I got the impression that they had not felt it would be otherwise.

The warrant of appointment of the CJI is issued well in time to enable the CJI-designate to familiarize himself with all matters concerning the Supreme Court and its administration. Once the CJI-designate is appointed, as a matter of convention, the outgoing CJI attends only to routine matters. In the event the outgoing CJI is required to take any major decision or one regarding a matter of policy, he is expected to do so in consultation with the CJI-designate. These are all healthy practices that have been established over a long period.

On and from the day the warrant of appointment was received, work started in the Registry of the Supreme Court and my home office for the oath-taking ceremony on 3 October. On being queried, I had indicated to the president's Secretariat that, subject to the convenience of the president, 10.45 a.m. would be a suitable time for administering of the oath. The Supreme Court Registry was informed by Rashtrapati Bhavan that about 250 personal guests could be invited by the CJI-designate for the oath-taking ceremony. Friends, acquaintances and members of the extended family came all the way from Assam. Similarly, people I had known, particularly the PGI doctors in Chandigarh as well as the doctors in Delhi who had so kindly looked after me were invited. They all came. There were lawyers and a few persons from Assam living in Delhi who were present. My court staff and my office staff, some with their families, also participated in the event.

The official gathering on the occasion was impressive, as usual.

The vice president, the prime minister (PM), cabinet ministers, the leader of the opposition and former PMs attended. Except for the customary namastes, there was no interaction with any of the dignitaries. There could have been none, given the clockwork precision with which the dignitaries, in order of precedence, entered the Durbar Hall.

Exactly a minute before the scheduled time, President Ram Nath Kovind arrived and at 10.45 a.m. administered the oath of office to me. In less than a minute I had become the 46th CJI. I had no idea that it would be as tumultuous as it turned out to be. Until then life had been relatively simple; I had not heard of or had any occasion to read *Live Law* and *Bar and Bench*, etc. I had little knowledge of what was going on in the world of activists (retired judges and practising lawyers) or in the world of people who claim to be the judicial intelligentsia. It was an altogether different world that I had stepped into, on and from 3 October 2018. The journey of 13 months had begun.

Nine

BATTLES FROM THE BENCH

A judgment is a delicate product of the judge's understanding of the law and the dictates of his conscience. Every judgment is susceptible to contrary views which are important for course correction within the system. But that is how it should be. Analyses of judgments must act as windows for reflection and not to undermine or denigrate the judge or the institution. I feel it has become necessary to steer prevalent thinking towards adopting and conforming to such values.

Having said that, I would like to touch upon, very briefly, a few judgments authored by me on what I consider to be issues of substance, including the 'controversial' judgments delivered during my tenure as the CJI.

I started my innings with a dissent in the petition challenging the election of Pranab Mukherjee as the president of India.[29] My view, which was in the minority in a five-judge Bench headed by the then CJI, Justice Altamas Kabir, was to the effect that the allegations of the holding of an office of profit by Mukherjee on the date of filing of nomination required a full-fledged trial, a view that Justice Chelameswar also took. Interestingly, the petitioner, P.A. Sangma, was a teacher in Don Bosco School, Dibrugarh, in

---

[29]In *Purno Agitok Sangma vs Pranab Mukherjee* (2013) 2 SCC 239.

the early 1960s when I was studying there. I knew him but as I had not met him for a long time, I had no reservations in hearing the case and deciding the preliminary issue (whether the case should go for a full-fledged trial, as mandated by the Supreme Court Rules) in his favour. Not for a moment did I feel that I should not be hearing Sangma's case. This is why, time and again, while on the Bench, I have maintained that the inability of a judge to hear a case must be in the last resort, perceived by the judge himself, though the views of others, undoubtedly, must also receive due consideration and respect. But unless the judge himself really and honestly entertains such a feeling, he should not refuse to hear the case. This is what I had done in a petition filed by human rights activist, writer and researcher Harsh Mander in connection with detenus awaiting deportation from Assam. Mander wanted me to recuse from the matter on account of certain statements made by me in the course of some court proceedings, which, according to him, made me 'unsuitable' to hear the case. I thought otherwise.

Sitting with Justice N.V. Ramana in *Adi Saiva Sivachariyargal Nala Sangam vs Govt. of Tamil Nadu and Another*,[30] we tried to balance the Fundamental Rights of a religious denomination under Articles 25 and 26 of the Constitution to decide what constitutes its essential religious practices, with the overarching constitutional mandate under Article 14. Specifically, it was held by us that the appointment of archakas (priests) in the temples in question (in Tamil Nadu) on the basis of Agamas (treatises pertaining to construction of temples, installation of idols and conduct of worship of the deity) would prevail, subject to the same not being based on caste, birth or any other constitutionally offensive parameters, in other words, Article 14. Writing the judgment in the case afforded me great pleasure and I relished every moment of the exercise.

---

[30](2016) 2 SCC 725.

Sitting with Justice R.F. Nariman in *Ram Singh vs Union of India*,[31] we interfered with the Government of India's decision to notify Jats as a Backward Class in certain states of the country. In doing so, the Court held that the paramount principle for determination in such cases would be social backwardness. Identification would require adherence to contemporary data and not historical wrongs. We emphasized the necessity of continual evolution of the methods and yardsticks for identification of emerging groups in society deserving palliative action by the State. Haryana literally burnt for some time after the judgment. We remained unmoved while numerous review petitions were filed.

By a judgment dated 13 May 2015, at the instance of two NGOs, Common Cause and Centre for Public Interest Litigation, in *Common Cause vs Union of India*,[32] the Court, consisting of Justice Pinaki Chandra Ghose and me, prohibited printing of photographs of all political persons in government advertisements, except the president, PM and the CJI (later modified to include governors and chief ministers). Why CJI, was repeatedly asked. This is because on occasions when government advertisements are issued concerning the judiciary and its achievements, the CJI should not be excluded. Is it not an occasion for the people to know a little about the judiciary? That, apart from the PM and the law minister of India, there is somebody called the CJI?

On a lighter note, one evening, while returning from a meeting, I noticed the photo of the then CJI at several bus stands. The picture had some lettering which I could not read as I was in a moving car. Two days later, when I ventured out to read the advertisements, they had already been taken off. I must concede that newspapers are certainly a better place for the photograph of the CJI than Delhi's bus stops!

The Uttar Pradesh Ministers (Salaries, Allowances and

---

[31](2015) 4 SCC 697.
[32](2015) 7 SCC 1.

My mother, my strength: Shanti Gogoi in front of our home in Dibrugarh, Assam.

Son of a Congressman: My father Keshab Chandra Gogoi (in the background in dark sunglasses) with former Prime Minister Rajiv Gandhi and his wife, Sonia Gandhi.

A nostalgic vibe: With classmates at St Stephen's College in 1973. I am standing on the extreme left.

Those were the days: At a fancy dress party in the Air Force Officers' Mess in Bareilly in 1975. I am seated on the extreme left.

A mentor and guide: J.P. Bhattacharjee with his juniors. I am second from the right. Amitava Roy and Hrishikesh Roy, both of whom rose to become Supreme Court judges, are first and second from the left, respectively.

The making of a justice: Being sworn-in as a judge of the Gauhati High Court in February 2001 by Chief Justice N.C. Jain.

The next chapter: Being administered the oath of office of the Chief Justice of the Punjab and Haryana High Court by Jagannath Pahadia, Governor of Haryana, in February 2011.

Welcome to the club: Chief Justice of India Sarosh Homi Kapadia congratulating me after my swearing-in as a judge of the Supreme Court in April 2012. Also seen are (standing from left) Justices G.S. Singhvi, D.K. Jain, T.S. Thakur and B.S. Chauhan. Justices Deepak Verma and Swatanter Kumar are standing behind them.

The Chief: President Ram Nath Kovind administers the oath of office to me as the 46th Chief Justice of India on 3 October 2018.

A visitor creates a flutter: Prime Minister Narendra Modi visits the Chief Justice's chamber in November 2018. Also seen (from extreme right): Justices S.A. Bobde, Madan Lokur, myself, my wife Rupanjali and Justice Kurian Joseph along with their spouses.

PM Modi listens intently as Justices Sharad Bobde and Madan Lokur engage in a conversation.

Protecting the rule of law: Participating in the First Judicial Conference of Constitutional and Supreme Courts/Councils of the OIC Member/Observer States in Istanbul, Turkey, in December 2018.

All in a day's work: With Prof. Zühtü Arslan, President of the Constitutional Court of the Republic of Turkey, in Istanbul, in December 2018.

A colossal place of worship: Rupanjali and I visit the Sheikh Zayed Grand Mosque in Abu Dhabi in December 2018.

'Elevated' conversations: With Rupanjali at the Burj Khalifa, Dubai, in December 2018.

Comparing notes: Presenting a memento to Justice Vyacheslav Lebedev, Chief Justice of the Supreme Court of the Russian Federation, at Sochi, in June 2019.

Speaking my mind: At Sochi in June 2019. To my right is Dr Justice D.Y. Chandrachud.

'Peppered' with Russian flavours: Enjoying a meal with Rupanjali in a restaurant in Sochi, Russia, in June 2019.

On top of the world: With Rupanjali on the 148th floor of the Burj Khalifa in June 2019.

Celebrating the landmark Ayodhya verdict: In conversation with my brother judges at Taj Mansingh on 9 November 2019. To my right is Dr Justice D.Y. Chandrachud; to my left is Justice S. Abdul Nazeer. Facing us (from right) are Justices Sharad Bobde and Ashok Bhushan.

The five men behind the anonymous Ayodhya verdict (from left): Justices Ashok Bhushan and Sharad Bobde, myself, Dr Justice D.Y. Chandrachud and Justice S. Abdul Nazeer.

Retirement retreat: Holidaying in Bali in January 2020.

Miscellaneous Provisions) Act, 1981 (as amended in 2016) made provisions for allotment of government accommodation to former chief ministers of the state for their lifetimes. In *Lok Prahari vs State of Uttar Pradesh and Others*,[33] sitting with Justice R. Banumathi, we held these provisions to be violative of the doctrine of equality. It was held that the Act, insofar as allotment of government accommodation is concerned, creates a special class of citizens for conferment of benefits and a CM, on demitting office, is on a par with any other citizen. The provision, therefore, was found to have failed to satisfy the test of reasonable clarification to save it from being ultra vires of Article 14. I remember some faint voices demanding application of the same logic to former PMs and presidents of the country also.

Judgments delivered in the CBI director's case, the Rafale case, Kashmir cases i.e. cases arising out of the abrogation of Article 370 and *habeas corpus* petitions challenging preventive detention orders passed by the competent authority, and, above all, the Ram Janmabhoomi case have been widely commented upon. But before I go to these judgments, let me touch upon one aspect which is interlinked—the independence of the judiciary. This has been judicially recognized as a basic feature of the Constitution, the bedrock of democracy and the ultimate saviour of life and liberty for citizens. Of late, however, it has become a convenient slogan that is being used very selectively by a group of activist lawyers and academics to judge the judges. The development, in my opinion, does not augur well for the institution.

I ask myself this question: independence of the judiciary from whom? The executive? I would not like to pretend that the judiciary is totally free from approach by the executive but, on the whole, I think that as an institution, we have been able to acquit ourselves well on this count. There are ways of dealing with the situation and our judges, over the years, have perfected the means of retaining

---

[33](2018) 6 SCC 1.

their independence without getting into any confrontation with the executive.

I am of the opinion that though attempts at executive control of the judiciary are real, the true danger, as strong, if not more, emanates from another quarter. This is based on my personal observations and experiences, and my reading and analysis of the public utterances/conduct of a group of people who hold out the card of judicial independence or lack of it. They do this through public speeches and writings in selective agenda-based publications which, at times, unfairly make personal attacks on judges based on misinformation. They are highly organized and though few in number, exert a powerful voice and a firm grip/control over the means of expression which includes a few newspapers and portals. They have devised novel ways of circulating what they write. A sentence or a paragraph in an article/write-up/news item with the author's jaundiced perception of a 'judicial wrong' is circulated in the social media and made to go viral.

Any judgment of a court or a view expressed, if it does not have the approval of this group, becomes a target, the stick to beat and discredit the judge. This leads to them saying that judicial independence has been surrendered to the executive. Every judgment on any important issue must necessarily be what this motley group desires. They prepare a report card at the end of the tenure of a judge. The message is clear: a good report card will come at a cost; if you are not ready to conform to a particular way of thinking and act accordingly, you will earn the dubious reputation of having compromised and surrendered the independence of the judiciary. The tragedy of the situation is that in the name of the independence of the judiciary, I believe, based on my experience, the institution is in danger of becoming dependent on the wishes, not necessarily of the executive, but of this group who are also the self-proclaimed champions of human rights and free speech or such other public causes.

This is the real danger and not even the Supreme Court is free from or immune to it. In fact, it is gaining strength every day. The danger of judges falling prey to this group of people either consciously or subconsciously is serious. Who would not like to leave the institution at the age of 65 unscathed and with a commendable report card that will be well circulated? Judges have to leave a legacy for their next generation which has to live and work in the prevailing ecosystem.

The danger of personal attacks on non-conformist judges is the greatest threat to the institution and in turn to democracy and the independence of the judiciary. In the name of saving democracy, there are veiled attacks that can kill democracy. A single narrative by this group of people is what is available today in the public domain. There is no other narrative to enable citizens to have the benefit of an alternative view of the matter. Enlightened citizens choose to stay away from confrontation, rendering the singular voice louder and more widespread. I believe the response of the judiciary in this regard and its efforts to handle the issue have been singularly lacking.

A judgment is the outcome of the conscious mind of the judge on any legal issue, free of bias and prejudice, independent of all external forces and agencies. The direction in which the final conclusion has gone is irrelevant. Merely because the view expressed or the conclusion reached has favoured the establishment will obviously not make the judgment wrong in law or amount to surrendering to the executive. Strong opinion is being circulated by the same group of people that key issues brought before the Court, usually by means of PILs, must necessarily be decided against the government, failing which the Court has to be understood to have been prompted by extraneous reasons or the influence of the executive. Such instances are gaining in frequency. The PILs in the 2G scam and the coal allocation cases, not to mention other PILs, were all decided against the State. Government action was interfered with. The authors of the judgments became the heroes of the moment. But what happened thereafter? It is a matter of record that colossal loss had been caused to the economy; foreign investment had become shy and investors' confidence had dwindled. Strangely, after the damage had been done, several criminal prosecutions arising out of those cases have ended in acquittal. Sadly, the damage is complete.

Let us examine the mining matters of the states of Odisha, Karnataka and Goa. True, extreme degradation of the environment was caused by the illegal mining, but was complete closure of the mines the solution to the problem? Has there been any quantification of the loss caused to the national economy? Has the impact of the closure on employment, income and quality of life been assessed? While the mines in Odisha and Karnataka have reopened partially and conditionally, the closure in Goa is still in force. I am not suggesting that the closure orders passed by the Supreme Court are for any other reason than legal necessity but cannot judges even of the apex court fall prey, even momentarily, to the strong temptation to become the man of the moment? Passing of interim orders against the establishment earns laurels. Refusal can bring about misery for the judge and even his family.

In an interview to a national TV channel in March 2020, in a lighter vein, I had said that retired judges do not talk about their judgments; they do not defend their judgments, they only attack the judgments of others. Today, what I write about any of my judgments is not to be construed as defence, rather as mere narration of my thoughts and experiences.

CBI Director

In the case of Alok Kumar Verma, Director, CBI, the challenge was against orders divesting him of his powers and duties as director, CBI, pending inquiry into certain allegations received in a complaint filed against him. The challenge was made by Verma himself and also by Common Cause. The impugned action was taken by the

Central Vigilance Commission (CVC) without reference to the high-powered committee (consisting of the PM, CJI and leader of the opposition) under Section 4A (1) of the Delhi Special Police Establishment (DSPE) Act, 1946. The orders divesting Verma of the powers, functions and duties of the director, CBI, were found by the Court to be in breach of the above mandatory requirement of law i.e. reference to the high-powered committee and were therefore set aside and the matter remitted to the high-powered committee for fresh consideration at the earliest. The appointment of M. Nageshwar Rao as the acting director, CBI, was also set aside by the Court. The order of the Supreme Court is dated 8 January 2019.

Verma's writ petition was allowed by the Court and he was reinstated in the post of CBI director with certain conditions. The activists called it a partial victory and found the condition imposed by the Court strange and unwarranted in law. The condition was the one that till his case is again considered by the high-powered committee, Verma would not take any policy decisions. Such conditions, I must state, are usually and always passed by a court when any executive decision is required to be reconsidered and retaken by the competent authority.

On 10 January 2019, the high-powered committee under Section 4A (1) of the DSPE Act, 1946 was convened by the appropriate authority to consider the matter, as directed by the Court. As the CJI, I could not have participated in the meeting as I had authored the judgment. Justice A.K. Sikri, the then senior most judge, was therefore nominated by me. The PM and Justice Sikri were of the view that Verma ought to be replaced/transferred whereas the third member, Mallikarjun Kharge (leader of the opposition) dissented. On the basis of the majority view of the high-powered committee, Verma was replaced by an acting director. Verma's term expired on 31 January 2019. Rishi Kumar Shukla was selected as the new director on 2 February 2019.

Interestingly, Verma's initial appointment as the CBI director in 2016 was challenged before the Supreme Court by the same NGO i.e. Common Cause in a proceeding registered as W.P(C) No.984/2016, which was dismissed on 20 January 2017. Two years later, the same group of people who had initially challenged Verma's appointment as the CBI director had resisted his transfer from the post. They had succeeded in the challenge made. Yet they criticized the judgment of the Court. It is difficult, well-nigh impossible, for me to understand how the minds of these people work. Obviously, there is more than what meets the eye.

As far as Verma is concerned, I must acknowledge that in certain quarters he enjoys the reputation of being an officer of high integrity and dedication. The perception of the political executive with regard to his suitability to continue as the CBI director is a matter with which we as judges are not concerned. What had to be judged by us is the legality and not the necessity of the executive actions and it was so done and decided.

Rafale

In the Rafale case, the main prayer in the four writ petitions that were filed was for a Court-monitored CBI investigation into allegations of corruption and wrongdoing in the award and execution of the contract for procurement of 36 Rafale fighter jets. The broad view of the Bench was that defence procurement contracts like aircraft acquisition, submarine procurement and so on, if challenged, ought not to be judged by the same yardstick as applicable to grant of building or road construction contracts. The Bench took the view that this principle should guide its consideration of the specific prayers made in the writ petitions.

All issues raised were considered and decided from the standpoint of limited judicial review under Article 32 of the Constitution under which the writ petitions were filed and entertained. Though many would have liked the Court to act as an appellate or investigative body, the Bench did not believe that it would be correct to exercise any such jurisdiction. Judicial decisions are rendered on the basis of materials brought before the Court and not on perceptions or expectations of any person or group of persons. That is how Rafale was decided.

The unilateral interactions with high-ranking air force officials in open court were intended to lend assurance to the Court about the need and quality of the aircraft. The highest court of the land cannot be understood to be entrapped by any particular procedure and must always be left with the freedom to develop its own procedures from time to time and from case to case, if need be, particularly while considering matters of vital importance to the nation, especially national security.

There was a demand raised before the Court for divulging the cost details of the aircraft, including the price of the armaments. The Court considered such information to be dangerous to the country's security as it would have made all, including the enemies of India, aware of the armoury that the aircraft was intended to carry. Thus, the Court asked for and received those details in a sealed cover.

This procedure, which kept certain information from the parties and the public, was adversely commented upon. As the Chief Justice, I was called the innovator of the sealed cover procedure, which was claimed to be inimical to sound judicial practice. However, the sealed cover procedure had been in vogue much before my time as the CJI. In fact, documents had been submitted in a sealed cover in connection with the 2009 contempt case against Prashant Bhushan which was recently sought to be heard by the Supreme Court. The sealed cover procedure was adopted in the 2G and the coal scam cases before the Supreme Court. In fact, in the Shaheen Bagh case, Sanjay Hegde, one of the critics of the sealed cover procedure, had himself submitted a report to the Court in a sealed cover. Is it not a case of double standards?

Reports of investigations are usually submitted in sealed covers. Are the defence secrets of the country less important than the mediation reports in the Shaheen Bagh case or investigation reports in the 2G or coal scam cases? Not only can reports be submitted in sealed covers, if necessary, in public interest, the Supreme Court can hold and has, in fact, held PIL proceedings in camera—for instance, in the Vineet Narain case while examining the Jain hawala diaries. I strongly feel that, using the transparency card, people cannot be allowed to bring into the public domain information and records that the interests of the nation or public order would require to be kept confidential.

The main judgment in the Rafale case is dated 14 December 2018. The review petition filed was also dismissed by a reasoned order dated 14 November 2019 authored by Justice S.K. Kaul. Justice Joseph wrote a separate order with an added direction but the ultimate conclusion i.e. that the review petitions should be dismissed, was unanimous. All issues and questions raised were dealt with and answered by the Bench.

The judgment drew much attention and was widely and violently attacked. The main judgment was delivered by three judges unanimously, so also the review judgment on whether the review should be allowed. But the attack was directed solely at the CJI who, by virtue of his position, headed the Bench. It was mounted by people who know that on the judicial side i.e. while sitting on the Bench, the Chief Justice enjoys no additional judicial power. His judicial powers are the same as any other judge of the Supreme Court.

Closely connected with the Rafale case was the contempt proceeding initiated against Rahul Gandhi with regard to certain statements he had made in respect of PM Narendra Modi, dubbing him the dishonest chowkidar of the nation. In a public statement, Mr Gandhi had said that such an attribution had been made by the Supreme Court. Obviously, his statement regarding the Supreme

Court was wholly incorrect. In the affidavit dated 29 April 2019, he, inter alia, said that the statement made by him was '... made by the answering respondent in Hindi in a rhetorical flourish in the heat of the moment. It was during a political campaign without a readable copy of the Supreme Court order being available on its website and, therefore, without the answering respondent having seen or read the order and relying upon electronic and social media reportage and the version of workers and activists surrounding the Respondent...'

In his affidavit, Mr Gandhi further stated, 'My statement was made in the heat of political campaigning. It has been used (and misused) by my political opponents to project that I had deliberately and intentionally suggested that this Court had said *Chowkidar Chor Hai*.'

While Mr Gandhi denied that any such attribution was made by the Supreme Court, yet there was no categorical regret for the wrong impression given; neither was there any hint of an apology. It was a 20-page affidavit which was placed before the Court by his lawyer, Abhishek Manu Singhvi. In the course of the hearing, Singhvi kept repeating that Mr Gandhi had apologized to the Court for the incorrect attribution but there was no such statement in the affidavit. On being asked to read out the said statement, Singhvi kept beating about the bush, reading everything else but not the one sentence that the Court wanted to hear. He could not have done so as there was no such statement by Mr Gandhi in the affidavit either apologizing to the Court or expressing regret over the matter in any way. Thereafter, the case was adjourned and a fresh affidavit dated 8 May 2019 was filed by Mr Gandhi, tendering an unconditional apology. With a final judgment dated 14 November 2019, the Court closed the proceedings with the observation that Mr Gandhi should be careful in future. Paragraphs 29 to 33 of the Court's judgment authored by Justice Kaul record the above facts. I do not think the Congress party, as a whole, was happy about the incident.

Sabarimala

In the Sabarimala temple case, the law in force denying entry of women (of a particular age group) into the Sabarimala temple was set aside by the Supreme Court in a 4:1 verdict. Justice Indu Malhotra disagreed and passed a dissenting judgment. After Justice Dipak Misra's retirement, all review matters pertaining to Justice Misra were to be heard by me. That is how the review petitions in the Sabarimala case came before a Bench consisting of myself (in place of Justice Misra) and the four other judges who were parties to the original order.

In the meantime, it came to my notice that the fate of women's entry into religious places of other denominations, on which issue other cases were pending before the Supreme Court, may have got pre-decided by the majority judgment in the Sabarimala case. I was, therefore, of the tentative view that to overcome such an undesirable situation (cases getting pre-decided without hearing the contesting parties), the legal issues decided in Sabarimala needed rehearing along with the other cases. In the meetings held with the members of the Bench, Justice A.M. Khanwilkar expressed the view that he was in favour of rehearing of the larger issues arising in the case without disturbing the correctness of the majority judgment in the Sabarimala case to which he was a party. Justice Malhotra and I agreed. It was accordingly decided by a 3:2 majority that questions of law decided in Sabarimala would now be reheard by a larger Bench. Neither has the original order of the Constitution Bench been doubted nor have the review petitions been decided finally. All questions have been kept open to be argued. But reopening of what was considered a concluded issue and that too of vital importance for Hindu faith and society was not taken too kindly by a lot of people.

To my mind, there was nothing extraordinary about the CBI director, Rafale or Sabarimala cases. They were routine adjudications made in the normal course of business of the Court. I wonder what would have been the scenario if the decisions of the Court had been the reverse. 'Unfortunately', my judgments could not be tailored to suit any particular group. A judge has no cause to espouse; no case to further. He has to decide in accordance with law and the dictates of his conscience and not the dictates of any particular group.

Kashmir cases

On 5 August 2019, Article 370 of the Constitution which conferred a special status on the then state of Jammu and Kashmir was revoked. The process leading to the exercise came to be challenged before the Supreme Court in a number of writ petitions. On the very first day of the petition being listed before my Court, the Bench referred the matter to the Constitution Bench as required under Article 145 of the Constitution when constitutional issues of grave importance are raised. As of date, the bunch of writ petitions is still pending consideration by the Court.

A couple of *habeas corpus*[34] petitions challenging the preventive detention of members of civil society also came to be filed directly under Article 32 before the Supreme Court. Three such petitions were listed in my Court. There may have been other *habeas corpus* petitions filed around this time which may have got listed before other Benches. Details of the progress of such cases would, therefore, not be known to me. I can only mention the cases that came up before my Bench.

In W.P. (Crl.) No.225/2019 *Mohammad Aleem Syed vs Union of India*, by order dated 28 August 2019, the Court permitted the petitioner to go to Anantnag in Jammu and Kashmir to meet his parents and after ascertaining their welfare, to report back to the Court. This course of action has been criticized as being curious and unusual. It may appear to be so but was adopted to enable

---

[34]Habeas corpus literally means produce the body. A high prerogative writ, it enables the court to entertain challenges against allegedly unlawful orders of detention by the State and, in a given case, even by a private individual, say, a father illegally detaining a married daughter.

a son (the petitioner) to meet his parents forthwith and satisfy himself about their welfare and apprise the Court accordingly. It was an attempt to cut short lengthy procedures of law. The report came promptly and on 5 September, the Bench presided over by me issued notice. The writ petition in question was closed as infructuous on the statement made by the counsel for the petitioner on 19 November (after my retirement).

◆

In Sitaram Yechury's case [W.P. (Crl.) No.229/2019], some elaborate orders were passed by the Court. As the petition was in respect of an aged person, Mohammed Yousuf Tarigami, who, the petitioner, Yechury, himself admitted to be not in good health, the Bench deviated from the practice of production of the detenue that is normally done in *habeas corpus* matters and instead proceeded to pass orders on 28 August 2019, inter alia, permitting Yechury to go to Jammu and Kashmir to meet the detenue and ascertain the state of his health and the need for specialized medical treatment. On 5 September, the bench ordered shifting of Tarigami to AIIMS in New Delhi. He was discharged from hospital on 13 September with advice to report back to AIIMS or any other hospital after a month. It was stated before the Court by the government that Tarigami was free to go to Srinagar whenever he desired. All this is recorded in the Court's order dated 16 September wherein the Court, while declining Tarigami any anticipatory orders with regard to his movement once he went to Srinagar, permitted him to move the Jammu and Kashmir High Court in this regard, if the situation so necessitated.

The emphasis in the case of Yechury's challenge to the detention of Tarigami was the need for urgent medical attention for the detenue which was provided by the Court. The detention order also seemed to have worked itself out, as evident from the Court order of 16 September.

In the case filed by the daughter of Mehbooba Mufti, former CM of Jammu and Kashmir, i.e. W.P (Crl.) No. 250/2019, the writ petition was closed on the very first day (5 September 2019) with the following order:

> We have heard learned counsel for the petitioner, Mr K.K. Venugopal, learned Attorney General for India, as also, Mr Tushar Mehta, learned Solicitor General of India.
>
> From the deliberations that have taken place, we are of the view that the State Government has not and does not intend to prevent the petitioner from coming back to Srinagar from Chennai, where she is presently staying and meeting her mother. The petitioner may accordingly return to Srinagar on a date of her choice. She would be free to meet her mother in private.
>
> So far as moving around in other parts of Srinagar is concerned, the petitioner would be free to do so subject to requisite permission from the district authorities as and when necessary.
>
> With the aforesaid observations, the writ petition is disposed of.
>
> Pending interlocutory applications, if any, shall stand disposed of.

I have reproduced the order as much has been said about my reported reaction asking why the petitioner wanted to move around freely in Srinagar since the weather there at that time of the year would be cold. I did make such a statement but it was on a lighter note. Judges need to lighten matters at times in view of the strenuous and serious nature of the work they undertake. The effective order that was passed in the matter is that the petitioner therein, Iltija, was free to move around in Srinagar subject to permission from the district authorities, if so required. Slight deviations from the set procedure in larger public interest and in the pursuit of substantial justice would always be permissible and in fact expected, especially from the top court of the country.

◆

A prominent political leader of Jammu and Kashmir belonging to the Congress and a former CM of the state, Ghulam Nabi Azad, had also filed a writ petition before the Supreme Court i.e. W.P(C) No.1164/2019. His petition was for directions to enable him to go to Kashmir and move around to find out for himself the conditions prevailing in the state. On 16 September 2019, the Bench headed by me entertained the petition and permitted Azad to visit Jammu, Srinagar, Anantnag and Baramulla. He had undertaken before the Court that while visiting the above places, he would not indulge in any political activity. This is recorded by the Court in its order dated 16 September.

◆

The proceedings registered and numbered as W.P. (C) No.1031/2019—*Anuradha Bhasin vs Union of India & Ors*—and W.P.(C) No. 1166/2019—*Enakshi Ganguly & Anr. vs Union of India & Ors*—pertained to protection to be afforded to juveniles, who had been detained, and for restoration of internet and 4G services in Kashmir, which had been discontinued. Both the petitions were entertained by my Bench on 10 August 2019 and 16 September 2019, respectively.

Soon after the Kashmir petitions were filed, entertained and preliminary orders were passed, I realized that it was not feasible for me to keep entertaining and hearing the Kashmir matters as I was in the midst of the Ayodhya hearing. Therefore, by an administrative order on 30 September, I assigned all the Kashmir cases to the Bench of the senior most judge available. (Justice Bobde was a part of the Ayodhya Bench.)

The administrative order assigning all Kashmir cases to another Bench read:

TABLE 3
Matter for 01.10.2019

S.No./ Sec.	Case No. & Title	Subject Category & Issue
1. X	W.P.(CRL.) No. 229/2019 Sitaram Yechury Vs. Union of India & Anr.	1300: (Habeas Corpus Matters)
2. X	W.P.(CRL.) No. 262/2019 Asifa Mubeen Vs. State of Jammu & Kashmir & Ors.	1300: (Habeas Corpus Matters)
3. X	W.P.(C) No. 1164/2019 Ghulam Nabi Azad Vs. Union of India & Anr.	1807: (Ordinary Civil Matters-Others)
4. PIL	W.P.(C) No. 1166/2019 Enakshi Ganguly & Anr. Vs. Union of India & Ors.	0812: (Letter Petition & PIL Matters-Others)
5. PIL	W.P.(C) No. 1188/2019 Dr Sameer Kaul & Anr. Vs. Union of India & Ors.	0812: (Letter Petition & PIL Matters-Others)
6. X	W.P.(C) No. 1031/2019 Anuradha Bhasin Vs. Union of India & Ors.	1807: (Ordinary Civil Matters-Others)

It is submitted that all the matters mentioned above have been filed after the abrogation of Article 370 of the Constitution from the State of Jammu & Kashmir. The same were listed before the Special Bench comprising Hon'ble the CJI, Hon'ble Mr Justice S.A. Bobde and Hon'ble Mr Justice S. Abdul Nazeer today i.e. on 30.09.2019 when the Hon'ble Court directed to list the matters tomorrow i.e. 01.10.2019.

Under the circumstances, orders of Hon'ble the CJI are solicited as to whether:

(A) Special Bench comprising of Your Lordship, Hon'ble Mr Justice S.A. Bobde and Hon'ble Mr Justice S. Abdul Nazeer may be constituted tomorrow i.e. on 01.10.2019 (Tuesday) at 10:30 A.M. for listing the instant matters and the same may accordingly be listed through the Supplementary List.[35]

OR

(B) Your Lordship may like to grant fresh coram[36] for listing the instant matters and the same may accordingly be listed before the Bench so nominated on 01.10.2019 (Tuesday) through the Supplementary List.

OR

any other directions as may be given by Your Lordship.

Sd/-

Addl. Registrar (DeU)

30.09.2019

Ld. Registrar (J-I/J-II)

Hon'ble the Chief Justice of India

Alternate Bench headed by Justice xxx Sd/-

30/9

The aforesaid administrative order is self-evident and would also enlighten persons who are often told that the business of the

---

[35]Supplementary List means supplementary/additional cause list.
[36]Coram means Bench.

Supreme Court is always shrouded in secrecy and mystery. It is not so in reality. There is complete in-house transparency which for good and adequate reasons is not put in the public domain.

My statement in court on 30 September that I did not have time to hear the Kashmir cases was correct. I was in the midst of the Ayodhya hearing. What would have been the credibility of the Supreme Court as an institution if the Ayodhya matter was to remain inconclusive on the date of my retirement? I did make such a statement but as the administrative order extracted in the previous page shows, all the Kashmir matters were assigned to another Bench and were to be listed on the very next day.

However, what was thrown into focus was that the CJI had no time for the Kashmir matters. What was deliberately and selectively omitted was that all the Kashmir matters were assigned to the Bench of the senior most judge available on that day itself and were to come up before that Bench on 1 October 2019. There has to be a limit to misinformation. It can be destructive and, at times, have disastrous consequences.

If a person is to be faulted and belittled, come what may, reasons cease to be relevant. It is the ferocity and viciousness of the attack that replace logic and reason. Holders of high public offices are usually victims of such attacks and repetitive noise. It is an occupational hazard. The dearth of response is not due to absence of rejoinders so much as the lack of any necessity to reply to non-relevant logic or its non-existence in such attacks. Yet, at the right time and opportunity, a little retort is in order not for any other reason but just to put things in proper perspective. This is how I would like to be understood.

Ten

'SUPREME' ALLEGATIONS AND MY QUEST FOR TRUTH

In early 2019, certain unfounded, unfortunate and unprecedented allegations of sexual harassment were brought against me by a lady employee of the Supreme Court, who had worked in my home office for about two months from August to October 2018. Prior to that, she had worked in my Court as a library staffer for about three years.

I was informed of these allegations on the evening of 19 April 2019 when my wife and I returned to Delhi from Tirupati. The complaint of the staffer was sent to all the Supreme Court judges and to some websites such as *The Wire, Scroll, The Leaflet, The Caravan* and so on who, in turn, sent more or less similar questionnaires to me, demanding a response within a few hours, failing which they threatened publication of the allegations.

Later that Friday night, I received information that an Article 32 petition was likely to be filed in the Supreme Court the next day i.e. 20 April, a Saturday, seeking, inter alia, orders restraining the CJI from discharging his duties until he was cleared of the allegations levelled by the staffer. Obviously, the plan was to stop me, with immediate effect, from attending to any administrative or judicial work. The following morning, I rang up the Attorney

General, the Solicitor General and the president of the SCBA to inform them of the developments. The Solicitor General requested that a Bench be constituted to decide whether judicial orders, if any, should be passed in the circumstances. I reflected upon the matter and soon concluded that aggression would be the best form of defence in the circumstances. I had no options.

I, therefore, informed the Registry and all concerned that there would be a special sitting of the Court consisting of Justice Arun Mishra, Justice Sanjiv Khanna and me at 10.30 a.m. Accordingly, the Bench assembled in Court No. 1. The Attorney General, the Solicitor General, the president of the SCBA and a few lawyers who were present were informed of the details of the allegations and the antecedents of the staffer, as revealed by her service record. This unscheduled hearing on Saturday which has been much talked about, was extremely short. In fact, there was no hearing at all. I expressed my indignation at the allegations and maintained that it was an attempt by certain unknown quarters to jeopardize the functioning of the CJI. At the end of the hearing, a very innocuous order was passed:

SUO MOTO WRIT PETITION (CIVIL) NO. 1/2019

IN RE: MATTER OF GREAT PUBLIC IMPORTANCE
TOUCHING UPON THE INDEPENDENCE OF JUDICIARY—
MENTIONED BY SHRI TUSHAR MEHTA, SOLICITOR
GENERAL OF INDIA

ORDER

Having considered the matter, we refrain from passing any judicial order at this moment leaving it to the wisdom of the media to show restraint, act responsibly as is expected from them and accordingly decide what should or should not be published as wild and scandalous allegations undermine and irreparably damage reputation and negate independence of judiciary. We would therefore at this juncture leave it to the media to take off such material which is undesirable.

(Justice Arun Mishra)
(Justice Sanjiv Khanna)

New Delhi
April 20, 2019

The situation was unprecedented. For the first time in the history of the Supreme Court of India, such allegations had been levelled against the CJI. A reputation built over nearly 45 years in the Bar and on the Bench was sought to be destroyed. My presence on the Bench, which in hindsight could have been avoided, was the expression of indignation roused on the spur of the moment by an accusation which was beyond belief and comprehension. Though I was on the Bench, I did not sign the order (extracted above). In fact no effective judicial order was passed on that date.[37]

It is not that I gave a clean chit to myself authoritatively, as perceived and alleged by many. Rather, on the morning of 21 April, I wrote to the senior most judge, Justice Bobde, requesting him to take over the complaint of the staffer and deal with it in an appropriate manner as considered fit and proper:

April 21, 2019

Dear Brother Bobde,

My attention has been drawn to a complaint lodged by _____against me levelling certain charges and requesting for an enquiry into the allegations levelled. As the allegations

---

[37]On subsequent dates, Justices Arun Mishra, Rohinton Fali Nariman and Deepak Gupta were on the Bench. It is this Bench that dealt with the issues raised by Utsav Singh Bains and referred the matter to the Patnaik Committee. After the retirement of Justices Mishra and Gupta, the Bench was reconstituted and it was this reconstituted Bench that passed orders closing the matter on 18 February 2021, as narrated later.

Ranjan Gogoi

have been levelled against me, naturally, as the senior most judge you will be required to deal with the matter instead of the Chief Justice of India. Accordingly, I request you to look into the matter and take appropriate action as may be considered fit and proper.

With regards,

Yours sincerely,

Sd/-

(Ranjan Gogoi)

Hon'ble Mr Justice S.A. Bobde,
7, Krishna Menon Marg,
New Delhi

DUE PROCESS OF LAW AND LOGIC

On 23 April Justice Bobde constituted a committee consisting of Justice N.V. Ramana, Justice Indira Banerjee and himself to hold an inquiry into the allegations in accordance with the in-house inquiry procedure.

The in-house inquiry procedure[38] to inquire into allegations against a sitting High Court/Supreme Court judge has been evolved by a Judges' Committee constituted for the purpose. It has been approved by the full court of the Supreme Court in a meeting by a resolution dated 15 December 1999 and has since been and continues to be the procedure established by law.

It is the CJI who is the ultimate authority in an in-house inquiry (set out as part of the Annexures) and decides whether to initiate the process of inquiry or not and if so to what stage the matter should be carried. It is the CJI who decides on the composition

---

[38]In-house procedure is the procedure prescribed by law.

of the committee and what action, if any, should be taken after receipt of the inquiry report. Naturally, if the allegations were levelled against the CJI himself, the next senior most judge would step into the shoes of the CJI and perform all the duties of the CJI under the in-house procedure. This is not specifically spelt out, but would logically follow because whenever the CJI is incapacitated from performing any duty, the senior most judge steps in. This is axiomatic.

In terms of the laid-down procedure, in an in-house proceeding on receipt of a complaint, the CJI may dismiss it at the very beginning. Alternatively, he may ask the judge concerned for his views/comments and thereafter, on being satisfied, either drop the matter or proceed to hold an inquiry. The inquiry is to be conducted by three sitting judges nominated by the CJI. No outsider, including advocates, is to be allowed. I do not understand under what law or procedure high and mighty voices demanded an inquiry by retired Supreme Court judges and outsiders, or that the services of an advocate be made available or an amicus curiae be appointed.[39]

If the allegations are found to be devoid of merit, the complaint is to be dismissed. If the charges are found to have substance but are not serious enough to warrant the removal of the judge, he has to be spoken to by the CJI. In the event that the allegations harbour substance warranting removal of the judge from office, he is to be asked to step down. If he does not do so, the matter goes to the president and the PM, perhaps to thereafter take the impeachment route. The first step in that eventuality would be that a motion for impeachment would have to be moved, and if it is to be admitted by the Speaker of the Lok Sabha or the Chairman of the Rajya Sabha, as may be, a full-fledged inquiry under the Judges (Inquiry) Act, 1968, by a committee constituted by the Speaker or the Chairman will have to be ordered.

On 24 April, the lady staffer sent a communication to Justice

---

[39]Amicus curiae refers to a person (often an advocate) appointed by the court to assist it.

Bobde that she would like Justice Ramana to stay away from the committee, inter alia, on the ground that he was like a member of my family! To my disappointment (only regarding the matter of principle), Justice Ramana recused. Though Supreme Court judges are a part of one family and meet and interact with one another every day, yet an in-house procedure wherein sitting judges alone would hold inquiries against brother judges has been evolved and approved by the full court. After Justice Ramana's recusal, the committee was reconstituted by Justice Bobde on 25 April, replacing Justice Ramana with Justice Indu Malhotra. The reconstituted committee, therefore, consisted of Justice Bobde (the senior most judge at that time) and Justices Indira Banerjee and Indu Malhotra. Both decisions of Justice Bobde constituting and reconstituting the committee on 23 April and 25 April, respectively, were approved by all the judges of the Supreme Court (full court) in writing (included in the Annexures)—an important fact that did not get reported or highlighted anywhere.

Though the complaint was entrusted to Justice Bobde to be dealt with by him as he thought fit, I was happy when Justice Bobde straightaway went to the third stage of the in-house procedure and ordered an inquiry. The inquiry commenced on or around 26 April. The lady staffer initially participated in the inquiry for three days. Thereafter, she reportedly requested the presence of an advocate. This is not permissible under the in-house procedure and was declined. At that stage, she walked out of the inquiry in the presence of three Hon'ble Judges of the Supreme Court of India.

Justice Bobde, through a polite letter, invited me for a cup of tea with the members of the committee. No matter what guise one might try to shroud it in, I recognized the invitation to tea as nothing else but a notice to me to appear before the committee. I complied but felt somewhat belittled. I submitted materials in my defence.

The Bobde Committee came to the conclusion that the charges were unsubstantiated. The inquiry report—an exhaustive 70-odd pages—was dated 6 May. On the same day, it was submitted to Justice Arun Mishra, the next senior most judge competent in law to deal with the matter (allegations were against the CJI, Justice Bobde was a member of the committee, Justice Ramana had recused, so that left Justice Mishra). I was told he saw the report and ordered it to be placed in a sealed cover. In view of the conclusion of the Bobde Committee, I would like to refrain from any comment on the merits of the charges or speculation on reasons behind the episode and the identity of the person(s) propping the staffer, if so.

The in-house procedure read with the judgment of the Supreme Court in *Indira Jaising vs Registrar General, Supreme Court of India & Anr.* reported in (2003) 5 SCC 494 requires the inquiry report to remain confidential because, as observed by the Supreme Court, if made public, it has the potential to do more harm than good. There is great wisdom in this view. A copy of the report was furnished to me; not in my capacity as the CJI, but as the judge against whom the allegations were levelled. This requirement is enshrined in the Resolution of the full court dated 15 December 1999, accepting the in-house procedure. I have, therefore, kept the report confidential.

The confidentiality attached to the in-house inquiry procedure perhaps, inter alia, for reasons mentioned above, have recently been reiterated by the Supreme Court in a press release dated 7 January 2021 in the following terms:

SUPREME COURT OF INDIA
(PUBLIC RELATIONS OFFICE)

No. PR/SCI/2021/01/01   Date: 07.01.2021

PRESS RELEASE

Media has recently been reporting about complaints making insinuations against members of the higher judiciary, and the action likely to be taken by the Chief Justice of India. Supreme

Court is being quoted as the source of the information. It is clarified once and for all that inquiries under the 'In-house Procedure' being totally and wholly confidential in nature, Supreme Court never releases information in matters incidental thereto.

PRESUMED GUILTY?

The findings and conclusions of the Bobde Committee have attained finality in law. The lady staffer, who had brought the allegations, has been reinstated in service. She was dismissed from service sometime in December 2018 after an *ex parte* departmental proceeding in respect of certain specific charges which were in no way connected with the allegations levelled by her. The reinstatement was during my tenure as the CJI and not after my retirement, as many believe or want believed because the reinstatement was made by Justice Bobde. It is little known that the reinstatement by Justice Bobde was made on humanitarian grounds, following the below petition submitted by the staffer to him on 1 November. He proceeded in the matter only after placing the petition before me and after I had passed orders requesting him to deal with the matter according to his discretion.

Dated: 1-11-19

To,
HMJ S.A. Bobde,
Hon'ble the Chief Justice of India designate,
Supreme Court of India,
Tilak Marg,

Sir,
    With due respect, the applicant humbly pray to Your Lordship to reconsider the penalty of dismissal from service

with effect from 21st December, 2018 as the applicant is finding extreme difficulty in finding a job and is facing hardship in the absence of employment.

This great institution has given me so much and an opportunity to learn for which I am grateful.

It is humbly prayed to Your Lordship to reconsider/review the order of punishment so that the undersigned can get employment and also to get relieved from the present state of hardship and financial stringencies.

Put up before CJI,   Yours faithfully,

Sd/-   Sd/-

(Justice Bobde)   (....................)

Justice Bobde is requested to deal with the matter. Rule 23 of the S.C. Employees (Conditions of Service) Rules may be brought to his Lordship's notice.

Sd/-
CJI
5/11

Rule 23 of the Supreme Court Officers & Servants (Conditions of Service and Conduct) Rules, 1961 states:

23. Powers of Chief Justice: Nothing in the rules in this part shall be construed to limit or abridge the power of the Chief Justice to deal with the case of any Court servant in such manner as may appear to him to be just and reasonable:

Provided that where any rule is applicable to the case of a Court servant, his case shall not be dealt with in a manner less favourable to him than that provided by the said rule.

Views were also expressed that as the staffer had been reinstated subsequent to my retirement, the allegations must have been legitimate. This conclusion is wrongly drawn because the staffer's petition for reinstatement was filed on 1 November; I passed orders on 5 November, requesting Justice Bobde to take a decision in the matter. I understand that, pursuant to Justice Bobde's orders, consequential reinstatement orders were passed on 7 November and she rejoined duties on 13 November—all the dates were within my tenure. Could there have been anything in exchange, as alleged by certain other quarters? Obviously not. First of all, I had nothing to do with the reinstatement. The decision was taken by Justice Bobde. In any case, nothing was left for the CJI to gain; the damage had occurred much earlier. All that should not have been done had been done much earlier. The reinstatement made seven months after the closure of the inquiry could not logically have been the outcome of any quid pro quo, as many argued.

Compassion is an integral part of administrative decision-making. In another instance, the summary dismissal of two Supreme Court employees, ordered by me on 13 February 2019, because of their alleged involvement in forgery of a Court order pertaining to the contempt case of Anil Ambani was also modified, reportedly on humanitarian grounds, by my successor, Justice Bobde. The effect of this modification was that one of the two employees was reinstated and the other was granted all retirement benefits.[40]

A little before my retirement, a very prominent woman activist-lawyer visited me twice at 5, Krishna Menon Marg. She had come with her husband on one visit. On both occasions, she told me that the lady staffer had consulted her for legal advice. She had advised her that on the basis of the facts as narrated to her, no case of sexual harassment existed and the only issue on which a legal proceeding could be brought before the Court was the staffer's dismissal from

---

[40] R. Balaji, 'Anil Ambani contempt case: Sacked SC officials pardoned by Justice Bobde', *The Telegraph*, 12 May 2021, https://bit.ly/3k09yLt, accessed on 28 September 2021.

service. I was further told that the lady staffer was dissatisfied with this. Subsequently, the complaint dated 19 April 2019 was filed. I wish that those who worked for 'justice' for the staffer had met me to hear my version before plunging into an irreparable and irreversible course of action. This was the minimum expected of senior members of the Bar who claim commitment to the good of the institution.

The visits of the woman lawyer reminded me of the visit of a senior lady journalist of a prominent English daily that had been very vocal about the incident. She came to 5, Krishna Menon Marg on an evening immediately following the incident. The journalist, who writes frequently and very powerfully, did not specifically seek an interview and that is why, perhaps, I agreed to meet her. She remained quiet and kept smiling. On my part, I did not say anything specific. She left. Maybe I should have talked to her. I should have realized the enormous power of the media to do or undo, make or unmake. My passive response in the situation was perhaps due to my lack of exposure on this front.

What price did I pay for all these happenings? Look at the devastation caused. The first casualty could have been my family. That did not happen, perhaps due to divine intervention. My wife and children (including my son-in-law, Tanmaya, and daughter-in-law, Kakoli) tolerated the humiliation and dishonour, but refused to believe the story and leave my side. They were my only pillars of strength in those very traumatic days. People, including near and dear ones, distanced themselves. Many of my 'friends' and 'well-wishers' disappeared. Some of my colleagues, while putting up a facade of support and sympathy which I did not seek, actually worked against me behind my back. Articles, write-ups and views on the issue, all of them derogatory, became the order of the day, every day, several times a day. No seminar, symposium or law lecture failed to mention the incident. This continues even today, after two years, as if there is an agenda that public memory has to be kept alive. This is why I have been prodded to title my memoirs *Justice for the Judge*.

I believe that the wound was intended to scar me permanently and incapacitate me. But it did not go that way. I completed my tenure to my satisfaction. What was intended did not happen. I continue to live within a cocoon of solace, knowing what happened and what did not happen—with my family believing me. This is my greatest source of strength.

In the light of my narration, I would like readers to decide on the credence and weightage to be given to the oft-repeated criticisms levelled on this issue, and whether I would be right in answering the questions raised in the following manner:

1. That I presided over my own case.

   I did not. Neither were there any effective orders passed nor any clean chit given to me in the hearing on 20 April 2019.

2. Did I constitute the Bobde Committee to inquire into allegations levelled against me?

   No. In fact, it was the full court of the Supreme Court which constituted, and thereafter reconstituted, the Bobde Committee.

3. Was the procedure adopted (in-house inquiry) to inquire into the allegations an eyewash?

   No. The in-house procedure is the procedure prescribed by law and in vogue since 1999.

4. Does the reinstatement of the employee after my retirement (factually incorrect as it was during my tenure as the CJI) establish/prove the allegations levelled to be correct?

   Obviously not.

PENCHANT FOR PREJUDICE

Now look at the hypocrisy which is glaringly apparent. People well-versed in law do not seem to understand that for inquiry into allegations against judges of the higher judiciary (High Courts and the Supreme Court), there are two established procedures—the in-house procedure and the procedure under the Judges (Inquiry) Act, 1968. The latter can be invoked only after a motion of impeachment of the judge concerned is admitted in the Lok Sabha or the Rajya Sabha. The provisions of the Judges Inquiry Act had no application in the present case. The provisions of the Sexual Harassment of Women at Workplace (Prevention, Prohibition and Redressal) Act, 2013, and/or the Supreme Court Rules, 2013 also had no application. Certain provisions of these enactments such as the composition of the inquiry committee contemplated thereunder as well as the penalty/punishment to be imposed would clearly show that the same were not intended for and in fact cannot apply to members of the higher judiciary. Therefore, it is the in-house procedure alone that was applicable. This is the legal framework built on the constitutional principle of protection of judges against sundry allegations that may be levelled against them in the course of performance of their duties. It is a facet of the independence of the judges and the institution of the Judiciary.

Despite the above position in law, and though the Bobde Committee in its report held the allegations levelled against me to be unsubstantiated and the report has attained finality in law, criticism has continued unabated. The in-house procedure has been labelled/criticized as an incestuous exercise; retired judges should have been included in the committee; the complainant (staffer) was denied reasonable opportunity and legal representation; witnesses were not examined; and the inquiry report was not given. Obviously, the critics did not care to read the in-house inquiry procedure which is available on the Supreme Court website or, having read it, refused to acknowledge or accept it. They demanded an ad hoc procedure which has no precedent either in law or practice. If there is a procedure in force, it has to apply across the board.

Individual perceptions about the inadequacy of the prevalent procedure according to their own convenience and agenda cannot be a justification to deviate from it selectively. Change the law/procedure if you consider it to be inadequate but so long as the procedure prescribed holds the field, it has to be applied uniformly to all cases. Not to do so is a sure way of inviting anarchy. The law cannot change depending on who is involved and in respect of whom it is to be invoked. To my knowledge, till date about 13 to 14 inquiries have been held in respect of allegations of misconduct against judges by following the in-house procedure. No lawyers, no outsiders have been allowed to be a part of any such inquiry. What is shocking and mind-boggling is the sheer hypocrisy and selective outrage as the facts below would indicate.

A seismic eruption took place regarding the legitimacy of the in-house procedure adopted in the inquiry by the Bobde Committee. Justice A.P. Shah, a former Chief Justice of the Delhi High Court, was particularly vocal and expressed strong reservations about the procedure while delivering the 27th Rosalind Wilson Memorial Lecture.[41] However, during an interview to an English daily in October 2020, in connection with another complaint filed by a CM, he affirmed that all inquiries probing allegations against judges of the higher judiciary must be conducted through the in-house procedure as it bolsters the judiciary's position. It is heartening to know that the learned judge has realized the true meaning, value and effect of an inquiry under the in-house procedure even if belatedly and, upon such realization, has not hesitated to acknowledge it publicly.

But the damage had been inflicted. The misinformation that I had 'presided' over my own case (some even called it a trial and referred to me as the accused) and handed myself a 'clean chit' disseminated, as negative news does, fast, far and wide. Shah in

---

[41]Pradeep Thakur, 'Entire episode was shrouded in secrecy: Justice AP Shah on harassment charges against CJI', *The Times of India*, 28 July 2019, https://bit.ly/3mgdtFe, accessed on 28 September 2021.

his lecture had also accused me of nominating the members of the Bobde Committee. He stated that I had handpicked the judges who had decided on the allegations against me—an utterly false and incorrect accusation, as revealed by what I have explained earlier.

There is yet another incident deserving of mention. A complaint dated 25 January 2019 was filed by the Campaign for Judicial Accountability and Reforms (CJAR) before the CJI, demanding an inquiry into as many as six allegations against a then Chief Justice of a High Court (now a sitting Supreme Court judge with several years of tenure left). The complaint and its enclosures run into 96 typed pages. As the CJI, I dismissed the complaint within five days at the threshold i.e. at the first stage under the in-house procedure by a reasoned order dated 30 January. During my tenure as CJI, to the best of my understanding, the complainant, CJAR, did not bother to enquire, either under the RTI or otherwise, about the status of the complaint—something I find intriguing. Why have they acted thus? Are they waiting for 'better times' to rake up the issue?

I am not the only one who finds these outbursts or silence selective. Amongst various articles, the following one appeared in the Delhi edition of *The Times of India* on 3 June 2019:[42]

> Days before becoming Chief Justice of India, Justice Ranjan Gogoi in his Ramnath Goenka lecture had agreed that independent judges and noisy journalists were democracy's first line of defence but modified it slightly to say that 'not only independent judges and noisy journalists but even independent journalists and sometimes noisy judges' were needed to guard the ethos and values of democracy. Eight months before the lecture, Justices Gogoi, Madan B Lokur and Kurian Joseph led by Justice Jasti Chelameswar held an unprecedented press conference to accuse then CJI Dipak Misra of wrongdoing.

---

[42]Dhananjay Mahapatra, 'After retirement, judges preach what they seldom practised', *The Times of India*, 3 June 2019, https://bit.ly/3vOBQwP, accessed on 28 September 2021.

They provided no evidence. The then CJI endured the ignominy silently.

Captain of the rebel judges Justice Chelameswar and his 'johnnies' (as Justice Chelameswar had referred to the other three judges just before the January 12, 2018 presser) shook the pillars of the highest court, created cracks in the vaunted brotherhood among judges and provided activist lawyers the license to heap ignominy and create doubt about the judges' integrity.

The presser scripted no tangible reforms. Later, Justice Gogoi smelled a rat in the course being charted by Justice Chelameswar with help from politicians in Congress, Left parties and activist lawyers. By the time the design reached its inglorious finale, with the Congress-led opposition filing a historic notice of removal against the CJI in Parliament, Justice Gogoi had distanced himself from the flow of events. Justice Gogoi believes in the Orwellian concept of free speech: 'Freedom is the freedom to say that two plus two makes four.' When he said 'noisy judges' were needed in democracy, he meant sitting judges living up to their oath to do justice without fear and favour and having the courage to call a spade a spade.

In India, it has become a trend with some retired judges to make the loudest noise about perceived violation of procedures. As judges, they routinely advise all and sundry to practice what they preach but after retirement, they quickly forget the 'preach what you practice' sermon.

Recently, Justice Lokur, followed by Justice Chelameswar, wrote articles criticising the procedure adopted by the Supreme Court in setting up an in-house committee of Justices S A Bobde, Indu Malhotra and Indira Banerjee to inquire into an unprecedented sexual harassment complaint against CJI Gogoi.

Justices Chelameswar and Lokur became SC judges in October 2011 and June 2012, respectively. Both had spent considerable time as judges and chief justices of various high courts before joining the SC.

On November 6, 2013, a law intern wrote a blog accusing retired SC judge A K Ganguly of making inappropriate sexual advances towards her nearly a year earlier in December 2012. The then CJI set up an in-house inquiry panel of Justices R M Lodha, H L Dattu and Ranjana Prakash Desai to inquire into it. There were several glaring procedural lapses — a retired judge is not amenable to an in-house inquiry procedure, majority of male judges in the panel was not in sync with the Vishaka judgment guidelines to deal with sexual harassment complaints, lawyer's assistance was not extended to the complainant, the SC did not make public the in-house inquiry report which found prima facie truth in the complaint, and, the 'sexually harassed' law intern refused Delhi Police's repeated requests to lodge an FIR. Though Justices Lokur and Chelameswar were firmly entrenched as SC judges by November 2013, why did they not protest against the improper procedure followed by the in-house panel?

Procedure-sensitive Justice Lokur, while heading a bench hearing a case relating to Manipur fake encounter killings, had brushed aside the judiciary's golden dictum of 'innocent till pronounced guilty' to rap the CBI for allowing 'murderers' (Army personnel) to loaf around. Probably, he had intended to say that the CBI was not expediting investigation against those accused of fake encounters. But in one verbal shot from the bench, he branded all the accused as murderers, without trial. Justice Lokur has been associated with computerisation of the judiciary and headed the SC's E-committee. In November 2016, then CJI T S Thakur unceremoniously replaced him with retired Rajasthan HC CJ Sunil Ambawani. Justice Thakur's successor Justice J S Khehar reinstated him. What procedure was followed on both occasions, no one knows.

Justice Lokur retired on December 31, 2018. At his farewell, CJI Gogoi had fondly recalled his more than 50-year friendship with Justice Lokur and referred to him as his 'right hand'. To make the 'right hand' happy, CJI Gogoi allowed Justice Lokur to continue in the E-committee despite the latter ceasing to be an SC judge. Justice Lokur did not question the procedure under which he was allowed to continue in the E-committee. The CJI has sanctioned him an official car, 200 litres of petrol per month, a driver and a peon for being part of the committee. Though Justice Lokur was sanctioned these perks since January, not a single meeting of the E-committee has been held since January.

We had earlier written about how Justices Chelameswar and Lokur bartered transfer of their favourite judges from one HC to another in the collegium meetings. Procedure and transparency was far from their minds when they were part of the SC collegium which wields the power to select persons for appointment as judges and transfer of judges.

Nearly 11 years ago, an FIR was lodged by a jeweller with a police station in Delhi accusing a media personality, who was the wife of a then powerful politician, of taking jewellery without paying for it. The complainant said the media personality told him that some of the jewellery was meant to be 'gifted to Mr Chelameswar in Hyderabad'. Procedurally, there should have been an inquiry into it. It could still be done, with the precedent of the Justice Ganguly incident.

I am not commenting or voicing any opinion on the accuracy or otherwise of the contents of the article or the assertions made in it; I only wish to point out that notably known and otherwise very vocal people committed to the cause of 'purity' in public life have ironically and selectively been vocal or have remained totally silent in matters of importance. They rise to speak only when it suits them regardless of how hollow they may appear to sound. Some write-ups on the recent controversy over the Pegasus spyware are a case in point.

A sensational report appeared in some newspapers that, along with the mobile phones of certain politicians, bureaucrats, journalists and public functionaries, that of the Supreme Court staffer who levelled the allegations of sexual harassment, and also her family members, may possibly have been placed under surveillance by use of the Pegasus spyware. Many of the news reports, after mentioning the alleged surveillance or snooping, had gone on to reiterate the details of the unfortunate incident as if there was an agenda to reopen a closed chapter with the intent to vilify and humiliate me. This is evident from the fact that this part of the news items has been, in most cases, a cut-and-paste exercise (lifted from an earlier news item and inserted verbatim). Insinuations have been made that the alleged snooping on the mobile phones had affected the sanctity of the Bobde Committee inquiry, as the defence of the staffer may have been compromised. This imaginative thinking has even burgeoned to question judgments of such import as Rafale and Ayodhya.

I think the time has come for the right-thinking majority to speak up. They can no longer enjoy the comfort of a non-confrontationist approach, staying clear of issues and being content that they have been spared the unfortunate. For, if unchecked, tomorrow the monster may devour them too. Can anything be more preposterous and derogatory than saying that secret material allegedly collected by illegal snooping on mobile phones was actually shared with the three sitting judges of the Supreme Court who constituted the committee and that they relied on such materials, knowing them to be illegally obtained? That apart, the snooping is alleged to have taken place after the complainant had submitted her affidavit on 19 April 2019. Her best case, which was disbelieved, had already been put forth before the alleged snooping took place.

Ranjan Gogoi

The insinuation of a link between the snooping and the judicial verdicts does enormous harm to the institution as it questions the integrity of the other judges on the Bench. Even if my opinion is to be excluded, what about the opinion of the other judges which was unanimous? Are they also tainted? Allegations of these kinds, based on perverse thinking, must be vociferously resisted and such resistance and protests must come from the vast silent majority for whom I have undertaken the present endeavour.

UNEARTHING THE LARGER CONSPIRACY

On 19 April 2019, on my return from Tirupati, when I was informed of the complaint by the lady staffer, I was also informed by Harish Juneja, principal private secretary to the CJI, that one Utsav Singh Bains, an advocate from Chandigarh, had come to meet me the previous day. As Bains had come without an appointment and I happened to be out of Delhi, he was refused entry to 5, Krishna Menon Marg.

A few days later, I learnt from social media that Bains had suggested a conspiracy had been hatched to defame me. He had suggested the involvement of several persons, including two Supreme Court employees who were summarily dismissed from service by me on 13 February 2019 following a complaint lodged with me orally by a sitting judge. The complaint was with regard to forgery and manipulation of an order passed by the judge. The order necessitated the personal presence of Anil Ambani in court in a contempt proceeding alleging disobedience of a judicial order requiring payment of a huge amount of money by him. Later, Bains had filed an affidavit in the Court, giving details of the alleged plot to defame the CJI and the involvement of several persons, including the two Supreme Court employees I had dismissed.

Bains's affidavit led to the constitution of the Patnaik Committee to look into the allegations of conspiracy against the CJI. The allegations of sexual harassment, as many have projected, were not the subject matter of inquiry by the Patnaik Committee; they were at that time being inquired into by the Bobde Committee under the in-house procedure. The clear difference between the matters of inquiry by the two Committees was, according to me, deliberately distorted in public perception by certain quarters to create an impression that the allegations of sexual harassment were still alive despite the Bobde Committee report holding them to be unsubstantiated. Nothing could have been more irresponsible and unfortunate.

Justice Patnaik's report was submitted to the Secretary General of the Supreme Court sometime in August-September 2019. It was during the tenure of my successor (Justice Bobde) that the matter attained finality. By order of the Court dated 18 February 2021, the report of Justice Patnaik was accepted and the *suo moto* case was closed in the following terms:

SUO MOTU WRIT PETITION (C) NO. 1/2019

IN RE: MATTER OF GREAT PUBLIC IMPORTANCE
TOUCHING UPON THE INDEPENDENCE OF JUDICIARY-
MENTIONED BY SHRI TUSHAR MEHTA, SOLICITOR
GENERAL OF INDIA Petitioner(s)

O R D E R

1. The enquiry report of Hon'ble Mr Justice A.K. Patnaik, Retired Judge of this Court has been placed before us. On perusal of the report, we find that it is quite comprehensive which has dealt with the scope of the enquiry, the materials and the findings and the conclusions along with the list of annexures and articles.

2. We have to keep in mind that the remit of the Committee was not to enquire into the merits of the allegations made by the complainant against the then Chief Justice of India

and this aspect has been noted in the report itself. The learned Judge has thus, recorded in the report that he has confined his examination to only one aspect i.e. the veracity of the version put forward by Mr Utsav Singh Bains. The report has also taken note of the limited investigative powers and access to records which it had and based on those materials and evidence before him, it has been opined that it is not possible to find corroborative material qua the allegations of Mr Utsav Singh Bains made in the affidavit. Simultaneously, the report also acknowledges that the existence of a conspiracy cannot be completely ruled out and this has been so opined as Justice A.K. Patnaik has not been able to obtain various records including electronic records of Whatsapp, Telegram etc. The learned Judge has recorded in the final paragraph that the Director of IB in his letter dated 05.07.2019 has stated that on account of the then Chief Justice of India taking series of tough decisions like in the case relating to National Register of Citizens (NRC), there was strong reason to believe that persons who were unhappy with those decisions hatched a conspiracy against the then Chief Justice of India. A reference has also been made to certain tough administrative decisions taken to streamline the process in the Registry.

3. We are also of the view that two years having passed and the possibility of recovery of electronic records at this distance of time is remote, especially since the scope of the enquiry and the power of the learned Judge is limited, no useful purpose will be served by continuing these proceedings.

4. As a result of our observations aforesaid, the proceedings are accordingly closed and the Suo Motu petition is disposed of.

5. The report which has been opened be placed back in a

sealed cover.

....J.
[SANJAY KISHAN KAUL]
....J.
[A.S. BOPANNA]
....J.
[V. RAMASUBRAMANIAN]
NEW DELHI
FEBRUARY 18, 2021

I wish the matter could have been taken up earlier for the conclusions in the report (discernible from the above order) do vindicate, to an extent, Bains's allegations regarding a conspiracy to defame me.

Eleven

NRC: A DOCUMENT FOR THE FUTURE

History has its own reasons for remembering certain people. One such name is that of R.B. Vaghaiwalla, ICS, the Superintendent of Census Operations for Assam, Manipur and Tripura when the 1951 Census operations were conducted. This gentleman got the census figures, which are usually destroyed after completion of the operations, entered into a register. This is how the famous 1951 National Register of Citizens (NRC) was prepared. There are two opinions as to why Vaghaiwalla acted in this manner. One says the purpose was to create a list of Indian citizens, as he and the administration at that point of time had been witness to how in the previous decades migration from the Mymensingh area (in erstwhile East Bengal or East Pakistan, and now Bangladesh) had changed the demographic pattern in the state of Assam, posing a threat to the very existence of the Assamese people. The other reason, according to sources, could be a request from the Central Ministry of Rehabilitation to find out the precise number of refugees who had entered India from East Pakistan to enable an exercise of account taking of supply of rations to them.[43] Both reasons are, in

---

[43]Mrinal Talukdar, *The Game Called NRC*, Nanda Talukdar Foundation, 2020.

a way, connected and it is evident that, even at that point of time in history, the number of immigrants into Assam from erstwhile East Pakistan must have been considerable. That it was indeed so is also evident from the fact that important and responsible voices of the then British census officers spoke to the effect that such 'immigration was likely to alter permanently the whole future of Assam, and [...] the whole structure of Assamese culture and civilization.'[44] In fact, C.S. Mullan, British census commissioner, in his Census Report of 1931, warned of 'an invasion of vast horde of land hungry Bengali immigrants, mostly Muslims, from the districts of East Bengal.'[45] History has taught us that one of the biggest threats a people would feel is a threat to their culture and language—their mother tongue. Religion comes only thereafter.

Why was no attempt made to stop infiltration? The answer is simple—because of vote bank politics. Immigrants translated into votes and a large number of immigrants spelled a large number of votes. In an environment where the indigenous population strongly opposed such immigration, exploitation of the fears of the immigrants led to a captive vote bank. And such vote bank politics led to extremely strong support and promotion of immigration from the powers that be. The people of Assam were always sceptical about the authenticity of the electoral rolls. In fact, in March 1979, during the build-up to the by-election for the Mangaldoi Lok Sabha constituency, the discovery of a large number of illegal Bangladeshi voters (about 70,000)[46] turned out to be the last straw as far as the forbearance of the people of Assam was concerned and eventually triggered the six-year-long Assam agitation. The scepticism was not confined to the people of Assam but extended to even the then Chief Election

---

[44]Dinesh Kotwal, 'Insurgency in Assam: The Demographic Dimensions', *Strategic Analysis,* May 2001 (Vol. XXV No. 2), https://bit.ly/3Gu2wYF, accessed on 1 October 2021.
[45]Ibid.
[46]Pranab Mukherjee, *The Turbulent Years: 1980-1996*, Rupa Publications India, 2016.

Commissioner, S.L. Shakdher, who in a conference of State Chief Electoral Officers in September-October 1978 had said:

> In one State (Assam), the population in 1971 recorded an increase as high as 34.98 per cent, over the 1961 figures and this increase was attributed to the influx of a very large number of persons from the neighbouring countries. The influx has become a regular feature. I think it may not be a wrong assessment to make, on the basis of the increase of 34.98 per cent between the two census, the increase that is likely to be recorded in 1991 Census would be more than 100 per cent over the 1961 census.
>
> In other words, a stage would be reached when the State would have to reckon with the foreign nationals who may probably constitute a sizeable percentage, if not the majority of the population of the state.
>
> Another disturbing factor in this regard was the demand made by the political parties for the inclusion in the electoral rolls of the names of such immigrants who are not Indian citizens, without even questioning and properly determining the citizenship status.[47]

SUSPICION AND HOSTILITY: THE NEW NORMAL

The Assam agitation, from 1979 to 1985, was ostensibly a movement which had three demands—detection, deletion (from the voters' lists) and deportation of foreigners. It was construed as a fight for survival. People made sacrifices, martyrs were born out of the movement (close to 700 people died), students lost several years of academic life, there was flight of capital from the state, industries came to a grinding halt, extremism was spawned by the movement,

---

[47]Dilip Gogoi, *Making of India's Northeast: Geopolitics of Borderland and Transnational Interactions*, Routledge India, 2019.

and ideas of separation from India and an independent Assam struck root.

It was at this stage that the Assam Accord, a tripartite agreement between the Government of India, the Government of Assam and the AASU, the student body that had spearheaded the movement, came to be signed on 15 August 1985. Pursuant to the Assam Accord, Section 6A was inserted in the Citizenship Act, 1955, by an amendment Act (Act 65 of 1985), making special provisions for citizenship for persons covered by the Assam Accord. Section 6A (1) (d) defines a person of Indian origin thus: ... 'if he, or either of his parents or any of his grandparents was born in undivided India'. Such persons of Indian origin coming to Assam before 1 January 1966 were declared to be Indian citizens whereas those coming between 1 January 1966 and 24 March 1971 were to be registered and became entitled to citizenship and all rights flowing therefrom, including political rights, after 10 years.

Elections were held to the state Assembly in December 1985 and the AGP, which was formed by the student community, swept the polls. Though now in power, the student body which had spearheaded the Assam agitation with the three demands did nothing regarding detection, deletion and deportation. The first step to achieve this, logically, would have been to identify citizens and non-citizens. This would have necessitated updating of the NRC of 1951, an exercise that continued to remain buried.

In the meantime, the influx continued unabated—so much so that Lieutenant General S.K. Sinha, then governor of Assam, sent a report dated 8 November 1998 to the president of India which pointed to an alarming situation. Some portions of it are worth reproducing, making for interesting reading:

1.   The unabated influx of illegal migrants from Bangladesh into Assam and the consequent perceptible change in the demographic pattern of the State has been a matter of grave concern. It threatens to reduce the Assamese people to a

minority in their own State, as happened in Tripura and Sikkim.

2. Illegal migration into Assam was the core issue behind the Assam student movement. It was also the prime contributory factor behind the outbreak of insurgency in the State. Yet we have not made much tangible progress in dealing with this all-important issue.

3. There is a tendency to view illegal migration into Assam as a regional matter affecting only the people of Assam. Its more dangerous dimensions of greatly undermining our national security, is ignored. The long cherished design of Greater East Pakistan/Bangladesh, making inroads into strategic land link of Assam with the rest of the country, can lead to severing the entire land mass of the North-East, with all its rich resources from the rest of the country. They will have disastrous strategic and economic consequences.

20. The growth of Muslim population has been emphasised in the previous paragraph to indicate the extent of illegal migration from Bangladesh to Assam because as stated earlier, the illegal migrants coming into India after 1971 have been almost exclusively Muslims.

21. Pakistan's ISI has been active in Bangladesh supporting militant movement in Assam. Muslim militant organisations have mushroomed in Assam and there are reports of some 50 Assamese Muslim youths having gone for training to Afghanistan and Kashmir.

CONSEQUENCES

22. The dangerous consequences of large-scale illegal migration from Bangladesh, both for the people of Assam and more for the nation as a whole, need to be emphatically stressed. No misconceived and mistaken notions of secularism should

be allowed to come in the way of doing so.

23. As a result of population movement from Bangladesh, the spectre looms large of the indigenous people of Assam being reduced to a minority in their home State. Their cultural survival will be in jeopardy, their political control will be weakened and their employment opportunities will be undermined.

24. The silent and invidious demographic invasion of Assam may result in the loss of the geo-strategically vital districts of lower Assam. The influx of these illegal migrants is turning these districts into a Muslim majority region. It will then only be a matter of time when a demand for their merger with Bangladesh may be made. The rapid growth of international Islamic fundamentalism may provide for driving force for this demand. In this context, it is pertinent that Bangladesh has long discarded secularism and has chosen to become an Islamic State. Loss of lower Assam will sever the entire land mass of the North-East, from the rest of India and the rich natural resources of that region will be lost to the Nation.[48]

In *Sarbananda Sonowal vs Union of India & Another* (2005) 5 SCC 665, while considering the constitutional validity of the provisions of the Illegal Migrants (Determination by Tribunals) (IMDT) Act, 1983, the Supreme Court by its judgment dated 12 July 2005, inter alia, observed that the state of Assam was facing an 'external aggression and internal disturbance' on account of large-scale illegal migration of Bangladeshi nationals. The apex court further observed that the Union government had failed to carry out its constitutional duty mandated by Article 355.[49]

---

[48]Report on Illegal Migration into Assam; submitted to the President of India by the Governor of Assam, 8 November 1998, https://bit.ly/3CmDJ6z, accessed on 1 October 2021.

[49]'Duty of the Union to protect States against external aggression and internal disturbance: It shall be the duty of the Union to protect every State against external aggression and internal disturbance and to ensure that the government of every State is carried on in accordance with the provisions of this Constitution.'

Ranjan Gogoi

The issue of updating the NRC remained buried till 2005, when in a tripartite meeting between PM Manmohan Singh, CM of Assam Tarun Gogoi and the AASU, a decision was taken to update the NRC.[50] The decision was nothing but lip service as nobody wanted to extinguish the fire sparked by the immigration issue as it afforded political warmth to everybody. The decision to update the NRC taken in 2005 was half-heartedly implemented in 2010 as a pilot project in two districts of the state and was soon abandoned due to eruption of violence. All the beneficiaries of the immigration issue heaved a sigh of relief and insisted that their stand that the NRC updation was an impossible exercise stood vindicated.

But the fire has to be stoked from time to time. Any event related to immigration from Bangladesh would be ideal for extracting political mileage, and no political party would ever want to let go such an opportunity. This is a necessity for all, including the student force, to remain relevant in contemporary Assamese politics. After all, heroes are produced by agitations and chaos.

The immigration issue or, rather, the failure to resolve it is an asset that could draw votes in favour of and to the benefit of all political parties, as exemplified by the open declaration of CM Tarun Gogoi as late as in December 2012: 'Where are the illegal Bangladeshis? Show me if there is any.'[51]

Battening off public emotion and succumbing to the intoxication of vote bank politics, politicians across the spectrum have exploited to the hilt the absence of any reliable figures of the number of illegal immigrants. While one set of political outfits has exploited the fear amongst the immigrants and fed upon their votes, another set of political parties has exploited the emotions of the Assamese

---

[50]This was the 12th tripartite meeting held on the issue and the immediate trigger was the threat by the AASU to disrupt the Indo-ASEAN Car Rally that was to be flagged off by PM Manmohan Singh. As quoted in Mrinal Talukdar, *The Game Called NRC*, Nanda Talukdar Foundation, 2020.
[51]Kaushik Deka, 'Tarun Gogoi's U-turn: Not a single Bangladeshi national in Assam', *India Today*, 2 December 2012, https://bit.ly/3jMcxqq, accessed on 1 October 2021.

locals and garnered their votes with promises to deport the illegal immigrants.

Further, in order to ensure that the confusion spawned by speculative figures doesn't ebb, important leaders have deliberately made lofty statements on the issue, only to withdraw them later. Former CM Hiteswar Saikia is on record, informing the state assembly in 1992 that there were 30 lakh illegal foreigners in the state. However, following pressure from some quarters, he made a U-turn two days later.[52] Parliament has also witnessed statements by various home ministers that there are around 50 lakh illegal immigrants in Assam. But after being successful in triggering speculation such statements were quietly withdrawn. In 1997, the then Union home minister, Indrajit Gupta, was on record, saying that India, including Assam, had one crore illegal foreigners.[53] Another such statement was made by Minister of State for Home Sriprakash Jaiswal who stated in Parliament in July 2004 that 'estimated number of illegal Bangladeshi immigrants in India as on 31.12.2001 were 50 lakhs in Assam, 57 lakhs in West Bengal, 3.25 lakhs in Tripura, 4.79 lakhs in Bihar and 3.75 lakhs in Delhi, 100 in Gujarat and 550 in Haryana, total 1.20 crores in India.' Jaiswal, too, subsequently withdrew his statement, saying the figure was based on hearsay.[54]

Though, under the Assam Accord, all Bangladeshis who had come to Assam up till the cut-off date of 24 March 1971 became legally eligible to be Indian citizens, which they did become, the AASU would like people to believe that since submission of their

---

[52]Anupam Bordoloi, 'Even Hindus Are "Illegal Immigrants" in Assam's Ambitious National Register Of Citizens! BJP on Backfoot?', *Outlook*, 16 September 2019, https://bit.ly/30ZonqI, accessed on 1 October 2021.

[53]Ibid.

[54]Bharti Jain, 'Two crore Bangladeshi immigrants illegally staying in India, Centre informs Rajya Sabha', *The Times of India*, 17 November 2016, https://bit.ly/3jJNvIq, accessed on 1 October 2021.

Shruti Menon, Sreenivasan Jain, "No Accurate Data", Centre Said on Illegal Immigrants 7 Times in 4 Years', NDTV, https://bit.ly/3vQ78DA, accessed on 1 October 2021.

first memorandum to PM Indira Gandhi in February 1980, the number of illegal immigrants in Assam has magically remained at 50 lakh, despite legalization of around 22 lakh such persons coming in between 1951 and 1971, following the Assam Accord and consequential changes in the Citizenship Act. Though the AASU leaders turned themselves into a political outfit—the AGP—and formed the government in 1985, they did nothing substantive for updating the NRC or finding out the truth. The figure of 50 lakh continues to be assiduously promoted by them even today.

Undoubtedly, the issue of immigration in Assam has always been the most important cash cow for all political activities in the state. The issue is the biggest king-maker in the state. The overt ideology of all political parties has remained remarkably solicitous about the people of Assam with the matter of immigration being described as the most important issue ever and the NRC update or anything similar being the most sacrosanct of acts for them. But those knowing the actual truth would never want a sincere and authentic NRC update to happen for it would expose everybody. And yet, the NRC update was one of the most crucial exercises linked to this festering issue. Who could have grasped this better than the Supreme Court, which took cognizance of the issue.

FROM COURT NO. 13 TO COURT NO. 1

In April 2013, I was sitting on a Bench presided over by Justice H.L. Gokhale in Court No. 13. A writ petition, No. 274/2009 *(Assam Public Works vs Union of India & Ors.)*, came to be listed before the Bench wherein, inter alia, deletion of the names of all foreigners (post-1971 immigrants) from the voter lists of the state was sought. On 8 May 2013, another connected writ petition i.e. W.P (C) No. 562/2012, wherein the provisions of Section 6A of the Citizenship Act were challenged and the issue of updating the NRC was raised, was ordered to be heard together with W.P(C) No. 274/2009. During the course of the proceedings before the Court, statements were made to the effect that the state of Assam was committed to updating the NRC for which purpose Prateek Hajela, an IAS officer, was being appointed the State Coordinator of NRC (SCNR). On behalf of the Union of India, a promise was made to make available the requisite funds and an initial amount of ₹25 crore was sanctioned and released as a first step in the exercise.

Justice Gokhale retired from the Supreme Court on 10 March 2014. Thereafter, and once I started presiding over Benches, this case along with the other connected cases came up before a Bench consisting of Justice R.F. Nariman and me. This is how I came to deal with the matter until the day of my retirement. The journey from Court No. 13 to Court No. 1 with Justice Nariman by my side, to say the least, was a remarkable experience. What was correct was not spoken and what was spoken was not correct. This was in respect of both the Union and the state of Assam.

Sometime in 2013, during the course of the Court proceedings, modalities for preparation of the NRC were finalized. The first step in this direction was to carve out a list of documents by which the citizenship of the applicants was to be determined. The said documents were to be utilized by an applicant to trace his lineage to a name appearing either in the 1951 NRC or any of the electoral rolls up to 24 March 1971. This was required to be done in view of Rule 4A of the Citizenship (Registration of Citizens and Issue of National Identity Card) Rules, 2003, which provided a special procedure for NRC preparation in Assam as distinguished from any such exercise in the rest of the country, which is dealt with by Rule 4 of the aforesaid Rules.

Under Rule 4A, the basic eligibility for inclusion in the NRC emanates from proof of residence in India up to the midnight of 24 March 1971, which is the cut-off date arrived at as per the Assam Accord and thereafter included in Section 6A of the Citizenship Act. In fact, there is a schedule prepared under Rule 4A which provides for 'special provisions as to manner of preparation of National Register of Indian Citizens in the State of Assam'. The process prescribed is one of inviting applications instead of house-to-house enumeration for verification of citizenship status, as contemplated for the rest of India by Rule 4 of the Rules.

The concept of digitized legacy data was the cornerstone of the NRC project. The statutes required publication of the (hard) copies of the 1951 NRC and electoral rolls up to 24 March 1971, as available with the government, to enable people to look up the particulars of their ancestors to establish their eligibility for inclusion in the NRC. Actual implementation of this, however, was an extremely complex and gigantic exercise. During the NRC pilot project carried out in 2010, this statutory provision was sought to be implemented in exactly the same manner as provided for in the statute i.e. by generating printouts of the legacy data for scrutiny. It failed. It was not possible for thousands of people to search for the names of their ancestors in hundreds and thousands of hard copies. Firstly, there was no fixity of the location where the ancestors would have stayed as over such a long period of around 60 years (1951 to 2010) it was but natural that large-scale movement of people would have happened. Scrutiny at multiple locations was required, which was impossible. Secondly, there was no index of names which could be easily created to ease the scrutiny as the name of the same person can appear with huge variations. For instance, Abdul Ali or Md. Abdul Ali or Ali Abdul or Mohammed Abdul Ali. Any physical search presupposes accurate data entry which is an assumption far removed from the ground reality. The old data had a large number of variations and even typographical errors. Further, such data is almost completely in vernacular i.e. either Assamese or Bengali and a substantial portion was handwritten. For the public also, it was impossible to get certified copies of the legacy data from the offices of district magistrates in large numbers as there was no mechanism to easily locate the requisite page, and even if it was located, so much handling of the old paper would have led to its disintegration. Digitization was thus the only way out. Not only was it done; software was also created to facilitate the scrutiny.

Submission of application forms started in April/May 2015. Public response to the legacy data scrutiny was positive. On successful scrutiny, the person was provided with the particulars as a unique 11-digit legacy data contained in a piece of paper called the Legacy Data Slip.

With the success of the legacy data publication, the process moved on to another very difficult but known area which was the application submission process. The application form was in three languages—Assamese, Bengali (for Barak Valley districts) and English. Based on demands by the All Bodo Students Union (ABSU), applicants were allowed to fill the forms in Bodo too. House-to-house distribution of blank application forms commenced during the third week of May 2015, and receipt of completed application forms at NRC Seva Kendras (NSKs) started by the end of that month.

Another extremely important part of the verification, unique to the Assam NRC, is the Family Tree Verification system. This system, designed by Hajela, was placed for approval before the Supreme Court Bench in a presentation made on 14 February 2017, in the presence of the chief secretary, Assam, the registrar general of India (RGI), and the counsel for the Union and the state. After witnessing and examining the presentation, the Bench approved it. The Bench considered it a novel and ingenious method to determine the accuracy of NRC eligibility.

Most of the NRC applicants were young people who had to establish their NRC eligibility based on the names of their ancestors; the link was required to be proved by way of documentary evidence. Declaration of descent from an ancestor was checked by consistency in statements about siblings from each applicant. This is the Family Tree Verification system. The SCNR informed the Bench that it had been found that it was quite easy to procure documents to prove lineage as most of the issuing authorities did not undertake any verification of the authenticity of the claimed parent-child relationship. A number of persons providing valid Electoral Photo Identity Cards (EPICs) or PAN cards, however, could not make it to the final NRC as they had used somebody else's legacy. The basic principle of Family Tree hearings is that descendants need to recognize one another to be genuine unless there are justified grounds for non-recognition. Recognition is established through mentioning of names in their family tree statements, called Manual Family Tree (MFTs) and matching of the MFTs. Each applicant had to declare his MFT beforehand. This was filled in after completion of the application form submission on 31 August 2015, as part of field verification. The MFT form was designed to list the details of different generations of the family, comprising the names of the legacy person(s), his/her spouse and the children and grandchildren of the legacy person. Such forms were submitted by all the NRC applicants and, therefore, the NRC authorities had knowledge of the family trees of all applicants.

These were then scanned and made into a centralized database. Thereafter, once the digitization of the application forms was completed, another database was created based on the legacies claimed. A comparison of the two databases permitted identification of likely cases of false links claimed and such cases were further investigated. As an illustration, let's take a hypothetical case where I am the only child of my father and have used his legacy (residence in India before 1971) for getting my name included in the NRC. However, there is another mischievous impostor who doesn't have a proper legacy before 1971 but he also shows my father as his father while applying for the NRC. Now, after comparison of the two databases, NRC authorities will get to know that I have not declared this impostor as my brother. To ascertain the truth, NRC authorities will call both of us for a hearing and we will be asked to explain the mismatch. As a law-abiding person, I will refuse to recognize the impostor and he will be identified. However, there is a possibility that I am also a mischievous person and for a consideration had sold my legacy and so will attempt to accept the impostor as my brother in front of the NRC authorities. However, at this stage, it would not be possible for me to do this as I have already declared in my MFT earlier that I do not have any sibling.

The naysayers and detractors of the NRC used this to claim that legacies had been traded but little did they know that the system itself provided for identifying such trade. Usually, the number of descendants was many; even if an impostor could successfully bargain with one or two of the descendants, such bargaining with all the other descendants was not reasonably possible. Before the development of this system, nobody even knew whether his/her legacy was already being misused by some other impostor. During the implementation of this verification system, lakhs of mismatches were found and only after satisfactory explanation was the applicant included. In the absence thereof, the applicant was kept out of the NRC. Satisfactory explanation included cases of nicknames and genuine absence of knowledge of official names of nieces/nephews. Some cases of mismatch also happened due to name changes after marriage and existence of more than one spouse who was unknown, among others. All the above details were very elaborately laid before the Court by the SCNR in the 59 reports (including the sealed cover reports) submitted from time to time.

Timelines were set by the Court, which were revised from time to time. These timelines were necessitated, however unjustified they may appear to be, due to the fact that slowly but surely the Bench was convinced that neither the Union nor the state government wanted the NRC exercise completed. One day, a very senior serving bureaucrat of the Government of India came to meet me at my residence (10, Tees January Marg). To my utter shock, he indicated that I go slow on the NRC matter. I told him with all the politeness at my command that I did not like interference in my judicial work.

So far as the state authorities were concerned, once it was realized that the NRC exercise was likely to succeed all kinds of obstructions were sought to be created in the functioning of the SCNR, details of which are on record at the Supreme Court, mainly in the sealed cover reports. This is the reason the Court was constrained to pass orders for reports to be submitted in sealed covers.

Even though all such attempts at obstructing the NRC updation exercise were quashed with an iron fist by the Supreme Court, it was but natural for politicians to harvest the most out of whatever happened next. Political functionaries, both of the Congress and the BJP, during the currency of the NRC updation, tried to extract their own political mileage, though they ostensibly had diametrically opposing ideologies. Around mid-2015, when the NRC updation process had progressed significantly and NRC application forms were being submitted by applicants, CM Tarun Gogoi, already rattled by the imminence of the NRC, was confronted with an IA filed in the Supreme Court by his most significant political rival, Himanta Biswa Sarma. He sought certain reliefs for the original inhabitants of the state and for the Indian citizens who had come to Assam post-1971. Not to be outdone, soon we had the chief secretary of the state filing an affidavit to the effect that the NRC updation was the most important exercise ever for the state and pleading that the NRC be prepared based on the 2014 electoral rolls. Political expediency had plumbed newer depths. A year later, when Sarbananda Sonowal came to power, he also sought to derive mileage on his part by swearing that the NRC updation was his top-most priority and sought to demonstrate it by making the state NRC office the first office visited by him after taking oath as the CM.

Even before publication of the draft list, the date for which was set as 31 December 2017, as late as November, law officers of the Union warned of the possibility of violence if the draft NRC was published. They also argued on behalf of the Government of India that the Supreme Court had encroached upon the domain of the executive and that the Court had transgressed the constitutional boundaries by ordering publication of the draft NRC on 31 December 2017. A year and a half later, in March 2019, another argument was put forward by the Union government that due to parliamentary elections in the country, around 165 companies of paramilitary forces deployed specifically for the NRC exercise were required to be withdrawn and, therefore, the final NRC publication should be deferred. The Court had to threaten ordering personal appearance of the Union home secretary and it was only thereafter that things fell in line.

By an order dated 13 August 2019, the Court turned down the request of both the Union and state governments for reverification. This was done since the process of verification at multiple layers, inherent in the verification module designed, obviated the necessity for any further verification or reverification. Strangely, the issue of reverification has been kept alive, at least in the public domain.

This mammoth exercise, which was beyond the scope of human endeavour and could only be accomplished by skilful use of software, was completed successfully, leading to the publication of the final NRC on 31 August 2019. But it was only after my retirement that politicians of the ruling party criticized it as erroneous on the ground that eligible persons were excluded and ineligible persons included. Himanta Biswa Sarma (now CM) reportedly said that the NRC prepared was fundamentally wrong (no reasons cited) and that after the elections in Assam of March-April 2021, a new exercise would start if the Supreme Court permitted it.[55] In what seems to be a follow-up move, on 8 December 2020, local media channels reported that an affidavit had been filed in the Gauhati High Court with regard to illegal entry of about 4,700 names in the NRC.

The stand of the opposition parties was no different though

---

[55]Abhishek Saha, 'NRC fundamentally wrong... new one after polls if SC allows: Himanta', *The Indian Express*, 6 November 2020, https://bit.ly/3CqXcmK, accessed on 1 October 2021.

their reasons may have been different. A few instances of human error were pointed out to discredit the entire exercise involving over three crore applicants. Apart from very general criticism, no specific flaw(s) were pointed out or recorded in writing and communicated/exchanged by and between authorities till date.

I understand that immediately after assumption of office by the new government in Assam in May 2021, an IA has been filed in the Supreme Court for permission to undertake reverification of the NRC to the extent of 20 per cent or so, on the ground of errors in the published NRC. Such a request had already been declined by the Supreme Court on 13 August 2019. There can be no dispute that if errors are found and proved they must be corrected for the endeavour of all concerned, including the Court, is to have an error-free NRC. But criticisms and accusations on general terms and in undignified language do not befit the huge human effort employed. I do not think that the people who have criticized the NRC preparation are even remotely familiar with the intricacies of the exercise undertaken. Neither do they have the time, the inclination or perhaps even the capacity to understand the complex process.

I do not know why the follow-up and consequential action, as required in law, have not been forthcoming. Rejection slips have not been communicated to enable the aggrieved persons to move to the Foreigners' Tribunal; the RGI has not carried out publication of the final NRC, as required under Clause 7 of the schedule containing the special provisions for preparation of NRC in Assam. Though orders have been passed by the Supreme Court for NRC data protection on the same lines as the Aadhaar data, I doubt if any steps have been taken in this regard.

RISE OF ARMCHAIR COMMENTATORS

Much criticism has been levelled against the manner of preparation of the NRC and the role of the Supreme Court in the process. In an interview, Faizan Mustafa, Vice-Chancellor of NALSAR University of Law, Hyderabad, inter alia, has said that the NRC exercise (because of the cut-off date of 24 March 1971) was contrary to Section 3(1) (a) of the Citizenship Act, 1955 under which citizenship by birth is acquired by all persons born in India between 26 January 1950 and 1 July 1987.[56] The exercise, therefore, has been called unconstitutional. Not only has Dr Mustafa entered into an ex parte legal debate on the purport and effect of the provisions of Section 6A of the Act vis-à-vis Section 3(1)(a) inasmuch as Section 6A deals with 'Special provisions as to citizenship of persons covered by the Assam Accord', what has been overlooked is that by an order dated 21 July 2015 passed in W.P (C) No.311 of 2015, the scope and validity of Section 3(1) (a) of the Act has been referred for consideration by a Constitution Bench along with the constitutionality of Section 6A of the Act. Both issues are at present pending in the Supreme Court.

There are many others who have criticized the exercise of updation of the NRC. Such criticism has been built on an entirely academic basis, ignoring the decades of struggle and sacrifice of a race to preserve and protect its culture and linguistic identity. These critics, ensconced in comfortable spaces in Lutyens' Delhi, have no connection with ground realities. They ignore the feelings and aspirations of the people of a Northeastern state which still reels under a strong wave of anti-national feeling and of separation from the rest of the country. It is a state which has only recently recovered from insurgency. It is such criticism and thinking that generate and nurture sentiment which is contrary to the nation's interests and integrity.

Some retired judges constituted a jury or a people's court to hear the matter. They alleged unfair procedure, hasty process and judicial overreach in the NRC exercise, resulting in loss of hearth and home for almost 19–20 lakh people. Many critics have cited

---

[56]'NRC violation of Citizenship Act, says Faizan Mustafa', *The Statesman*, 11 September 2019, https://bit.ly/3EpXhr8, accessed on 1 October 2021.

adverse international opinion, terming the exercise a perversity and unwarranted in human rights law. I do not give the aforesaid views any credence as they ignore the realities of life in Assam and the Northeast. They overlook the fact that the NRC is a document of identification contemplated by the laws in force. The exclusion of a name from the NRC is not the end of the road. Such exclusion is subject to a well laid down judicial process i.e. challenge before the Foreigners' Tribunal followed by resort to the courts of law. That apart, by itself, the NRC does not contemplate expulsion (from the country) of those not included. Any such action is an altogether separate process based on a completely independent exercise of decision-making by the political executive.

At the local level, personal attacks on the SCNR and veiled attacks on the judges, particularly me, by local politicians and specifically by Abhijit Sharma, the president of Assam Public Works (petitioner in W.P(C) No.274 of 2009) left us (the Bench) convinced that orders should be passed to protect Hajela from undue harassment and calculated harm. The Bench passed the order dated 18 October 2019 for his deputation on inter-cadre transfer to Madhya Pradesh, his home state. Subsequent events like filing of FIRs against Hajela and other NRC officials; allegations of corruption and threats to order CBI probes besides enormous misinformation to the media and wide publicity thereof leave me convinced that the Bench was thoroughly justified in passing the rather unusual order for the inter-cadre transfer of Hajela by invoking Article 142 of the Constitution.

In conclusion, I would like to quote from my speech delivered on 3 November 2019 at the launch of the book, *Post Colonial Assam (1947–2019)* by Mrinal Talukdar:

In the above context, the present effort by Mrinal Talukdar titled *Post Colonial Assam (1947–2019)* is laudable for it revolves around facts and perceptions that display a chain of events over decades which have been perceived as discriminatory, regressive and unconstitutional by the wider section of the citizenry in Assam, with a palpable undercurrent of detachment from the national discourse that has been fuelling a sense of isolation and alienation in the Assamese minds. On the one hand, Mrinal's book seeks to bring to the fore the sheer lack of understanding and acceptance of the enormity of the geo-political turbulence that was unleashed amongst the peace-loving citizenry of Assam and other North-Eastern states, by the waves of human migration triggered in the aftermath of the partition of the sub-continent by the retreating colonial power. The contents of the book need not be thought of as any rhetoric, as it is nothing but core reality—and a living truth. Added to this are the unexploited and undeveloped avenues of tourism potential; lack of state assistance in tea research though Assam produces 50 per cent of Indian tea; the neglected mineral resources and the impoverished academic institutions. All speak for themselves.

[...] At this crossroads, we need to keep in mind that our national discourse has witnessed the emergence of armchair commentators who are not only far removed from ground realities, but also seek to present a highly distorted picture. The emergence of the social media, and its tools, have also fuelled the intent of such commentators, who thrive through their 'double-speak' language sitting in the confines and comforts of their spaces. They launch baseless and motivated tirades against democratic functionalities and institutions, seeking to hurt them and bring down their due processes. These commentators, and their vile intentions, do survive well in situations where facts are far removed from the citizenry, and rumour mills flourish.

Assam and its development agenda too have been victims of such armchair commentaries, wherein the 'due processes' have been questioned and challenges have been thrown at vital initiatives that were aimed at ushering in a new era of peaceful co-existence, leading to overall progress and prosperity of the entire region. It is here that Mrinal's work, together with the backdrop of events narrated therein, would help the knowledgeable and the discerning readers understand the socio-economic and geo-political realities of Assam and its neighbourhood, upon which all well-meaning future endeavours would require to be based. This is an occasion to put things in proper perspective—the NRC as it will finally emerge is not a document of the moment—19 lakh or 40 lakh is not the point. It is a base document for the future—a kind of a reference document to determine future claims. This is its intrinsic value, in my comprehension.

[...] And while so pondering, I would request a little insight as to what might be the expectations from various stakeholders, in particular, the fourth estate. Given the composition of this august gathering, I believe this is an appropriate forum to discuss the issue. It is our duty to participate in the political life of the community, the society and the state as public citizens. Without such involvement, there remains the danger of becoming irrelevant and sinking into cynicism, endlessly creating and diagnosing problems without playing any part in solving them. One can see this happening these days, in the manner in which workings of the institutions are assessed, especially by the media and particularly on social media. A case in point would be the nature of reporting about the whole NRC process, and institutions engaged therein. One has to ask, is this a constructive manner of engaging with any institution, particularly one tasked with the crucial responsibility of protection of basic rights of all? We must resist the urge to find wrongs and shortcomings everywhere we look and merely for the sake of finding one. The constant desire to play to the gallery by demeaning institutions and all their efforts must be resolutely avoided. This, of course, must be a self-check. At no point is this a suggestion for uncritical affiliation, for public scrutiny and critical engagement are an absolute imperative for attainment of a vibrant and meaningful democracy. But where is the critical meeting, when unrestrained mudslinging, casting unsubstantiated aspersions and launching personal attacks against both the institution and its members, masquerade as public discourse? We all will do well to remember that it does not take long to tear down an institution, but it takes eons to build an effective one.

Today, it seems that Assam with its irredeemable past is being saddled with an unpresentable present. Do we run the risk of an unimaginable future as well? What lessons must we draw on to avoid such an eventuality? It is often said that those who forget history are bound to repeat its mistakes.

I delivered this speech with great satisfaction, considerably more than when I have addressed various national and international events. I have, therefore, provided the link to the entire speech to enable readers to derive complete insight into my thoughts on the matter.[57]

---

[57]Pratidin Bureau, CJI Ranjan Gogoi defends NRC: SPEECH IN FULL https://bit.ly/3bPHwO8, accessed on 3 November 2021.

Twelve

AYODHYA: FIVE MEN AND AN ANONYMOUS VERDICT

Faith and religious beliefs are matters of conviction and not proof. Yet, they bond humans and human communities. At the same time, they also occasion what is diverse and different. Homogeneity and oneness continue to remain elusive notwithstanding the claimed efforts of the leaders amongst us to bind humanity together. Driven by the diverse and the different, nation states have been engaged in centuries-old disputes revolving around religious faith and beliefs.

One such dispute that drew wide attention from most Indians as well as from the international community was a centuries-old structure located in Ayodhya in the state of Uttar Pradesh in respect of which members of two different religious denominations had been making claims and counterclaims based primarily on their perceived right of worship to the exclusion of all others. One of the denominations (Hindus) had claimed that the present construction stood on the ruins of an earlier structure of faith, which had been demolished in a measure of religious persecution several centuries ago. Ironically, the Hindus who claimed to have been so persecuted by the alleged demolition centuries earlier came to be blamed for the demolition of the present-day structure in the late twentieth century. Though civilization had undergone several transformations, irreversibly influencing human life on the planet, the dispute on the structure appeared to have survived through the centuries.

Against this backdrop, some amongst the faithful knocked on the doors of the judiciary, seeking legal redress to the dispute from an institution whose processes and pursuits are guided by the values enshrined in the Constitution of India. By the time the dispute reached the apex judicial institution, only images and descriptions were left of the present-day structure upon which the original judicial proceedings had begun. In the course of the journey through the Court, spanning half a century, the dispute ceased to centre around the structure or the right of some to worship there to the exclusion of others, but became an issue of deeper faith, affecting millions of Hindus and Muslims, the possible outcome of which could leave a deep impact on the multi-cultural and multi-religious socio-economic canvas of the young nation, creating distrust amongst its citizenry. Meanwhile, contemporaneous governments had also passed ordinances and executive orders, the effects of which appeared to have added layers of uncertainty to various aspects of the dispute.

The approach to the courts and finally the Supreme Court was a challenge to India's constitutionalism as well as to the dynamism of an institution in which the Indian people repose faith as the guardian of their Constitution—the Supreme Court of India. Within the institution, decision-makers were awake to the various challenges that would need to be overcome to take the judicial process to its logical end.

Expectations were high, and the tools of judicial dispensation had to be employed with 'complete justice' acting as the beacon. The Ayodhya case was an occasion for India's judiciary to make an invaluable contribution to the odyssey of mankind as, through its verdict, it was expected to lay out a vision and inspire the will in communities across the world to seek closure of such inter-faith

Ranjan Gogoi

conflicts through peaceful and judicial ways. It would also guide the faithful to discover the ability to accept and co-exist with what may be different or diverse or perceived to be so.

ANATOMY OF THE DISPUTE: CLAIMS AND COUNTERCLAIMS

The Ayodhya case decided by the Supreme Court on 9 November 2019 is a chronicle of a protracted legal battle, inter alia, for recognition of the claim that Ayodhya is the birthplace of Lord Ram and that he was born at the sanctum sanctorum or 'garb-grih' right below the central dome of the three-domed mosque demolished on 6 December 1992. The Hindu version, which was hotly contested, was, further, to the effect that in that birth spot of Lord Ram there had existed an ancient Ram temple which was demolished to build the mosque which came to be known as the Babri Masjid.

The contrary version was to the effect that the mosque was constructed in the sixteenth century during the reign of Emperor Babar on vacant land and that no pre-existing Hindu temple was demolished to construct it. Whether either version is mere belief or historical fact, documented and demonstrated by legal evidence, was the issue that confronted the Supreme Court. Complex facts buried in history had to be unearthed to decide simple claims of right to the land made by the parties.

The land under the central dome measured approximately 1,500 sq. yards—less than one-third of an acre. Along with the adjacent land, on which according to the Hindu claim other places of worship had existed, the total disputed area measured about 2.77 acres. A fierce battle of claims over a seemingly tiny parcel of land had been raging between the two principal religious groups of the country since the medieval era. The claims and counterclaims came to be crafted on a legal framework during British rule and continued to simmer after Independence, leading to inflamed sentiments on both sides. The issue was a fount of perennial conflict, which degenerated into violence on at least three occasions—in 1856-57 (when riots broke out), in December 1949 when the mosque was desecrated and idols of Lord Ram were placed under the central dome, and in December 1992, when the entire mosque was brought down by a horde of kar sevaks. This sparked communal violence in the country as well as in neighbouring Pakistan and Bangladesh, and led to the fall of the elected government in Uttar Pradesh.

The claim and counterclaims of the parties were raised in four suits filed between 1950 and 1989.[58] They were transferred by the Allahabad High Court in 1989 to be heard by a full bench of the High Court (three judges)—perhaps in view of the sensitivity of the matter. The High Court delivered its judgment on 30 September 2010, which ran into almost 4,000 printed pages (bound in four thick volumes). There were three separate judgments and the judges also differed in the final operative relief granted. While all the three judges held the area covered by the central dome in favour of the Hindu parties, Justice Dharam Veer Sharma (who died recently) declared the entire premises as belonging to the Hindu deities who were the plaintiffs in Suit No. 5. Justice Sudhir Agarwal

---

58

1.	Original Suit (O.O.S) No.1 of 1989 (Regular Suit No. 2/1950	Gopal Singh Visharad (since deceased and survived by Rajendra Singh) Versus Zahoor Ahmad and others
2.	Original Suit No. 3 of 1989 (Regular Suit No. 26/1959	Nirmohi Akhara and others Versus Baboo Priya Datt Ram and others
3.	Original Suit No. 4 of 1989 (Regular Suit No. 12/1961	The Sunni Central Board of Waqfs, U.P. and others Versus Gopal Singh Visharad (since deceased) and others
4.	Original Suit No. 5 of 1989 (Regular Suit No. 236/1989)	Bhagwan Sri Ram Lala Virajman and others Versus Rajendra Singh and others

Ranjan Gogoi

recognized the partial rights of all the contesting parties over the rest of the disputed property (except the area under the central dome). Justice S.U. Khan, on the other hand, declared all the three parties (including the Nirmohi Akhara) as joint title holders of the disputed property while declaring the Hindu parties to be entitled to allotment of the portion below the central dome in the final decree of partition.

Obviously, the decision could not satisfy any of the parties. Twenty-one appeals were filed before the Supreme Court and collectively came to be known as the Ayodhya case. A large number of intervention applications by parties claiming to be interested also came to be filed before the Supreme Court, enabling it to hear a large number of counsel, some of whom, I must acknowledge, provided valuable assistance to the Court.

Attempts to hear the appeals had been going on for quite some time. For one reason or another, every time the case would come up for hearing it would get deferred. Take 5 December 2017: the matter was fixed for hearing before a Bench of three judges headed by CJI Dipak Misra. When the matter was called, Kapil Sibal wanted the case to be heard in 2019 (presumably after the Lok Sabha elections). Rajeev Dhavan, counsel for one of the contesting parties, submitted that the decision of the Constitution Bench in *Dr M. Ismail Faruqui and Ors. Vs. Union of India & Ors.* (1994) 6 SCC 360 required reconsideration by a larger Bench and until then, the hearing should be adjourned. According to the counsel, what required consideration by a larger Bench were the observations of the Constitution Bench in Faruqui's case to the effect that '...a mosque is not an essential part of the practice of the religion of Islam and namaz (prayer) by Muslims can be offered anywhere, even in open...'

CJI Misra, who was presiding over the Bench then hearing the case, declined to adjourn the hearing to 2019. In his own way, he made attempts to go ahead with the case. But sometime in April-May 2018, the impeachment episode cropped up. Many believed that the impeachment move was calculated to prevent CJI Misra from hearing the Ayodhya case. Whether there is any substance in this is not within my knowledge. However, I find some commonality between such thoughts and the views expressed in certain quarters that the events narrated in an earlier chapter could have been similarly calculated with not only the Ayodhya hearing that was due shortly, but also the ongoing hearings in sensitive cases like Rafale and NRC in mind. The only difference was that while the first move (involving CJI Misra) succeeded, the second (involving myself) did not.

The three-judge Bench decided the question of reference to a larger Bench on 27 September 2018 by refusing a reference. Instead, it directed the Registry to list the cases for hearing on 27 October 2018. Two things must be noted. The first is that 27 September i.e. the date of the decision by the three-judge Bench was one of the last days of Justice Misra's tenure as the CJI and the date fixed for hearing i.e. 27 October was after the commencement of my tenure as the CJI. Second, the process of hearing of the Ayodhya case really commenced during the tenure of my predecessor, Justice Misra. This should settle all speculation as to whether I had resurrected the cases to hear them out of turn, as alleged by many. What I did was to let the case take the usual procedural course.

A NEW YEAR, A NEW DAWN

The date fixed by Justice Misra's Bench for hearing i.e. 27 October 2018 was a Saturday. The matter, therefore, came up on 29 October 2018 (Monday) before a Bench of Justice Sanjay Kishan Kaul, Justice K.M. Joseph and myself. An order was passed that the matter would be listed for hearing before the appropriate Bench in the first week of January 2019. There was no specific date chosen. I, therefore, expected that before the cases were listed, my permission would be sought. This was not done and, suddenly, without my knowledge, the case got listed on 4 January 2019. At the time, I had not even constituted the Bench that would hear it. Also, my assessment of the state of readiness of the case for hearing was yet to be completed. Neither the Secretary General nor any of the registrars could explain how the case got listed without my knowledge and permission. Be that as it may, on 4 January, the Bench consisting of Justice Kaul and myself, in the above situation, had no alternative but to pass the following order:

> Further orders in the matter will be passed on 10.1.2019 by the appropriate Bench, as may be constituted.

Thereafter, as the CJI, I took the decision that the appeals should be heard by a five-judge Bench headed by me and with Justices S.A. Bobde, N.V. Ramana, U.U. Lalit and D.Y. Chandrachud. All the other four members of the Bench were future Chief Justices of the country. On 10 January 2019, the matter came up before the five-judge Bench. Rajeev Dhavan pointed out that sometime in the year 1997, Justice Lalit had appeared in a connected matter and therefore the learned judge may decide whether he would like to continue on the Bench. Justice Lalit, naturally, expressed his disinclination to continue. We, therefore, had no option but to adjourn the case to another date as I had to reconstitute the Bench. Dhavan also raised a question as to why the appeals had been fixed for hearing before a five-judge Bench when a reference to a larger Bench had been refused by the Court on 27 September 2018. This was answered by the Court with its order dated 10 January 2019 holding that, following the provisions of the Supreme Court Rules, the Chief Justice (myself) had decided that the cases (appeals) would be heard by a Bench of five judges and the constitution of the larger Bench had nothing to do with the earlier order of the Court on 27 September 2018.

The following observations of the Court, in its order of 10

January 2019, are worth noting to show how, in the meantime, the ground work for readying the cases for hearing had been progressing:

> The Secretary General of the Registry has informed the Chief Justice that in the four suits, out of which these appeals have arisen, in all, 120 issues have been framed for trial. A total of 88 witnesses were examined. The depositions of the witnesses run into 13,886 pages. A total of 257 documents were exhibited (according to Dr Rajeev Dhavan the number of Exhibits is 533 including 3 Archaeological Reports). The judgment runs into 4304 printed pages (according to the Registry, 8533 typed pages). The Bench has been informed that the original records are lying in 15 sealed trunks in a room which has also been sealed. Whether the depositions and documents which are in Persian, Sanskrit, Arabic, Gurumukhi, Urdu and Hindi, etc. have been translated is not clear.
>
> The orders of this Court, particularly, the order dated 10th August, 2015 indicate that though the learned counsel for the parties had attempted to submit some translated version of the evidence, there is a dispute with regard to the correctness of the translations made.
>
> In these circumstances, the Registry of this Court is directed to physically inspect the records which are lying under lock and key; make an assessment of the time that will be taken to make the cases ready for hearing by engaging, if required, official translators of the requisite number and give a report thereof to the Court. The said report will be submitted to this Court by the Registry on 29th January, 2019 when the reconstituted Bench (without Uday Umesh Lalit, J), as may be, will assemble once again to take up the matter for further orders.

In the meantime, Justice Ramana (number three judge on the Bench) met me and requested that he should be excluded from the Bench when it was reconstituted. I asked why and he indicated his difficulties. As my original plan that the appeals should be heard by a five-judge Bench consisting of the current Chief Justice and the four future Chief Justices had, anyway, to be abandoned with the recusal of Justice Lalit (there were no more future Chief Justices available at that point of time), I reconstituted the Bench by excluding Justice Ramana and including Justice Ashok Bhushan and Justice S. Abdul Nazeer who had been members of the three-judge Bench that had passed the order of 27 September 2018.

In terms of the order of the Court dated 10 January, the Registry submitted its report on 29 January i.e. the fixed date. The report is extracted in the order of the Court dated 26 February 2019 passed by the reconstituted Bench of Justices Bobde, Chandrachud, Bhushan, Nazeer and myself. The report makes interesting reading. It indicates the enormity of the cases before us and their state of readiness for hearing by the Bench. An extract from the report is reproduced as part of the Annexures.

In the order dated 26 February, the Bench noted that 'pursuant to the several orders passed by this Court indicated above it appears that the State of Uttar Pradesh has submitted translation of the oral evidence in the cases which runs into about 13000 pages. Some of the Exhibits have been translated by the parties who propose to rely on the said documents in terms of the orders of this Court'. However, pending verification of the translation, the Bench recorded the necessity for grant of two months' time to the parties to satisfy themselves with regard to the accuracy of the translations of the relevant documents filed in court by the state of Uttar Pradesh. At the suggestion of Justice Bobde, we sought the views of the counsel for the parties regarding the feasibility of Court-monitored mediation, by Court-appointed mediators, if the mediation was to be completed within two months, which time we were even otherwise allowing to enable the Registry to ready the appeals for hearing. As the parties were broadly in agreement that such an exercise could be attempted, we fixed 6 March 2019 for further orders.

The matter came up on 8 March on that date, we appointed a mediation panel consisting of Justice Fakkir Mohamed Ibrahim Kalifulla, former Supreme Court judge, as the Chairman, Sri Sri Ravi Shankar, the spiritual and yoga guru, and Sriram Panchu, a senior advocate and an acknowledged mediator. We also directed that the mediation proceedings should be held at Faizabad, Uttar Pradesh, and that the proceedings, including the views expressed therein by any of the parties as well as by the mediators, should be kept confidential. We also expressed our reservations regarding reporting of the mediation proceedings in the print or electronic media, but left it to the mediators to pass necessary orders, if so required, restraining publication of the proceedings. The mediation proceedings were directed to be conducted in camera.

On 7 May (two months after the order dated 8 March constituting the mediation committee), the Court received a report from the Chairman of the Mediation Committee indicating the progress made and seeking further time until 15 August. This was granted by the Court on 10 May. Coincidentally, the Supreme Court was scheduled to go on its long vacation from 13 May and reopen on 1 July. After the summer recess, the Bench assembled on 11 July to consider an application filed in the meantime by one of the contesting parties stating that the mediation process had failed and the matter should be heard on merits. A report was sought from the mediation committee while permitting it to continue with the proceedings. A report was duly submitted, intimating the failure of the mediation attempt. On 2 August, the Court assembled to consider the report, after which orders were passed that the cases/appeals would be heard on and from 6 August, on a day-to-day basis.

'ENOUGH IS ENOUGH!'

The hearing of the Ayodhya case(s) commenced at 10.30 a.m. on 6 August. There were not too many advocates in the Court. Sushil Kumar Jain, senior advocate, appearing on behalf of the Nirmohi Akhara, the appellant in one of the cases i.e. C.A. No. 4905-4908/2011, began the arguments. I did not think he was very well prepared. Perhaps he had not expected the hearing to really commence. The hearing dragged on until fireworks emanated from Dhavan who, during Jain's arguments, looked at me and said that these cases could not be heard in the manner that I would 'normally' hear cases coming before me. This was without any provocation, and only because we had urged Jain to step up the pace of his arguments. Everything will have to be considered and everybody will have to be given a full hearing, Dhavan said. All documents would have to be scrutinized. Dhavan indicated that he may himself take about six weeks to complete his arguments. At one point, he also mentioned that none of the judges except Justice Chandrachud had either read the papers or understood the case. I requested all my brother judges to remain silent and not to respond as it could have resulted in scuttling of the hearing.

Such incidents kept occurring in court frequently and increased with time. But the hearing continued. Many of the questions put to the counsel by the Court were elaborately answered and some of the replies were insightful and knowledgeable, though, at times, unconnected with either the question raised or the issues arising in the case. Equally, at times, the questions by the Court too were academic and unconnected with the case. As the CJI, I had to constantly bring the ship back to course.

About a week after commencement of the hearing, I found a huge change in the atmosphere in court. The courtroom became more crowded; lawyers who may have harboured scepticism about the possibility of any sustained hearing of the case became cooperative. Our decision to have five days' continuous hearing (Monday to Friday), which had initially met with stiff resistance, became more accepted. Dhavan, who had insisted on a mid-week break at least while he would be arguing, agreed to remain on his legs all five days when I pointed out that he could take a mid-week break on a Wednesday—with the consequence that somebody else would argue a separate appeal or IA on that day. As the hearing progressed and my retirement drew closer, I suggested that we could continue the sessions until 5 p.m. All the counsel agreed and for a considerable number of days we heard the matter until 5 o'clock.

Apart from Sushil Kumar Jain, arguments were offered by K. Parasaran, C.S. Vaidyanathan, Ranjit Kumar, P.S. Narasimha (now a judge of the Supreme Court), Jaideep Gupta, Vikas Singh, Hari Shankar Jain, V.N. Sinha and several others whose names I do not recollect. They argued on behalf of the Hindu parties whereas Dhavan, Meenakshi Arora and Zafaryab Jilani principally argued on behalf of the Muslim parties. The judges acknowledged in open court the valuable assistance rendered by the counsel of both sides.

The arguments that commenced on 6 August were heard for 40 days and concluded on 16 October. On the last date of hearing, at about 11.30 a.m. or 12 noon, I received a slip of paper from the Secretary General of the Supreme Court stating that a representative of one of the litigants was seeking permission to enter the Supreme Court. Justice Bobde, who was to my right, and Justice Chandrachud, on my left, asked about the note as receipt of notes from registrars in the midst of hearing by a five-judge Bench is somewhat unusual. Since it pertained to an administrative matter, I told them accordingly. I sent a handwritten reply to the Secretary General saying that under no circumstances was the person to be allowed entry. A bona fide visitor to the Supreme Court in connection with his case is always entitled to a visitor's pass through his Advocate-on-Record. Since this person was approaching the Registry or the Secretary General for entry, I sensed that his objective was not well-intended but aimed at disrupting the hearing. Had he been able to do that, the court proceedings would have been affected and the case may have had to be adjourned. The Secretary General acted as he was instructed.

During the lunch recess, he sought further instructions. I enquired whether he could maintain status quo for another two hours. He assured me he could. The hearing resumed at 2 o'clock and a little after three, I closed the hearing by saying, 'Enough is enough' and 'Judgment is reserved'. This is how the hearing of one of the longest disputes in legal history and one of the most fiercely contested cases in the Supreme Court came to an end.

I must confess that the conduct of business in court, never for a moment, reflected the ongoing stress, anxiety and trauma within me. The years of training and self-discipline as a judge were pressed into service. But, at every moment, I was conscious that the oral hearings, the discussions amongst the judges, the preparation and delivery of the judgment—all had to be completed within a time frame in view of my impending retirement on 17 November 2019.

I often carried the surcharged emotions home. My wife was the only person with whom I could share the turmoil within me and lay bare the highly disturbed man behind the cool and calm exterior exhibited in the courtroom. One particular day, I refused to go to court. Rupanjali eventually won with her enormous persuasive powers. On another day, though she succeeded in pushing me out of the house (5, Krishna Menon Marg), once I reached the Court, I refused to budge from the chamber. Justice Bobde called off the hearing that day, telling the other judges that I was unwell.

While the hearing was progressing, negative statements by activists and lawyers on one or another unrelated issue kept getting published, perhaps to disturb the peace which was required to decide a case of such magnitude.

I do not remember getting more than three to four hours of daily sleep during the entire period of the Ayodhya hearing.

Negative comments on the feasibility of completion of hearing; statements by activists about the misplaced priority of the Supreme Court in taking up the case and wasting judicial time and, to top it all, the Damocles' sword-like deadlines for completion of the different stages of the case kept reminding me what was at stake— the consequences to me and the institution, and its reputation if the case was to remain inconclusive before my retirement. Even some of my colleagues were highly sceptical. Why has this madman put the reputation of the Supreme Court at stake, was the topic of several private conversations amongst the judges. But the way things progressed and ended convinced me that there was a divine force which made the conclusion of the case, regardless of the way the judgment went, possible.

A somewhat unusual feature of the three-month hearing was that no judge on the Bench availed of casual leave even for a day. No judge on the Bench suffered even from a common cold or fever that kept him away from the hearing. Equally inexplicable was another occurrence. One of the judges told me that he might have to take leave for a few days as a close relative was seriously ill and in the ICU of a hospital. I told him that he might not require to do so as his relative would recover. This was in order to console and comfort him. The judge did not take any leave, and I too did not ask about his relative as presumably he had recovered.

While I must acknowledge and appreciate the role of all my brother judges on the Bench, Justice Bobde's part in bringing the Ayodhya case to a logical conclusion, in spite of the multiple hurdles, is significant. Without his contribution, the Bench could not have succeeded in completing the case within the available time frame.

Every day, after the hearing, all five judges would meet in the Chief Justice's chamber for a cup of tea. We used to talk about many other things and only generally about the case and the arguments made in the course of the day. Never did we discuss which way the verdict should eventually go.

It was only in the last few days of the hearing that there appeared to be unanimity of opinion building up that the disputed land should go in favour of the Hindu parties for constructing the Ram temple and the Muslim parties should be allowed a five-acre alternative plot in a suitable and prominent place in Ayodhya for building a mosque. It was agreed that relief would be moulded accordingly.

About a week before the hearing concluded, I suggested that the opinion of the Court should not only be unanimous, which it was going to be as the trend of discussions and mutual exchanges indicated, there should also be only one judgment and the name of the author of the judgment should not be disclosed. The judgment to be pronounced would be finalized once all the individual judgments were received and necessary editing and merger carried out to turn the draft judgments into the final one. I do not know about the others, but I started writing my judgment and wrote about 300 pages. I received two separate judgments with the same conclusion authored by two of the judges. All the draft judgments received were handed over to a third judge on the Bench for editing and merger.

In Supreme Court practice, the judge who has authored a judgment sends it to the other judge(s) on the Bench for consideration and approval. The other judge(s), if he agrees with the draft judgment, sends it back usually with the remark 'I respectfully agree'. This practice was followed in the Ayodhya case also. The draft judgment was circulated by me to all the brother judges not as the author, but as the presiding judge of the Bench. The written approval of all the four judges was received by me. The acknowledgments/approvals make very interesting reading and perhaps settle all doubts and questions raised by 'investigative journalists' and pessimists, activists and detractors about the authorship of the judgment. The practice followed is in consonance with the legal concept of per curiam, meaning the order of the court. I believe it was recently followed in the judgment in the One Rupee Contempt case.

Some logistical issues, however, remained to be resolved. These were discussed during the last meeting on 8 November in my official chamber at 5, Krishna Menon Marg. After the discussions, the judges emerged after about an hour, smiling and holding hands, having resolved the logistics. I immediately called the registrar in charge of listing, who, as instructed, was waiting. He was told to list the case for pronouncement of judgment the next day at 10.30 a.m. This was around 8.30 p.m.

I had very little sleep that night. Though I had a prepared text of the operative part of the judgment, I kept thinking about what I should read from that so as to shorten the court proceedings to the minimum.

AYODHYA'S HOUR OF RECKONING

The following morning—9 November—on entering the courtroom, we found it overflowing with advocates, some litigants and, of course, mediapersons. Every inch of available space was taken up, all entry and exit points had been opened and curtains lifted out of the way. There was a spillover of the assembly in the corridor in front of the CJI's court.

After we had taken our seats, I was the first to sign the judgment. Then the other judges signed it in order of seniority. Within a few seconds, the ink dried and the Ayodhya judgment had become etched in judicial history for posterity to read. I told the packed courtroom that the judgment was unanimous and per curiam (authorship undisclosed). A spontaneous roar arose.

Thereafter, I commenced reading the operative parts which, in spite of my best efforts, took about 45 minutes. The judgment was pronounced on a Saturday as the next three days were holidays. I felt that this was one judgment that should not be kept pending for even a minute once it was ready for pronouncement. In fact, prior to the pronouncement, I had met the chief secretary and the

Director-General of Police of Uttar Pradesh. This was dictated by prudence in view of the judgment's importance and the impact it was bound to have, whichever way it went.

After the judgment, the Secretary General organized a photo session in the judges' gallery outside Court No. 1, below the Ashoka Chakra. In the evening, I took the judges for dinner to Taj Mansingh Hotel. We ate Chinese food and shared a bottle of wine, the best available there. I picked up the tab, being the eldest.

Early the next morning, we (Rupanjali, my mother and I) left for Dibrugarh. Dropping off my mother there, we went to Guwahati to attend an event during which I released the Assamese version of *Courts of India*, published by the Supreme Court. We returned to Delhi the following day (11 November) despite 11 and 12 November being holidays. The Sabarimala, Rafale and Rojer Mathew cases were still to be finalized and the judgments were due for pronouncement in the remaining days prior to my retirement. I was, therefore, back to work, which continued until the last day in office.

This is how one of the most protracted and fiercely contested cases in India's judicial history came to an end. I was least worried about the possible ramifications that the Court's verdict would have, if any, on India's political, religious or social canvas. To me, the Ayodhya case was a challenge inherited by me from my predecessors, a challenge I chose not to avoid or shirk but to face head-on and complete within a time frame. In fact, I was due to visit Egypt, Brazil, the US, Canada and Indonesia from 18 October to 2 November (26 October to 2 November 2019 were Court holidays on account of Diwali) for official meetings but thought it fit to cancel the trip to ensure that the Ayodhya judgment was delivered before my retirement. In hindsight, I would call my decision absolutely the right one.

I succeeded in what I had set out to achieve. This is my enduring satisfaction: a job done and not left incomplete.

Thirteen

....

THE MANY FIRSTS

The cherished dream of most advocates (it was mine as well) is to be designated a senior advocate by the High Court in which he is practising or by the Supreme Court, if he happens to have the bulk of his practice there. And why not? The Advocates Act, 1961, recognizes only two classes of advocates—senior advocates and other advocates. Under Section 16 of the Act, an advocate can be designated a senior advocate if the Supreme Court or High Court 'is of the opinion that by virtue of his ability, standing at the Bar or special knowledge or experience, is deserving of such distinction'.

A litigant, particularly before the Supreme Court, would naturally prefer to have the services of a senior advocate who has been recognized by the Court itself as a lawyer of standing and ability. Not only is there an immediate upgradation of status with the designation, it is also financially rewarding as the fees charged go up several-fold. Advocates have only one upgradation in their career, namely, the designation as senior advocate. A judgeship has a different footing and many successful advocates do not wish to become judges. Thus, I am not wrong in saying that designation as a senior advocate is much sought-after by advocates.

The practice and procedure leading to designation as senior

advocate used to vary from court to court. In my parent High Court, the designation was accorded on the basis of unanimity of opinion; in the Punjab and Haryana High Court, voting by the judges is resorted to. In the Supreme Court, when I joined in 2012, designation was by consensus amongst judges. In 2013, during the tenure of CJI Justice P. Sathasivam, suddenly, in the course of deliberations in a full court on the subject of designation of senior advocates, one or two judges insisted that we should follow the practice of secret ballot. The full court was adjourned, and in the next meeting, votes were cast and designations accorded. Between the two meetings, hectic lobbying by advocates, including visits to the judges' chambers in the Supreme Court, was noticed. A practice which is definitely not healthy seemed to have crept in.

At the next meeting in April 2015, during which the designation of senior advocates was taken up by the full court, only five advocates were designated. This time, too, lobbying and canvassing were witnessed at full force. The system was at odds. While the secret ballot had its own drawbacks, the earlier practice of decision by consensus led to divisions within the small judicial family in the Supreme Court. The views of individual judges on advocates seeking the designation came to be known in the Bar. I do not know if the viability—or lack of it—of either procedure was the reason why designations were not granted for a considerable time.

In the meantime, senior advocate Indira Jaising filed an Article 32 petition with regard to designation of senior advocates. The matter was extensively considered by a Bench of three judges with me presiding. By a judgment dated 12 October 2017, the Court, after an elaborate discussion on the practice prevailing in many other countries and after considering the pros and cons of the matter, decided the issue by setting guidelines to regulate the procedure to be followed for designating senior advocates.

Following the order, the guidelines were notified by the Registry of the Supreme Court and applications were invited on

6 August 2018. A total of 105 applications were found to be in order and were put up before the committee which consisted of the CJI, the next two judges in order of seniority, the Attorney General and a member of the Bar nominated by the other four members of the committee (Soli Sorabjee was the nominated member). Interactions were held in five different batches and suitable names were shortlisted. The full court on 27 March 2019 considered the cases of all the 105 applicants along with the assessments made by the committee and resolved to designate 37 advocates or advocates-on-record (AsOR) as senior advocates; 46 names were deferred for consideration at the next full court meeting, whereas the remaining 22 cases were dealt with according to the guidelines in force, namely, the cases were to be considered after two years. The issue of designation has not been taken up by the Supreme Court since. Jaising has filed another IA in the writ petition, seeking directions for fresh consideration of cases for designation.

I reckon the judgment pertaining to the designation of senior advocates to be one of the important judgments concerning the courts and the Bar of the country. Many High Courts have framed their own guidelines in conformity with the judgment and have undertaken and completed the designation exercise. Yet, strangely, the judgment is yet to acquire the status of a 'noteworthy' judgment.

Another case that came before my court that I consider to be of great significance pertained to the setting up of a crèche in the Supreme Court for the convenience of working mothers belonging to the staff as well as the Bar. Once again, Indira Jaising played a pivotal role as she had conducted the case in this regard filed by one Dr Anindita Pujari. It took a lot of effort and time to put the facility in place and a series of judicial orders had to be passed after several rounds of consultation with domain experts and physical visits to the site. The crèche became operational in May 2018 and started functioning in an area of about 2,000 sq. ft for 30 children between six months and six years at a very nominal fee. The response was very good. During the time it was temporarily shut on account of COVID-19, there were 27 children coming to the facility every day. As the CJI, I had visited the place on several occasions and found the facility to be very well managed.

QUEST FOR REFORM

There are, however, some other decisions on the administrative side of the Supreme Court that, I believe, have had a far-reaching impact on the institution. The raising of the strength of the Supreme Court from 31 to 34 by Gazette notification of 9 August 2019 was a result of my letter of 21 June to the PM with detailed reasons and justification for seeking an increase in the number of judges.

Critics may argue that while the Supreme Court of the United States of America has nine judges, as a constitutional court should the Supreme Court of India continue to enhance its judge strength? They forget that the population of the US is one-fourth that of India. The Indian Supreme Court is a constitutional court as well as an appellate court. Apart from its constitutional jurisdiction, it also hears civil, criminal and taxation cases and appeals covering a wide range of other subjects. There can be no comparison.

I had no difficulty in transacting Collegium business. All my colleagues were extremely cooperative. Consequently, 14 judges came to be appointed to the Supreme Court in about a year. Similarly, 28 Chief Justices of High Courts were appointed. The names of the Supreme Court judges and High Court Chief Justices so appointed are given on the next page:

TABLE 4
Supreme Court Judges Appointed

S. No.	Name	Date of Appointment	Date of Retirement	Remarks
1.	Hemant Gupta	02.11.18	16.10.22	
2.	R. Subhash Reddy	02.11.18	04.01.22	
3.	M.R. Shah	02.11.18	15.05.23	
4.	Ajay Rastogi	02.11.18	17.06.23	
5.	Dinesh Maheshwari	18.01.19	14.05.23	
6.	Sanjiv Khanna	18.01.19	13.05.25	Will be CJI w.e.f. 10.11.2024
7.	B.R. Gavai	24.05.19	23.11.25	Will be CJI w.e.f. 14.05.2025
8.	Surya Kant	24.05.19	09.02.27	Will be CJI w.e.f. 24.11.2025
9.	Aniruddha Bose	24.05.19	10.04.24	
10.	A.S. Bopanna	24.05.19	19.05.24	
11.	Krishna Murari	23.09.19	08.07.23	
12.	S. Ravindra Bhat	23.09.19	20.10.23	
13.	V. Ramasubramanian	23.09.19	29.06.23	
14.	Hrishikesh Roy	23.09.19	31.01.25	

TABLE 5
Chief Justices Appointed

S. No.	Name	High Court	Date of Apptt.	Date of retirement	Tenure	Parent High Court
1.	Surya Kant	Himachal Pradesh	05.10.18	09.02.24	5.04	Punjab and Haryana

2.	N.H. Patil	Bombay	29.10.18	06.04.19	0.05	Bombay
3.	A.S. Bopanna	Gauhati	29.10.18	19.05.21	2.06	Karnataka
4.	D.K. Gupta	Calcutta	30.10.18	31.12.18	0.02	Calcutta
5.	V.K. Bist	Sikkim	30.10.18	16.09.19	0.10	Uttarakhand
6.	Ramesh Ranganathan (AP)	Uttarakhand	02.11.18	27.07.20	1.08	Telangana and Andhra Pradesh
7.	S.K. Seth	Madhya Pradesh	14.11.18	09.06.19	0.06	Madhya Pradesh
8.	Govind Mathur	Allahabad	14.11.18	13.04.21	2.04	Rajasthan
9.	Sanjay Karol	Tripura	14.11.18	22.08.23	4.08	Himachal Pradesh
10.	A.P. Sahi	Patna	17.11.18	31.12.20	2.01	Allahabad
11.	S. Ravindra Bhat	Rajasthan	05.05.19	21.10.20	1.05	Delhi
12.	P.R. Nair Ramachandra Menon	Chhattisgarh	06.05.19	31.05.21	2.00	Kerala
13.	A.S. Oka	Karnataka	10.05.19	24.05.22	3.00	Bombay
14.	D.N. Patel	Delhi	07.06.19	12.03.22	2.09	Gujarat
15.	A.K. Mittal	Meghalaya	28.05.19	29.09.20	1.04	Punjab and Haryana
16.	R.S. Chauhan	Telangana	22.06.19	23.12.21	2.06	Rajasthan
17.	V. Ramasubramanian	Himachal Pradesh	22.06.19	29.06.20	1.00	Madras
18.	Vikram Nath	Gujarat	10.09.19	23.09.24	5.00	Allahabad
19.	Ravi Shankar Jha	Punjab and Haryana	06.10.19	13.10.23	4.00	Madhya Pradesh
20.	Indrajit Mahanty	Rajasthan	06.10.19	10.11.22	3.01	Orissa
21.	L. Narayana Swamy	Himachal Pradesh	06.10.19	30.06.21	1.08	Karnataka
22.	J.K. Maheshwari	Andhra Pradesh	07.10.19	28.06.23	4.00	Madhya Pradesh
23.	Ajai Lamba	Gauhati	07.10.19	20.09.20	0.11	Punjab and Haryana
24.	S. Manikumar	Kerala	11.10.19	23.04.23	2.05	Madras

25.	Arup Kumar Goswami	Sikkim	15.10.19	10.03.23	3.04	Gauhati
26.	Mohd. Rafiq	Meghalaya	13.11.19	24.05.22	2.06	Rajasthan
27.	A.A. Kureshi	Tripura	16.11.19	06.03.22	2.04	Gujarat
28.	Dr Ravi Ranjan	Jharkhand	17.11.19	19.12.22	3.01	Patna

In addition, 127 High Court judges were appointed and 60 names cleared by the Collegium under me were pending before the government at the time of my retirement. These facts are hardly known to anybody. There is absolutely no focus on these aspects in any forum. Even in seminars/webinars on contemporaneous issues like pendency and the need for more judges or timely appointment of judges, there is an ominous silence regarding these facts.

In yet another letter dated 21 June 2019 to the PM, I had suggested that the retirement age for High Court judges be raised to 65. I did not recommend raising the retirement age of Supreme Court judges. If my suggestion had been accepted and acted upon, there would have been a freeze on retirements for three years which would have helped in dealing with the abnormal number of vacancies in the High Courts that exist at any given time. Bringing the retirement age of judges of the higher judiciary i.e. High Courts and the Supreme Court on a par (65 years), may in turn have resolved many consequential issues, benefitting the institution. If the retirement age of High Court judges had been increased to 65, some incumbents may have preferred to continue till that age as Chief Justices of High Courts instead of opting to come to the Supreme Court for a three-year tenure.

The issue of a large number of vacancies in the district and subordinate courts (over 5,000 out of the sanctioned number of about 25,000) as also that of inadequate infrastructure, including residences/accommodation for the judges and the availability of support staff was taken up by the Supreme Court on the judicial side. A suo moto writ petition, No. 2/2018, was registered in this regard and directions issued from time to time. Progress was also monitored by the Court periodically. I believe that a substantial number of vacancies have been filled in the meantime. Many states, however, have lagged behind in performing their constitutional duty of providing the required physical infrastructure (courtrooms) to enable the courts to function. The issue of inadequate infrastructure has gone largely unnoticed as such newly added courts (without courtrooms) have been functioning virtually, like most courts in the country due to the pandemic.

The Supreme Court administration has to evolve to keep pace with the growth in volume of business. Hence, as many as 292 posts of Supreme Court employees were created during my tenure. One significant decision was the merger of four posts of Senior Assistant Librarian with the post of Librarian i.e. upgradation. This was done to overcome the stagnation that had affected the morale of the library staff. After all, the Supreme Court Judges' Library is one of the richest and largest law libraries in Asia. One person who used to spend a lot of time in the library is Fali Nariman, who would be seen browsing through the many foreign journals that were subscribed to. I do not know if he still does so.

Law clerks provide valuable assistance to judges. Provision was made for an additional law clerk (increase from three to four) for each judge. The remuneration of law clerks was also raised to ₹65,000 per month to enable them to work efficiently and live comfortably in Delhi.

When I found a large number of cases pending in the Supreme Court which did not justify consideration by a Bench of two or three judges, I initiated a proposal to vest jurisdiction in a single judge to hear certain matters like bail/anticipatory bail or transfer. If such matters are being heard by a sessions judge on his own or by a single Bench in a High Court, why are two or three judges of the Supreme Court required to hear appeals arising out of orders of the High Court passed in bail/anticipatory bail matters? This, however, required an amendment of the Supreme Court Rules. The proposal for amendment of the relevant Rules was approved by the full court on 27 March 2019 and the matter sent to the government under Article 145 of the Constitution. Order VI Rule 1 of the Supreme Court Rules was amended on 18 September by insertion of a proviso enabling a single judge of the Supreme Court to hear and decide certain categories of cases. The much-hyped transfer petition of Rhea Chakraborty, the actor whose name came to be associated with another actor's unnatural death (the case is still under investigation), was heard by a single judge of the Supreme Court, according to the amendment of the Supreme Court Rules.

COURT COMPLEX AND BEYOND

Constitution Day (26 November) in 2018 was observed as a joint event of the executive, legislature and judiciary of the country. A function was organized in Vigyan Bhawan, which was inaugurated by the president. The head of the judiciaries of the Bay of Bengal Initiative for Multi-Sectoral Technical and Economic Cooperation (BIMSTEC) countries, consisting of Bangladesh, Bhutan, Myanmar, Nepal, Thailand and Sri Lanka, and other dignitaries were present. The participation of the BIMSTEC Chief Justices was the Indian judiciary's contribution to the country's good neighbourly relations. At the dinner held that evening on the Supreme Court lawns, amongst other members of the executive, the vice president and the PM were also present. PM Narendra Modi visited the Chief Justice's Court and the Chief Justice's chamber for, I understand, the first time. There was, as usual, some criticism and controversy over this. Is the PM of the country not entitled to come and see the courtroom and the chamber of the Chief Justice?

Even though the fate, fortunes and future of the country are at times decided within the closed portals of the Supreme Court, the complex has remained largely out of bounds for the general public. As the Chief Justice, I took the decision that from November 2018, the general public should have access to the Supreme Court Complex. A guided tour was arranged for visitors in batches every Saturday for which bookings were to be made through the official website of the Court. I believe there has been a positive response. Another significant decision was to provide a free newspaper to all the Supreme Court staff of the rank of Senior Court Assistant and above.

The foundation of the additional building of the Supreme Court was laid on 27 September 2012 by the then CJI, Justice S.H. Kapadia. By the time my tenure as the CJI commenced, the complex with six multi-storied buildings had been built. Some work like underpasses connecting the new and old buildings, certification by the Fire Service and some other statutory authorities and some minor aspects were left to be completed. I gave a gentle nudge to the ongoing process, the building became ready and was inaugurated by the president of India on 17 August 2019. Today, over 80 per cent of the Supreme Court Registry operates from the additional building which has two auditoria and a conference room with state-of-the-art facilities.

A month before my tenure was to end, on 18 October 2019, I recommended that bungalow numbers 5 and 7 on Krishna Menon Marg be merged to form the Chief Justice's complex, housing the residence, secretariat and home office, including the Confidential Branch. The proposal appears to have been accepted.

Thereafter, on 16 November, I recommended that the CJI should use a special aircraft for official travel. I was careful to do this at the end of my tenure so as not to be seen as recommending something for my own benefit. I made this recommendation as I believe that the vacant seat beside or proximate to the Chief Justice on a commercial flight is a highly coveted and expensive seat. That apart, the CJI cannot be expected to rub shoulders with people who may be either high-profile litigants or interested in some pending litigation in the Supreme Court or a High Court. Such situations are best avoided. Apparently, my recommendation has not found approval from the government.

On 9 February 2019, President Ram Nath Kovind invited all judges of the Supreme Court along with their families to visit the famed Mughal Gardens of Rashtrapati Bhavan. A special tour was organized and all the judges and their family members, including grandchildren, had a leisurely and extensive tour of the splendid Gardens. This was followed by brunch in the banquet hall of Rashtrapati Bhavan where we were served with memorable elegance and pomp. This was the first time that such an event was held and I am thankful to Kovindji for his kindness. The event was held again in 2020. I am sure it is going to be an annual occasion.

I could list a few more little-known events but I do not wish to go on unnecessarily as I feel I have been able to give an idea of 'the unnoticed events' in the Supreme Court during my tenure. This is rewarding enough for me.

Fourteen

THE NEXT CHAPTER

There were several periods during my tenure as the CJI that were utterly dreadful and seemed a thankless call of duty with no end in sight. At the same time, these were among the most challenging assignments that came my way and this was possibly the case with many of my predecessors. During these periods, every moment was fraught with stress and anxiety. Problems of any sort could arise at any juncture, calling for immediate resolution. There were requests for hearing of cases beyond Court hours, even for midnight hearings. These were difficult calls to make for obvious reasons. I do not remember allowing any. Pending judgments in cases deeply impacting governance and the social and political life of the nation were perpetually at the back of one's mind.

In 2019, election year, the polls were spread over seven phases from 11 April to 19 May. This was a period of great personal distress for me on account of events already narrated and in the aftermath of the Bobde Committee report. A host of issues brought to the Court by activists had to be decided, including those relating to electoral bonds, a plea by 21 opposition parties demanding random checking of at least 50 per cent of the Voter Verifiable Paper Audit Trail (VVPAT) slips of each Electronic Voting Machine (EVM), petitions alleging violation of the model code of conduct by PM Modi and others, petitions raising issues of bribery in elections and cases raising questions of the entitlement of persons to vote if excluded from the NRC, among others.

At the same time, routine administrative matters kept flowing in as usual. Collegium business had to be transacted. Employees' grievances had to be heard. Requests by the SCBA and the AoR Association also had to be addressed. Meetings of the Permanent Committee for designation of senior advocates had to be convened and held. The Bar was, and rightly so, expecting the designation exercise to be completed at the earliest. Interactions with the eligible advocates had to be held by the Permanent Committee that consisted of the CJI, the next two senior most judges, the Attorney General and Soli Sorabjee. Foreign delegations had to be hosted and there were requests for interactions with the CJI and the senior judges.

Requests for appointments kept flooding the table of the PPS. Some of these requests had to be entertained. People had issues and grievances. Meeting people, after all, was one way of keeping your eyes and ears open. Requests to participate in seminars, lectures, convocations and so on had to be selectively entertained. There were invites to formal/State events in Rashtrapati Bhavan where the CJI's presence, at times, becomes a must if only to engage in conversations with senior constitutional functionaries. During the course of one such exchange, a government functionary told me that the 'latest' movie he had watched was *Ram aur Shyam*. More often than not, the conversations between members of the political branch and the Supreme Court judges at ceremonial functions are on such topics of 'mutual interest' and hardly on any serious 'business'.

Assessment of any situation or problem, evaluation of the pros and cons and the eventual decisions—all had to be immediate and could brook no delay. Every decision would leave one party, if not both, dissatisfied. Avenues for expression of disapproval were plentiful. Self-appointed spokespersons were circulating freely. There was no restraint either on misinformation or undignified language. Stress levels were, therefore, always high. Sleep was not easy. Yet one had to be fully alert at all times. There was no room for errors. Politeness and understanding were in high demand from the CJI but not vice versa.

For me, life as the CJI, to say the least, was lonely. I wish there was more camaraderie and brotherhood amongst the judges. There was this colleague who, during my troubled days in April 2019, came to me with some Ayurvedic preparation which he advised me to take to relieve stress. Behind my back, he was doing just the opposite by acting against me. I have been informed that the same brother judge tried to obtain a copy of the report of the Patnaik Committee. How and why he intended to use it is, of course, best known to him. At the same time, there are persons not connected to the legal world or the world of politics, whom I would not like to name, who stood by me at all times. I am grateful and indebted to them.

It was with feelings emanating from my recollection of such things that I handed over charge to Justice Bobde at 9.30 a.m. on 18 November 2019. I debated in my mind if, after the oath was administered to Justice Bobde, I should come back at all to the official residence of the CJI. I toyed with the idea of checking into The Claridges for the next two days as I would have had to remain in Delhi to take part in the protocol dinners that are hosted in honour of the incoming and outgoing CJIs by the president and the PM, in that order. I decided against moving to the hotel as I was likely to be misunderstood by setting a precedent. Late in the evening of 19 November, after the PM's dinner, I finally became free after my last official engagement as the outgoing CJI. I took a flight on 20 November to Guwahati, reaching in the afternoon. I was back in the place where the journey had begun almost two decades earlier.

I was looking forward to living in our new house in Guwahati, which we had occupied in September 2019. I was also looking ahead to a quiet life after retirement with a few friends and acquaintances, and occasional visits by my children and grandson (they live in

Delhi), at least for some time. But that was not to be.

Life as a retired CJI was an altogether different experience. We were on our own after nearly two decades with very little support from the system that I had parted company with—so much so that at times I wondered if the offer of support made by the Gauhati High Court pursuant to a full court resolution should have been accepted by me. Was my decision to authorize the letter below of the registrar (Admn.) of the Supreme Court correct in today's world?

Rajesh Kumar Goel
Registrar
Supreme Court of India

Phone : 011-23071057
Fax : 011-23383669

December 2, 2019

Dear Shri Phukan,

This has reference to e-mail dated 5th November, 2019 of Registrar [Vigilance], High Court of Gauhati.

This is to inform you that the Post retiral benefits of former Hon'ble Chief Justices of India are governed by the provisions of Rule 3 [3B(1)] of the Supreme Court Judges Rules, 1959.

In addition to the above, some High Courts have made provisions for certain additional benefits for Judges who have served in their respective High Courts. The High Court of Gauhati had not made any provision in this regard.

It is informed vide aforementioned e-mail dated 5th November, 2019 that the Full Court of the High Court of Gauhati vide its Resolution dated 30.10.2019 has sought to confer certain facilities to Hon'ble Shri Justice Ranjan Gogoi, former Chief Justice of India, which are in the following terms:

1) A dedicated Private Secretary to look after the day to day requirements of his Lordship and madam. The Private Secretary, in addition to discharging other responsibilities that may be entrusted to him, may also coordinate with the Registry for any protocol related requirements.

2) One Grade-IV peon and one Bungalow Peon be made available by the High Court to serve at the Guwahati residence of His Lordship.

3) A chauffeur driven vehicle belonging to the High Court in good condition be made available to his Lordship on fuel basis, as and when required.

4) A Nodal Officer be identified from the Registry so as to coordinate with the Private Secretary so appointed.

While appreciating the gesture shown by the Full Court of the High Court of Gauhati, Hon'ble Shri Justice Ranjan Gogoi, Former Chief Justice of India, has conveyed to this Registry that His Lordship will not accept the above-mentioned facilities conferred by the Full Court of the High Court of Gauhati.

This is for your kind information.

With kind regards.

Yours sincerely,

Rajesh Goel

[Rajesh Kumar Goel]

Shri Robin Phukan,
Registrar General,
High Court of Gauhati,
Guwahati,

2

Strangely, many have accused me of selling my soul in 'accepting' the above benefits/facilities.

Within a few days of my arrival in Guwahati, violent protests by the Assamese people against the Citizenship (Amendment) Bill erupted all over the state. People from all walks of life, including housewives and the elderly, joined the protests. Once it became an Act after it was passed by the Rajya Sabha on 11 December 2019, the protests grew louder, larger and more aggressive. The police had to resort to firing to control the crowds; roads were blocked and large-scale incidents of arson took place. Public and private vehicles were burnt. I could hear police firing from my bedroom. People from different walks of life came to meet me to seek my advice and guidance. I told them to adopt the legal route.

We had planned a holiday in Bali from 3 January 2020. Tickets had been purchased and hotel bookings made. We therefore left for Bali amidst the turmoil. Bali was a refreshing change, all the more so as it was the first trip on our own after my demitting office. We stayed at the Oberoi Beach Resort. Rashmi had booked a luxurious villa for us, which was a few hundred feet from the beach. The ambience was unbelievably pleasant. In the evenings, we preferred to have dinner in the hotel restaurant instead of going out. The restaurant was an incredible experience. The soft-spoken and well-mannered hotel staff and good food with the roar of the sea in the background made for a soothing experience after two decades of hectic work.

On the way back to Assam, as part of our pre-arranged schedule, we went to Bengaluru and then to Mysuru. We spent a night in a tiger reserve, staying in a log cabin, and succeeded in spotting several leopards. We visited the Suttur Shakha Mutt at BR Hills in Chamarajanagar and met many residents of the ashram, including children from the Northeast who were living there and being trained in different skills to be able to earn a living. We also visited the orphanage run by the Deenabandhu Trust. We took sweets for the residents and made a small donation to the secretary of the trust, G.S. Jayadev, a selfless worker devoted to the cause. A lady who had done her MTech from IIT, Bombay and another engineering graduate from Mysore University were working in the ashram. I was a little surprised. They told me they would like to continue what they were doing.

After returning to Assam, I found my table flooded with invitations and requests from various groups and bodies to take part in all kinds of events, covering a wide range of subjects touching on different aspects of national life. Invitations came for participation in the India Today Conclave in Delhi and the Arun Jaitley Memorial Lecture, from St Xavier's College, Kolkata, from Shri Ram College of Commerce, Delhi, and many other places. I was looking forward to meaningful participation in such events, but it was not destined to be so. The coronavirus had reached India. All the events were cancelled.

A NEW INNINGS

Around this time, I was offered nomination to the Rajya Sabha. I did not think twice before accepting, because the nomination was to be made by the president of India. True, the president performs his duties on the advice of the council of ministers headed by the PM. But that is the constitutional system. I did not even remotely think that there was anything wrong in accepting the offer or that it would be inviting the kind of adverse comments that eventually cropped up, including opinions that the Rajya Sabha seat was a quid pro quo for judgments delivered in the Rafale and Ram Janmabhoomi cases. Even in my wildest imagination, if it had occurred to me that people would have publicly aired their 'views' and 'thoughts' in such a manner, I would probably have thought twice before accepting the nomination.

My acceptance was primarily because it would give me the opportunity to project the problems of the judiciary before the representatives of the other two wings of the State even while retaining my independence as a nominated member. During my tenure as the CJI, I realized that the legislature and the executive do not have a very clear idea of the functioning of the judiciary, its problems and their resolution. As a nominated MP, I could make my own contribution in this regard to help build a judicial system in tune with the near-unanimous opinion of all and sundry that the country should have a more effective judiciary dedicated to serving the common man.

The other compelling reason, I must confess, is that it would give me opportunities to highlight issues pertaining to my home state, including the perennial and burning issue of recurring floods, the more recent issue of the Citizenship (Amendment) Act and meaningful and effective action in furtherance of Clause 6 of the Assam Accord, which deals with benefits to the indigenous people of Assam.

How many people in the country know that every year the rural population of Assam has to suffer five to six floods? Does the country know that a vast majority of villagers lose their homes and cultivation every year and depend on State relief? Do armchair intellectuals and activists, who talk about everything, know that till date Assam has lost about 4,000 sq. km of its land (more than the size of Goa) out of about 56,000 sq. km in the Brahmaputra valley alone due to erosion, that the annual loss of land due to erosion is about 80 sq. km? What has been done in this regard since Independence except distribution of substandard food to 'victims' of floods and distribution of building materials to enable them to rebuild their homes only to lose them again the following year? It was to highlight these and other such issues that I accepted the nomination to the Rajya Sabha. I must point out that I do not draw any salary, a decision I had intimated to the Secretary General of the Rajya Sabha in writing almost immediately after taking the oath of office on 23 March 2020.

My nomination as a Rajya Sabha member was protested against by members of opposition parties, particularly the Congress. It reminded me of the protests by a large number of advocates following the elevation of Justice V.R. Krishna Iyer as a Supreme Court judge, on the grounds that he was a Marxist.[59] But for this 'similarity', I can have no claim of being even remotely on a par with the great jurist. The protests and the boycott of my oath-taking did not hurt me as much as it disappointed me because immediately after the boycott, one or two members of the Congress came to my seat in the House and told me that this is how politics is played and that I should not take the boycott seriously! They, in fact, requested me to come to the Central Hall to meet some Lok Sabha members who were waiting. I demurred.

There are, however, some interesting facets about nominations to the Rajya Sabha. K.T.S. Tulsi, an advocate and nominated member of the Rajya Sabha, completed his term in February 2020 (my nomination in March 2020 was against that vacancy). Tulsi was thereafter 'nominated' by the Congress to contest the Rajya Sabha election from Chhattisgarh. He was elected unopposed as a Congress candidate. Swapan Dasgupta, another nominated member, unsuccessfully contested the Assembly election in West Bengal in May 2021 as a BJP candidate. He had resigned his Rajya Sabha seat to contest. After losing, he was renominated for the unexpired period of his earlier term. Mahesh Jethmalani, whose affiliation to the BJP is unequivocal, was also nominated to the Rajya Sabha under Article 80 of the Constitution.[60] As of today nine out of the 12 nominated members of the Rajya Sabha have declared their affiliation to the BJP.

---

[59]Upendra Baxi, *Courage, Craft and Contention: The Indian Supreme Court in the Eighties*, N.M. Tripathi, 1985.

[60]Article 80 states that the Council of States shall consist of:

    (a)   12 members to be nominated by the president in accordance with the provisions of clause (3); and

    (b)   not more than 238 representatives of the States and of the Union territories.

As far as I am concerned, I chose not to join any political party. The period prescribed for opting to join a political party by a nominated member i.e. six months, is also over. Therefore, my further continuance in the Rajya Sabha can only be as an 'independent' individual unattached to any political party, which is what is envisioned by Article 80 of the Constitution.

What strikes me as significant is that current political thinking appears to be far removed from the constitutional philosophy behind Article 80, a manifestation that has become startlingly apparent of late. The thinking and consequential actions of political parties and functionaries are not questioned for it is a two-way traffic. What is questioned and that too very selectively are bona fide individual decisions and actions.

Regardless of all this, a young High Court judge, who had come to see me around this time, earnestly remarked that the judicial fraternity wanted to see me in Parliament as strong as I had appeared in court. I am not too sure of that. Almost coinciding with my nomination (March 2020), mankind has faced one of its toughest challenges ever—the pandemic, which continues unabated. I have been medically advised to stay away from the House, if there is an option to do so. I have chosen to do so. The monsoon session (2021) of Parliament is over. The winter session is now due. I do not know what lies in store in the times ahead.

EPILOGUE

More than 18 months have passed since my retirement. This period has been most challenging as every human and every system has been put to the most severe test by the raging pandemic. Humanity's biggest challenge ever has also thrown the judicial system into a situation where the effects will be felt only in times to come. The pile-on of additional cases has made the arrears staggering. The 'inability' of the system to accord due heed to all cases and issues demanding its urgent attention has probably led to a fair measure of institutional setback that will require to be remedied in the coming years. But there are positive outcomes as well. Virtual courts and reliance on technology have given the system a boost in new areas. The technological innovations need to be carried forward even after the resumption of 'normal times'.

Qualitative additions of manpower; tweaking of training modules built on more result-oriented procedural jurisprudence and introduction of innovative measures to make a judicial career more lucrative so as to attract the best talent available are some short-term measures that could be introduced. Long-term innovations, including reforms in substantive law, could be entrusted to experts. There is an abundance of talent in our midst; the only requirement is to harness it. The net result of the much-awaited and necessary innovations, as and when introduced, will be a matter of close scrutiny.

Chief Justice Bobde has retired. The 'report cards', to which I have referred in the preceding chapters, came in large numbers.

They tended to be mostly negative. Articles and write-ups appeared in plenty, charging him for not doing what was expected and for doing what was unexpected. The venting appeared to have been just waiting for D-Day, 24 April 2021 (date of Justice Bobde's retirement).

Justice N.V. Ramana assumed office as the 48th CJI on 24 April 2021. His tenure has started on a different note—free of hostility from any quarter: an advantage that I am sure Justice Ramana will utilize in the best interests of the institution. The challenges are many and, in a way, more formidable. The pendency of cases has grown multifold (with nearly a crore of new cases); sitting of courts all over the country has not been as smooth and regular as before on account of the pandemic; and vacancies of judicial seats have increased. Above all, new and unforeseen legal issues have cropped up, requiring the courts to venture into 'new' areas of adjudication.

The judiciary, which has always enjoyed the trust and confidence of the majority of the people, will undoubtedly continue to offer solutions to the multiple problems that confront the system. Judges will continue to act as guardians of constitutional values and citizens' rights and freedom, a duty well performed at all times. Having been a part of this great institution for over 40 years, first as a lawyer and then as a member of the Bench, my dream is to see the institution at its strongest and best. It is this desire and the need to protect and safeguard the institution that prompted me to write about its working and the potential dangers confronting it. Of course, the institution has always been robust enough to check, control and overcome all such dangers.

While I was busy discussing with my publisher the first draft of the book in Delhi in February 2021, my mother was diagnosed with acute aortic valve stenosis or severe blockage of the aortic valve. She was advised to undergo a minimal invasive cardiological procedure called transcatheter aortic valve replacement (TAVR). It was an elective procedure which would enhance the quality of her life which otherwise, we were told, would progressively deteriorate.

We decided to take the risk and she too was keen on the procedure. But things did not go as expected and she passed away in a Delhi hospital on 9 April. Though she was 87 years old, she would still have been with us if not for our decision to go ahead with the procedure. She had walked into the hospital with her walking stick, only to leave it in a coffin. I feel devastated. All three brothers were with her until her last breath. There are several references to her in the book which I had mostly completed before her death. I preferred to keep most of them unchanged, retaining the present tense as if she were still with us.

I always recall what she told me when controversy after controversy had plagued me while in office as the CJI: 'The higher you go in life, the more ill people will speak of you. So long as you believe that what you are doing is right, there is nothing to worry.' Prophetic words, indeed, for she had not heard of Charles Mackay, who said:

> You have no enemies, you say?
> Alas! my friend, the boast is poor;
> He who has mingled in the fray
> Of duty, that the brave endure,
> Must have made foes! If you have none,
> Small is the work that you have done.
> You've hit no traitor on the hip,
> You've dashed no cup from perjured lip,
> You've never turned the wrong to right,
> You've been a coward in the fight.

I have lived and conducted myself as I have been moulded by divinity. Many a time, I was advised to go slow, to act soft, to alter my opinions and resultant action for the sake of expediency and peace. But then that would have meant succumbing, compromising. Had I been endowed with such traits, life would have been easier, less troubled and more peaceful, and non-controversial. I remained true to myself and led my life as I have narrated. Hopefully, the description of the many incidents in my life will lend readers a slightly different insight and perspective than that to be gleaned from what has been portrayed elsewhere. This has been my life—this is my story. There are many other secrets, opinions and sentiments that I may or may not take to my grave. Only time will tell.

ANNEXURES

REPORT OF THE COMMITTEE
ON IN-HOUSE PROCEDURE

This Committee has been constituted with a view to devise an In-House Procedure for taking suitable remedial action against Judges who, by their acts or omission or commission, do not follow universally accepted values of Judicial life including those included in the Restatement of Values of Judicial Life.

Complaints are often received containing allegations against a Judge pertaining to the discharge of his judicial functions. Sometimes complaints are received with regard to the conduct and behaviour of the Judge outside the court. The complaints are generally made by a party to the proceedings who feels dis-satisfied with the adverse order passed by the Judge or by persons having a personal grudge against the Judge. Most of these complaints are found to be false and frivolous. But there may be complaints which cannot be regarded as baseless and may require deeper probe. A complaint casting reflection on the independence and integrity of a Judge is bound to have a prejudicial effect on the image of the higher judiciary of which the Judge is an honoured member. The adoption of the In-House Procedure would enable a complaint against a Judge being dealt with at the appropriate level within the institution. Such a procedure would serve a dual purpose. In the first place, the allegations against a Judge would be examined by his peers and not by an outside agency and thereby the independence of the judiciary would be maintained. Secondly, the awareness that there exists a machinery for examination of complaints against a Judge would preserve the faith of the people in the independence and impartiality of the judicial process. The Committee has approached the task assigned to it in this perspective.

HIGH COURT JUDGE :

A complaint against a Judge of a High Court is received either by the Chief Justice of that High Court or by the Chief Justice of India (CJI) directly. Some times such a complaint is made to the President of India. The complaints that are received by the President of India are generally forwarded to the CJI. The Committee suggests the adoption of the following procedure for dealing with such complaints :-

(1) Where the complaint is received against a Judge of a High Court by the Chief Justice of the High Court, he shall examine it. If it is found by him that it is frivolous or directly related to the merits of a substantive decision in a judicial matter or does not involve any serious complaint of misconduct or impropriety, he shall file the complaint and inform the

CJI accordingly.   If it is found by him that the complaint is of a serious nature involving misconduct or impropriety, he shall ask for the response thereto of the Judge concerned. If on a consideration of the allegations in the complaint in the light of the response of the Judge concerned,   the Chief Justice of the High Court is satisfied that no further action is necessary he shall file the complaint and inform the CJI accordingly. If the Chief Justice of the High Court is of the opinion that the allegations contained in the complaint need a deeper probe, he shall forward to the CJI the complaint and the response of the Judge concerned along with his comments.

(2) When the complaint is received by the CJI directly or it is forwarded to him by the President of India the CJI shall examine it.   If it is found by him that it is either frivolous or directed related to the merits of a substantive decision in a judicial matter or does not involve any serious complaint of misconduct or impropriety, he shall file it.   In other cases the complaint shall be sent by the CJI to the Chief Justice of the concerned High Court for his comments.   On the receipt of the complaint from the CJI the Chief Justice

of the concerned High Court shall ask for the response of the Judge concerned. If on a consideration of the allegations in the complaint in the light of the response of the Judge concerned the Chief Justice of the High Court is satisfied that no further action is necessary or if he is of the opinion that the allegations contained in the complaint need a deeper probe, he shall return the complaint to the CJI along with a statement of the response of the Judge concerned and his comments.

(3) After considering the complaint in the light of the response of the Judge concerned and the comments of the Chief Justice of High Court, the CJI, if he is of the opinion that a deeper probe is required into the allegations contained in the complaint, shall constitute a three member Committee consisting of two Chief Justices of High Courts other than the High Court to which the Judge belongs and one High Court Judge. The said Committee shall hold an inquiry into the allegations contained in the complaint. The inquiry shall be in the nature of a fact finding inquiry wherein the Judge concerned would be entitled to appear and have his say. [But it would not be a formal judicial inquiry involving the examination and cross-

examination of witnesses and representation by lawyers.]

(4)   For conducting the inquiry the Committee shall devise its own procedure consistent with the principles of natural justice.

(5)   After such inquiry the Committee may conclude and report to the CJI that (a) there is no substance in the allegations contained in the complaint, or (b) there is sufficient substance in the allegations contained in the complaint and the mis-conduct disclosed is so serious that it calls for initiation of proceedings for removal of the Judge, or (c) there is substance in the allegations contained in the complaint but the mis-conduct disclosed is not of such a serious nature as to call for initiation of proceedings for removal of the Judge.

(6) In a case where the Committee finds that there is no substance in the allegations contained in the complaint, the complaint shall be filed by the CJI.

(7)   If the Committee finds that there is substance in the allegations contained in the complaint and the misconduct disclosed in the allegations is such that it calls for initiation of proceedings for removal of the Judge, the CJI shall adopt the following course :-

(i)   the Judge concerned should be advised to resign his office or seek voluntary retirement;

(ii)   In case the Judge expresses his unwillingness to resign or seek voluntary retirement, the Chief Justice of the concerned High Court should be advised by the CJI not to allocate any judicial work to the Judge concerned and the President of India and the Prime Minister shall be intimated that this has been done because allegations against the Judge had been found by the Committee to be so serious as to warrant the initiation of proceedings for removal and the copy of the report of the Committee may be enclosed.

Ranjan Gogoi

(8) If the Committee finds that there is substance in the allegations but the mis-conduct disclosed is not so serious as to call for initiation of proceedings for removal of the Judge, the CJI shall call the Judge concerned and advise him accordingly and may also direct that the report of the Committee be placed on record.

CHIEF JUSTICE OF THE HIGH COURT :

A complaint against the Chief Justice of a High Court is normally received either by the CJI or by the President of India who forwards it to the CJI. On receipt of such a complaint the CJI shall examine it and if it is found by him that it is either frivolous or directly related to the merits of a substantive decision in a judicial matter or does not involve any serious complaint of misconduct or impropriety, he shall file the complaint without any further action. In case it is found by the CJI that the complaint is of a serious nature involving misconduct or impropriety, he shall ask for the response of the Chief Justice concerned about the allegations contained in the complaint.   If, on a consideration of the allegations in the light of the response of the Chief Justice concerned, the CJI is satisfied that no further action is necessary he shall file the complaint.   If, however, he is of the opinion that the allegations contained in the complaint need a deeper probe, he shall constitute a three member Committee consisting of a Judge of the Supreme Court and two Chief Justices of other High Courts. The Committee shall hold an inquiry on the same pattern as the committee constituted to examine a complaint against a Judge of the High Court and further action in the light of the findings of the Committee shall be taken by the CJI on the same lines.

JUDGE OF SUPREME COURT :

If a complaint is received against a Judge of the Supreme Court by the CJI or if such a complaint is forwarded to him by the President of India, the CJI shall first examine it and if it is found by him that it is either frivolous or directly related to the merits of a substantive decision in a judicial matter or does not involve any serious complaint of misconduct or impropriety, he shall file the complaint without any further action. In case it is found by him that the complaint is of a serious nature involving misconduct or impropriety, he shall ask for the response thereto of the Judge concerned. If, on a consideration of the allegations in the light of the response of the Judge concerned, the CJI is satisfied that no further action is necessary he shall file the complaint. If, however, he is of the opinion that the matter needs a deeper probe, he would constitute a Committee consisting of three Judges of the Supreme Court. The said Committee shall hold an inquiry on the same pattern as the committee

Ranjan Gogoi

constituted to examine a complaint against a Judge of a High Court and further action on the same lines In the light of the findings of the Committee shall be taken by the CJI.

The Committee feels that the In-House Procedure suggested herein will allay the misgivings in certain quarters that the members of the higher judiciary are not accountable for their conduct. At the same time, it will also serve as a safeguard for the members of the higher judiciary from being maligned or being subjected to vilification by false and frivolous complaints. The Committee earnestly hopes that the occasions for invoking the In-House Procedure will seldom arise.

(S.C. AGRAWAL)   (A.S. ANAND)   (S.P. BHARUCHA)

(P.S. MISHRA)   (D.P. MOHAPATRA)

The Supreme Court of India at its Full Court Meeting held on December 15, 1999 to consider the Report of the Committee on **"In-House Procedure"** devised to take suitable remedial action against Judges who, by their acts or omission or commission, do not follow universally accepted values of Judicial life including those included in the **'Restatement of Values of Judicial Life'**, dated October 31, 1997 has unanimously adopted the Report of the Committee with the following addition to Para 5 of the Report. The amended Para 5 of the Report would now read thus :

"5(i) – After such inquiry the Committee may conclude and report to the CJI that (a) there is no substance in the allegations contained in the complaint, or (b) there is sufficient substance in the allegations contained in the complaint and the mis-conduct disclosed is so serious that it calls for initiation of proceedings for removal of the Judge, or (c) there is substance in the allegations contained in the complaint but the mis-conduct disclosed is not of such a serious nature as to call for initiation of proceedings for removal of the Judge.

(ii)   A copy of the Report shall be furnished to the Judge concerned by the Committee."

ORDERS DATED 23RD & 25TH APRIL, 2019 PASSED BY JUSTICE BOBDE CONSTITUTING AND RECONSTITUTING THE IN-HOUSE INQUIRY AND APPROVAL OF THE FULL COURT

In pursuance of the letter of Hon'ble the Chief Justice of India dated 21st April, 2019, I have examined the affidavit dated 18.4.2019 of the complainant, xxxxxx, ex-employee of the Supreme Court. Having perused the affidavit, I am of the view that it will be appropriate to have the matter gone into by a Committee of three Judges of this Court.

The Committee shall consist of myself, Hon'ble Mr. Justice N.V. Ramana and Hon'ble Ms. Justice Indira Banerjee.

All relevant papers be accordingly made available to the Members of the Committee.

The approval of all the Hon'ble Judges of this Court may be obtained.

Sd/-
(S.A. Bobde),J.
23.4.2019

Secretary General:

Respectfully submitted.
Sd/-
23.4.2019

Hon'ble Mr. Justice Sanjiv Khanna	Sd/-23.4.2019
Hon'ble Mr. Justice Dinesh Maheshwari	Sd/-23.4.2019
Hon'ble Mr. Justice Ajay Rastogi	Sd/-23.4.2019
Hon'ble Mr. Justice M.R. Shah	Telephonically approved
Hon'ble Mr. Justice R. Subhash Reddy	Sd/-
Hon'ble Mr. Justice Hemant Gupta	d/-
Hon'ble Mr. Justice K.M. Joseph	Sd/-
Hon'ble Mr. Justice Vineet Saran	Sd/-

Hon'ble Ms. Justice Indira Banerjee	Sd/-
Hon'ble Ms. Justice Indu Malhotra	Sd/-
Hon'ble Mr. Justice Deepak Gupta	Sd/-
Hon'ble Mr. Justice Navin Sinha	Sd/-
Hon'ble Mr. Justice S. Abdul Nazeer	Sd/-
Hon'ble Mr. Justice Mohan M. Shantanagoudar	Sd/-
Hon'ble Mr. Justice Sanjay Kishan Kaul	Sd/-
Hon'ble Mr. Justice L. Nageswara Rao	Sd/-
Hon'ble Mr. Justice Ashok Bhushan	Sd/-
Hon'ble Dr. Justice D.Y. Chandrachud	Sd/-
Hon'ble Mr. Justice A.M. Khanwilkar	Sd/-
Hon'ble Mr. Justice Uday Umesh Lalit	Sd/-
Hon'ble Mrs. Justice R. Banumathi	Sd/-
Hon'ble Mr. Justice Abhay Manohar Sapre	Sd/-
Hon'ble Mr. Justice R.F. Nariman	Sd/-
Hon'ble Mr. Justice Arun Mishra	Sd/-
Hon'ble Mr. Justice N.V. Ramana	Sd/-
Hon'ble Mr. Justice S.A. Bobde	Sd/-

Ref.: Complaint by Ms. X, former employee of the Supreme Court of India

The Committee to look into the affidavit dated 18.4.2019 of the complainant, Ms. X, former employee of the Supreme Court comprising myself, Hon'ble Mr. Justice N.V. Ramana and Hon'ble Ms. Justice Indira Banerjee was constituted and approved by the Full Court by circulation.

One of the members, Hon. Mr. Justice N.V. Ramana has recused himself from the duly constituted committee. A copy of his letter of recusal is enclosed herewith.

Now, the Committee is reconstituted as follows:-

(1) Myself
(2) Hon'ble Ms. Justice Indu Malhotra
(3) Hon'ble Ms. Justice Indira Banerjee

The approval of all the Hon'ble Judges of this Court may be obtained.

Sd/-

(S.A. Bobde), J.

25.4.2019

Secretary General:

Respectfully submitted.

Sd/-

25.4.2019

Hon'ble Mr. Justice Sanjiv Khanna	Sd/-25.4.2019
Hon'ble Mr. Justice Dinesh Maheshwari	Sd/-25.4.2019
Hon'ble Mr. Justice Ajay Rastogi	Sd/-
Hon'ble Mr. Justice M.R. Shah	Sd/-
Hon'ble Mr. Justice R. Subhash Reddy	Sd/-
Hon'ble Mr. Justice Hemant Gupta	Sd/-
Hon'ble Mr. Justice K.M. Joseph	Sd/-
Hon'ble Mr. Justice Vineet Saran	Sd/-
Hon'ble Ms. Justice Indira Banerjee	Sd/-
Hon'ble Ms. Justice Indu Malhotra	Sd/-
Hon'ble Mr. Justice Deepak Gupta	Sd/-
Hon'ble Mr. Justice Navin Sinha	Sd/-
Hon'ble Mr. Justice S. Abdul Nazeer	Sd/-
Hon'ble Mr. Justice Mohan M. Shantanagoudar	Sd/-
Hon'ble Mr. Justice Sanjay Kishan Kaul	Sd/-
Hon'ble Mr. Justice L. Nageswara Rao	Sd/-
Hon'ble Mr. Justice Ashok Bhushan	Sd/-
Hon'ble Dr. Justice D.Y. Chandrachud	Sd/-
Hon'ble Mr. Justice A.M. Khanwilkar	Sd/-
Hon'ble Mr. Justice Uday Umesh Lalit	Sd/-
Hon'ble Mrs. Justice R. Banumathi	Sd/-
Hon'ble Mr. Justice Abhay Manohar Sapre	Sd/-
Hon'ble Mr. Justice R.F. Nariman	Sd/-
Hon'ble Mr. Justice Arun Mishra	Sd/-

Hon'ble Mr. Justice N.V. Ramana   Sd/-
Hon'ble Mr. Justice S.A. Bobde   Sd/-

"REPORT

1.   This report is being submitted in compliance with Order dated 10.01.2019 passed by the Hon'ble Supreme Court in Civil Appeal Nos. 10866-10867 of 2010, titled as "M. Siddiq. (D) Thr. Lrs. Vs. Mahant Suresh Das and Ors.".

2.   By virtue of Order dated 10.1.2019 in C.A. Nos. 10866-10867 of 2010, the Hon'ble Court was pleased to issue following directions to the Registry of Supreme Court of India:

> "The orders of this Court, particularly, the order dated 10th August, 2015 indicate that though the learned counsels for the parties had attempted to submit some translated version of the evidence there is a dispute with regard to the correctness of the translations made.
>
> In these circumstances, the Registry of this Court is directed to physically inspect the records which are lying under lock and key; make an assessment of the time that will be taken to make the cases ready for hearing by engaging, if required, official translators of the requisite number and give a report thereof to the court. The said report will be submitted to this Court by the Registry on 29th January, 2019 when the reconstituted Bench (without Uday Umesh Lalit, J.), as may be, will assemble once again to take up the matter for further orders."

3.   It will be appropriate to mention here that prior to issuing aforesaid directions, the Hon'ble Court in its order had also observed that:

> "......The Bench has been informed that the original records are lying in 15 sealed trunks in a room which has also been sealed. Whether the depositions and documents which are in Persian, Sanskrit, Arabic, Gurumukhi, Urdu and Hindi, etc. have been translated is not clear."

4.   To comply above-mentioned directions, the Secretary General on 12.01.2019, has constituted two Committees. Copy of document showing constitution of Committee is enclosed herewith as Annexure I.

5.   Accordingly, all the members of both the Committees visited the room where the record is kept. The keys of the room and trunks were in the possession of Registrar (J-I). The same were kept in the sealed envelope. The envelope was opened in the presence of members of both the Committees. The lock with the seal of the room was found to be intact. Thereafter, the lock was opened, by breaking the seal, in the presence of Committee Members. There were 15 trunks in the room. Each trunk was having two locks and all the locks were found properly sealed. Report to that effect was prepared at the spot, and signed by the Committee Members. The charge of the room and sealed boxes was then handed over to the Committee No.2, for further compliance of the order.

6.   The members of second Committee with the assistance of officials of Registry, opened all the trunks one after the another. The record was physically inspected. It will be appropriate to mention here that Original record from the High Court of Judicature at Allahabad, Lucknow Bench was received in two consignments, consisting of 8 trunks (numbered 1 to 8) & 7 trunks (numbered 1 to 7) respectively. The first consignment was received on 24.3.2014 and the second on 17.8.2017.

7.   The officers and officials of the Registry have physically inspected the entire record kept in the trunks. It was found that the original documents were kept in Trunk Nos.1,2,4,5 & 6 of the first consignment. The scanned copies thereof were found placed in Trunk No.3,7 & 8 of the first consignment. In addition, 7 DVDs containing entire record in digitized form were found kept in Trunk No. 2 of first consignment. The evidence recorded during trial was found kept in Trunk No.1, 2 & 3 of the second consignment, while photocopies thereof were found kept in Trunk No.4. Trunks numbers 5 & 6 of the second consignment consisted of the impugned Judgment. A report of Archaelogical Survey of India was found kept in Trunk No.7 of the second consignment.

8.   It is revealed that the record consists of 38,147 pages of which 12,814 pages are in Hindi, 18,607 pages are in English, 501 pages are in Urdu, 97 pages are in Gurumukhi, 21 pages are in Sanskrit, 86 pages are in other language scripts, 14 pages contain images and 1,729 pages are in combination of more than one language script viz. Hindi, English, Urdu, Sanskrit and Gurumukhi. The record also includes 4,278 blank pages, though numbered yet not relevant for the purpose of translation.

9.   The Judgment runs into 8,170 pages. The deposition is in 14,385 pages, out of these 2,548 pages are in English and 10,907 pages are in Hindi. The deposition also includes various documents of which 97 are in Punjabi (Gurumukhi), 824 are in multiple languages, 5 are in Sanskrit, 2 are in Urdu and 2 are in other language scripts.

10.   There are 453 documents which have been marked with exhibits. The said exhibits consist of 3,609 pages which includes 2,188 pages in English, 572 in Hindi, 395 in Urdu, 402 in multiple language scripts and 52 in other language scripts. It has further been noticed that, barring few, the record received from the High Court does not include translation of vernacular documents in English. Thus, the documents/exhibits which are not in English will have to be translated.

11.   Thus, record received from the Hon'ble High Court is not in terms of Order XIX Rule 11(i) of Supreme Court Rules, 2013. In this context, it will be appropriate to refer to some of the relevant Rules of Supreme Court Rules, 2013, which are as under:

Order VIII :

Documents

Rule 2 : No document in language other than English shall be used for the purpose of any proceedings before the Court, unless it is accompanied by:

(a)   a translation agreed to by both parties; or

(b)   a translation certified to be true translation by a translator appointed by the Court; or

(c)   the said document is translated by a translator appointed or approved and notified by the Court.

Explanation – The provisions of this rule shall, so far as may be, apply also to a document in English of which a part is in a language other than English.

Rule 3 : Every document required to be translated shall be translated by a translator appointed or approved and notified by the Court:

Provided that a translation agreed to by both parties, or certified to be a true translation by the translator appointed or approved by the Court, may be accepted.

Order XIX :

Preparation of Record

Rule 11(1) : The record shall be printed in accordance with the rules contained in the First Schedule to these rules and, unless otherwise ordered by the Court, it shall be printed under the supervision of the Registrar of the Court:

Provided that where the proceedings from which the appeal arises were had in courts below in a language other than English, the Registrar of the Court appealed from shall within six months from the date of the service on the respondent of the notice of petition of appeal transmit to the Court in triplicate a transcript in English of the record proper of the appeal to be laid before the Court, one copy of which shall be duly authenticated. The provisions contained in rules 12 to 17 shall apply to the preparation and transmission to the Court of the said transcript record:

Provided further that where the records are printed for the purpose of the appeal before the High Court and the said record be in English, the High Court shall prepare 10 extra copies in addition to the number of copies required by the High Court for use in the Court.

12.   As stated earlier, the record received from the Registry of High Court of Judicature at Allahabad, Lucknow Bench is not in compliance with proviso to Order XIX Rule 11(1) of the Supreme Court Rules, 2013 nor is there translation certificate in terms of Order VIII Rule 2(b). The record received contains about 38147 pages, which includes 12814 pages in Hindi. The record in Hindi language includes the deposition of witnesses which runs into 10907 pages. The above information is tabulated herein under for explicit understanding.

(A)   Table showing details of Record received from Registry of Hon'ble Allahabad High Court, Bench at Lucknow, in terms of language scripts

Sl. No.	Particulars	Remarks
1.	Number of Pages in Hindi	12,814
2.	Number of Pages in English	18,607
3.	Number of Pages in other languages	2,434
4.	Pages, though numbered, have no contents (Blank Pages)	4,278
5.	Documents containing images	14
6.	Total number of pages found in 15 trucks	38,147

(B)   Table showing bifurcation of above record for the purpose of assessment of time to make case ready for hearing.

Sl. No.	Particulars	No. of Pages
1.	Deposition of witnesses in English	2,548
2.	**Deposition of witnesses in Hindi**	**10,907**
3.	Exhibited documents in English	2,188
4.	**Exhibited documents in Hindi**	**572**
5.	Exhibited documents in other languages	849

13.   The Supreme Court Registry has one Translation Cell for the limited purpose of translation of documents from Hindi Language to English language, if ordered by the Court. It has sanctioned strength of 10 translators, out of which 5 are Senior Translators and 5 are Junior Translators. At present, the working strength is 8 which includes 5 Sr. Translators and 3 Jr. Translators. Out of them 2 translators are on maternity leave and are likely to join duty in the last week of March, 2019. Thus, as on date, the effective strength of translators in Translation Cell is 6. As per prescribed standard a Senior Translator is required to translate 1600 words per day and a Junior Translator 1300 words per day. Approximately it comes out to be 6-7 pages/day. However, in view of the importance of matter, if the translators are asked to put in more working hours every day, each translator may translate about 12 pages/day.

14.   The Registry has also empanelled advocates and other persons for the purpose of translation of 14 vernacular languages in English which includes Punjabi (Gurumukhi), Sanskrit and Urdu. However, the Registry does not have any translator to translate the document which is either in Persian or in Arabic. Therefore, arrangements will have to be made to engage translators to translate the documents which are in Persian or Arabic. Nonetheless, for the purpose of assessment of time to make the matter ready, the Registry intends to take note of data of translation of only Hindi document into English because the documents in other language scripts could simultaneously be translated through the empanelled advocates / translators and by engaging translators. In that sense, translation 10,907 pages of deposition in Hindi and 572 pages of exhibited documents in Hindi will have to be carried out through official translators.

15.   In the circumstances, if entire strength of 8 official translators is utilised to translate 11,479 (10,907 + 572) pages, it is likely to take about 120 working days to make the case ready for hearing. The said time may be reduced if the Hon'ble Court permits the Registry to engage services of translators from other departments viz. various High Courts, Government Departments etc., e.g. if 16 translators (8 official translators of Supreme Court and 8 engaged from other sources) are deputed, the translation will be completed in about 60 working days. It may further be reduced by engaging more translators.

16.   With the above-mentioned details, the report is submitted for favour of kind perusal, consideration and necessary orders, please."

IN THE SUPREME COURT OF INDIA
CIVIL APPELLATE JURISDICTION
CIVIL APPEAL NOS.10866-10867/2010 ETC.

M. SIDDIQ (D) THR. LRS.   Appellant(s)

VERSUS

MAHANT SURESH DAS & ORS.   Respondent(s)

Dear Brother,

A draft judgment prepared on the basis of inputs furnished by me, Justice S.A. Bobde, Justice D.Y. Chandrachud, Justice Ashok Bhushan and Justice S. Abdul Nazeer is sent herewith for your kind approval.

With regards,

Sd/-
[Ranjan Gogoi]
07.11.2019

Hon'ble Mr. Justice S.A. Bobde
Hon'ble Dr. Justice D.Y. Chandrachud
Hon'ble Mr. Justice Ashok Bhushan
Hon'ble Mr. Justice S. Abdul Nazeer

Dear Chief,

I respectfully agree.
Sd/-
(S.A. Bobde)

M. SIDDIQ (D) THR. LRS.   Appellant(s)
VERSUS
MAHANT SURESH DAS & ORS.   Respondent(s)

Dear Brother,

A draft judgment prepared on the basis of inputs furnished by me, Justice S.A. Bobde, Justice D.Y. Chandrachud, Justice Ashok Bhushan and Justice S. Abdul Nazeer is sent herewith for your kind approval.

With regards,

Sd/-
[Ranjan Gogoi]
07.11.2019

Hon'ble Mr. Justice S.A. Bobde
Hon'ble Dr. Justice D.Y. Chandrachud
Hon'ble Mr. Justice Ashok Bhushan
Hon'ble Mr. Justice S. Abdul Nazeer

Respected Chief, I am in entire agreement. With warm personal regards.

Yours sincerely
Sd/-
(Dhananjaya Chandrachud)
7.11.2019

IN THE SUPREME COURT OF INDIA
CIVIL APPELLATE JURISDICTION
CIVIL APPEAL NOS.10866-10867/2010 ETC.

M. SIDDIQ (D) THR. LRS.   Appellant(s)

VERSUS

MAHANT SURESH DAS & ORS.   Respondent(s)

Dear Brother,

    A draft judgment prepared on the basis of inputs furnished by me, Justice S.A. Bobde, Justice D.Y. Chandrachud, Justice Ashok Bhushan and Justice S. Abdul Nazeer is sent herewith for your kind approval.

    With regards,

Sd/-

[Ranjan Gogoi]

07.11.2019

Hon'ble Mr. Justice S.A. Bobde
Hon'ble Dr. Justice D.Y. Chandrachud
Hon'ble Mr. Justice Ashok Bhushan
Hon'ble Mr. Justice S. Abdul Nazeer

I respectfully agree.

Sd/- (Ashok Bhushan)

08.11.2019

IN THE SUPREME COURT OF INDIA
CIVIL APPELLATE JURISDICTION
CIVIL APPEAL NOS.10866-10867/2010 ETC.

M. SIDDIQ (D) THR. LRS.   Appellant(s)

VERSUS

MAHANT SURESH DAS & ORS.   Respondent(s)

Dear Brother,

A draft judgment prepared on the basis of inputs furnished by me, Justice S.A. Bobde, Justice D.Y. Chandrachud, Justice Ashok Bhushan and Justice S. Abdul Nazeer is sent herewith for your kind approval.

With regards,

Sd/-
[Ranjan Gogoi]
07.11.2019

Hon'ble Mr. Justice S.A. Bobde
Hon'ble Dr. Justice D.Y. Chandrachud
Hon'ble Mr. Justice Ashok Bhushan
Hon'ble Mr. Justice S. Abdul Nazeer

Respected Chief Justice,

I agree with the above judgment.

Sd/- (S. Abdul Nazeer)

GLOSSARY

Any narration of the working of the Supreme Court would necessarily require use of terms and expressions with which a reader unconnected with law and the courts (for whom this book is primarily meant) would not be familiar. Let me therefore list these expressions and convey what they mean:

1. **Bench**—Judges sitting together in court to transact court business. Benches could be of two judges (most common); three judges (to hear matters where two Benches of two judges are in disagreement); five judges (Constitution Bench). Benches with greater strength (seven, nine judges) can also be constituted to hear specific matters. Usually, in the Supreme Court, judges sit on Benches of two.

2. **Roster**—The list of subjects assigned to a court. Cases pertaining to those subjects will come up before that particular court.

3. **Mentioning**—At 10.30 a.m., on every working day, lawyers have the liberty of making requests for early listing of their cases; to seek permission to file affidavits and documents beyond the time fixed by earlier orders of the court and to bring to the notice of the court any administrative bottleneck that may be holding up their cases. This is called mentioning which normally is to be made in the Chief Justice's Court unless the Chief Justice is sitting on a Constitution Bench in which case mentioning may be made in the court presided over by the senior most judge available. In the case of matters

that are tagged to a particular Bench, the CJI may ask the lawyer to make the mention before that particular Bench if the Chief Justice feels that the particular Bench may be more appropriate to deal with the matter. In practice, though, the bulk of the mentioning is made before the Chief Justice's Court; at times, some lawyers break the tradition and mention their cases before another court. The court before which such a mention is made may entertain the request or ask the lawyer to make the mention before the Chief Justice's Court.

4. **Defective**—A Special Leave Petition (SLP) or an appeal or any case filed with defects—defects could be of different kinds—from not filing requisite documents or not certifying a document when required or not paying full court fees, etc.

5. **Miscellaneous day**—Mondays and Fridays are miscellaneous days in the Supreme Court. On these days, fresh cases (about 30 to 35) are listed before the Court along with more or less an equal number of after notice cases. Regular cases are normally not heard on these days.

6. **Miscellaneous matters**—Fresh cases and after notice matters.

7. **Fresh cases**—Cases which are listed before the court for the first time for a preliminary hearing to decide whether the case is to be entertained or rejected/dismissed at the very threshold.

8. **After notice matters**—Cases where notice has been issued earlier and the opposite side has been served. These cases are primarily listed for grant/to vacate/to extend interim orders. A case can also be finally disposed of at the notice stage which often happens in the Supreme Court.

9. **Listed**—Appear in the cause list of the court. A cause list is a list of cases that a court will hear on a particular day. Cause lists are prepared daily and appear on the website of the Supreme Court in the evening of the previous day.

10. **Regular days**—Days where no miscellaneous work is supposed to be transacted and only regular hearings are to take place.

11. **Regular cases/Regular hearing**—Cases which are to be heard for final disposal.

12. **Interlocutory Application (IA)**—Interim applications seeking some interim orders or directions.

13. **Circulated/Circulation**—When a legal document/affidavit is given to the lawyer(s) of the opposite side or when a draft judgment is sent by one judge to the other(s) who has also heard the case(s) for approval.

Index

Dattu, H L, 148
Dave, Anil, 55, 72
Dave, A.S., 83
Delhi Faculty of Law, 23
Delhi High Court, 36, 53, 76, 77, 80, 81, 82, 89, 93, 145
Delhi Law Faculty, 15, 44
Delhi University (DU), 10
Desai, Ranjana Prakash, 148
Dhavan, Rajeev, 183
Dibrugarh, 1, 4, 5, 7
    airport, 9
    district bar association, 2
Director-General of Police, 193
Disqualification proceedings, 22
Division Bench, 20–21
Diwali mela, 50
Dutt, V.P., 14

E-committee, 149
Electoral Photo Identity Cards (EPICs), 167
Electronic Voting Machine (EVM), 205

'Foreigners movement,' 3,22

Gandhi Study Circle, 12
Ganguly, A K, 148
Gauhati High Court, 20, 21, 25, 27, 29, 30, 31, 32, 33, 38, 43, 53, 60, 170
Gauhati University, 8
Goel, A.K., 99
Gogoi, Anjan Kumar, 6
Gogoi, Nirjan, 6
Gogoi, Shanti, 1
Gogoi, Tarun, 34, 161, 169
Goswami, P.K., 21
Gujarat High Court, 83
Gupta, Rajan, 36

Hazarika, Lalit, 9
Himachal Pradesh High Court, 82
Hooda, Bhupinder Singh, 38
'Horizontal Transfer Policy,' 35–36

Indian Air Force, 6
Indian National Congress (INC), 13–14
Indian Police Service (IPS), 16
Indraprastha (I.P.) College, 12
Irwin College, 9

Jain, D.K., 36
Jain, N.C., 28
Jammu and Kashmir High Court, 81
Janata Party wave, 3
Jayadev, G.S, 211
Jethmalani, Ram, 27
Joseph, K.M., 74, 182
Joseph, Kurian, 75, 100
Jubilee Hall, 13, 14
Judicial office, 63

Kabir, Altamas, 43
Kalifulla, Fakkir Mohamed Ibrahim, 186
Kant, Surya, 82
Kapadia, S.H., 35, 44, 203
Karnataka mining judgment, 51
Katju, Markandey, 55
Kaul, Sanjay Kishan, 40, 182
Kaziranga, 7
Kerala High Court, 38
Khan, S.U., 181
Khanna, Sanjiv, 80
Khanwilkar, A.M., 124
Khehar, J. S., 73, 148
Krishna Iyer, V.R, 213
Kumar, Brijesh, 26, 27
Kumar, M.M., 43
Kureshi, Akil, 83